Think Positive, Live Happy

Chicken Soup for the Soul: Think Positive, Live Happy
101 Stories about Creating Your Best Life
Amy Newmark & Deborah Norville

Published by Chicken Soup for the Soul, LLC www.chickensoup.com
Copyright ©2019 by Chicken Soup for the Soul, LLC. All Rights Reserved.

The publisher gratefully acknowledges the many publishers and individuals who granted Chicken Soup for the Soul permission to reprint the cited material.

Front cover illustration of elephant courtesy of iStockphoto.com/Denis-Art (©Denis-Art)
Front cover illustration of coconut drink courtesy of iStockphoto.com/Floortje (©Floortje)
Interior photo courtesy of iStockphoto.com/Jacob Wackerhausent (©Jacob Wackerhausen)
Photos of Deborah Norville courtesy of Timothy White
Photo of Amy Newmark courtesy of Susan Morrow at SwickPix

Cover and Interior by Daniel Zaccari

Distributed to the booktrade by Simon & Schuster. SAN: 200-2442

Publisher's Cataloging-In-Publication Data
(Prepared by The Donohue Group, Inc.)

Names: Newmark, Amy, compiler. | Norville, Deborah, compiler.
Title: Chicken soup for the soul : think positive, live happy : 101
    stories about creating your best life / [compiled by] Amy Newmark &
    Deborah Norville.
Other Titles: Think positive, live happy : 101 stories about creating your
    best life
Description: [Cos Cob, Connecticut] : Chicken Soup for the Soul, LLC,
    [2019]
Identifiers: ISBN 9781611599923 | ISBN 9781611592931 (ebook)
Subjects: LCSH: Conduct of life--Literary collections. | Conduct of life--
    Anecdotes. | Happiness--Literary collections. | Happiness--Anecdotes. |
    Optimism--Literary collections. | Optimism--Anecdotes. | LCGFT:
    Anecdotes.
Classification: LCC BF637.C5 C45 2019 (print) | LCC BF637.C5 (ebook) | DDC
    158.1/02--dc23

Library of Congress Control Number: 2019940302

PRINTED IN THE UNITED STATES OF AMERICA
on acid∞free paper

25 24 23 22 21 20 19   01 02 03 04 05 06 07 08 09 10 11

Think Positive, Live Happy

101 Stories about Creating Your Best Life

Amy Newmark
Deborah Norville

Chicken Soup for the Soul, LLC
Cos Cob, CT

Changing your life one story at a time®
www.chickensoup.com

Table of Contents

❸
~Give It a Try~

❹
~The Power of Attitude~

❺
~The Words That Changed My Life~

6

~From Lemons to Lemonade~

7

~Step Outside Your Comfort Zone~

8

~Find Your Inner Strength~

9

~Make Every Day Count~

10

~Reboot Your Life~

⑪

~Make a Difference~

Introduction

There's a lot of truth to that old Yiddish saying: "Man plans… God laughs." Wouldn't it be wonderful if we could also find a way to laugh when the plans we have so carefully laid out go awry? To not be enraged, frustrated, and despondent — or worse — when the news isn't good, the prognosis grim, or the future seems bleak.

Sometimes you need an example to follow. There are times when a role model is required, someone to emulate as you try to pick yourself up, take that deep breath and find a way to move forward. Not move on — but move forward.

Moving forward. It's an important distinction — and very different from moving on. My friend who lost her husband in the terror attack of September 11th taught me that. I had said something about moving on and she quickly corrected me. You don't move on, she explained. You move forward from challenge or grief or disappointment.

Grief doesn't go away. That feeling of loss is always there — subdued perhaps, but ever present as you move *forward*.

Forward. To a new destination. Forward to happy. A place where it's different and where whatever left you *needing* to think positive and *hoping* to live happy, well that situation isn't there. IT stayed behind as YOU moved forward.

We've all been there. There are unlimited ways to be thrown for a loop: Your spouse is in love — but not with you. They've diagnosed your illness — but don't know how to cure it. Unemployment is at record lows — but you can't find a job and the bills keep coming.

Perhaps it's less dramatic: you just feel sad, your friends seem to have abandoned you, the days seem... pointless.

Years ago, my depression was there for the world to see. My high profile network job was over. I felt I would never work in television news again and the TV pundits agreed. "Left for dead by the side of the road," was how one newspaper critic described me. I might have remained by that career roadside if I hadn't gotten inside my own head and worked to change my mindset and get myself back on track.

The key word there is WORK. If you've ever experienced a melancholy moment, you know it's very easy to slide back to that unhappy place. (At this point, the journalist in me says that, for some, it's important to get professional help. In my own case, I got myself back on track by changing my outlook. I did my own brand of cognitive behavioral therapy.) Books like this one — *Chicken Soup for the Soul: Think Positive, Live Happy* — can be an important tool to help you change your outlook and get on the right track.

Somewhere among the 101 stories Amy Newmark and I have selected from the thousands that were submitted, you will find the message that's right for you. If you're just looking for a little pick-me-up to brighten your day, you'll find it. If you're feeling trapped and afraid to venture outside your comfort zone, we've got inspiration for you. And some of the stories in these pages will have you re-examining the way you look at the world.

Not everything's always the way it seems. That's the lesson Perry Perkins delivers in "Snapshots." He tells the story of an older gentleman sitting alone at the diner. A mother and daughter enter and spot him and Perry hears them talking in hushed tones about how sad the old man must be, sitting there by himself. What Perry knows, but the mother and daughter don't, is that twelve of the man's friends have just left the restaurant. They had shared a meal and the room had been filled with the sound of their laughter, jokes, and teasing. Now that old man is sitting alone, but he is basking in the afterglow of breakfast enjoyed with friends.

How often have you heard the word no? And how often have you said it to yourself: "No, I'll never do that." Whether it's the voice inside your head or some person trying to dissuade you, we've all had roadblocks put in front of us. Brenda Beattie's story called "Can't Is a Four-Letter Word" and Jennifer McMurrain's story "Yes, I Will" both remind us that we can prevail if we just keep going. Brenda persisted in the face of doubters who said she'd never land the government job that would provide financial security for her family. And Jennifer literally climbed a mountain of doubt as her skeptical family wondered how she'd complete a challenging hike. "Yes, I will," Jennifer repeated to herself as she put one foot in front of the other. You'll have a smile on your face as you read how that story ends.

Would being more bold bring you happiness? Lori Kempf Bosko's "The Bucket List" will inspire you to push your own limits. Some people have bucket lists of goals they hope to accomplish before they die. Lori makes a 100-item bucket list *every year!* Some goals might seem laughingly simple, while others, like a trip to Rome, seem impossible. By the time the new year rolls around, Lori has ticked off almost every item on her list and she's ready to make a new one.

But the most inspiring story might be our first. It's called "Facing the Fear" and it comes straight from the heart of the woman who embodies the spirit of the *Chicken Soup for the Soul* series. Her readers know Amy Newmark as the editor-in-chief and publisher of the books they love. She is also a soul sister among those of us who've had to face cancer.

Amy is one of the most organized people you'll ever meet and her very scheduled life called for her to edit *Chicken Soup for the Soul: Think Positive, Live Happy* along with five thousand other things. That's when God laughed and sent a challenging form of cancer her way. Fear goes hand in hand with cancer. Turns out, the positivity and gratitude that are the foundation of Chicken Soup for the Soul were exactly what the doctor ordered when Amy sought help to deal with the panic that sometimes swept over her. It takes courage to be as candid as Amy is. I think her story will help *you* be brave and remind you to savor every moment.

Relish each of these 101 happy moments that come from thinking positive. Go out and make your own memories and celebrate that happiness. Recognizing that you ARE happy today helps ensure that you will continue to live happy tomorrow and all the days after that.

—Deborah Norville—

Live in the Moment

Facing the Fear

We spend precious hours fearing the inevitable.
It would be wise to use that time adoring our families,
cherishing our friends and living our lives.
~Maya Angelou

The psychiatrist said, "Tell me why you're here. Do you need drugs?"

"No!" I said. "Even after my surgery I only took Tylenol and Advil. I'm here because I need some pointers on how to deal with the fear. The oncologist thought you might help me develop a strategy."

I was seeing this doctor at Memorial Sloan Kettering Cancer Center because I am in remission from a cancer with a high rate of recurrence... and when it recurs, that's basically it. You're going to be on chemo for the rest of your life, whether that's twenty years or twenty months.

My five months of chemo had ended two months earlier, and now I was in the waiting period. The kind of cancer I had — fallopian tube cancer — is rare, but it's basically like ovarian cancer; it's just that the tumor grows in a different place. My ovaries were actually clear, as were all my lymph nodes, but this type is treated exactly the same as ovarian cancer. And the statistics are the same, too — awful. One day, as I was sitting in the chemo chair waiting to start a six-hour treatment, the oncologist thought she was imparting good news when she said, "Twenty percent of Stage 3 and 4 patients don't have a recurrence!"

She left and I burst into tears, causing a flurry among the nurses. Of course, *every* time I walked into that building, no matter how nice the staff was, I cried.

But the fact that there was an 80% chance the cancer would come back was pretty daunting. Now, I'm a math person, and a negotiator. So I conducted a private negotiation with the statistics. It went like this: *The surgeon was surprised at how little cancer he found; the 20/80 statistics are for Stage 3 and Stage 4 combined, so it must be better for Stage 3ers with a light case like mine; my CA-125 [cancer marker] was extremely low when I was diagnosed and dropped to normal after the very first chemo.*

I explained my excellent reasoning to the oncologist at the end of my first post-chemo appointment, asserting my belief that I should only have a 50% chance of recurrence instead of 80%. She stopped as she exited the exam room and said in a pacifying way, "Sure, let's go with that."

So, I will. Even so, how do you deal with a 50% chance that you'll learn sometime in year two or year three of your remission that the cancer is back? That's where I am now — hoping to be in the lucky 50% who are cured. Hoping to never go through the exhausting, painful, debilitating, time-sucking process of chemo again. Hoping not to die in middle age.

The psychiatrist asked a bunch of routine questions about my life. When I talked about my late mother, and how I had understood the root causes of her moodiness and had accepted it, she said that she rarely saw patients who had worked through that kind of issue *prior* to seeing a psychiatrist. I explained that it was because of my work at Chicken Soup for the Soul, that reading all the stories has taught me a lot about forgiveness and what makes people act the way they do. She asked me about negative or toxic influences in my life, and I explained that, again because of Chicken Soup for the Soul, I had already removed all the toxic people from my life. So that was another box checked.

She moved on to gratitude. Was there anything I was grateful for? That unleashed a very long list. I told her that I was grateful that my cancer responded right away to the chemo; that I had a "cold cap" to wear during chemo that allowed me to keep most of my hair; that MSK's world-class care is only fifteen minutes from my home; that I have good health insurance and no financial worries. I was thankful that in-depth genetic testing showed no cancer genes — so I don't have to worry I passed something on to my children. I told her how supportive my incredible husband and children are; that I couldn't believe my luck that my doctor daughter chose OB/GYN as her specialty and could shepherd me through the process; and that my friends and co-workers have been wonderful.

At the end of our hour, the psychiatrist said that I already had the necessary tools and I didn't need to come back. I had explained my initial strategy for calm and happiness — four vacations during the first six months after treatment, plus the fortuitous arrival of a new grandchild at the end of that period. After that, my plan was to continue taking fabulous vacations every other month for as long as I could, or forever if I turn out to be in the lucky 50%!

I still needed a strategy for dealing with the waves of panic that were hitting me. I decided that I'm only allowed to panic between 8 and 8:10 each morning. If I want to think about all the scary stuff (usually at night), I have to wait until 8 the next morning. Of course, I never end up having such morose thoughts at 8 in the morning.

And I am exercising, which is a great way to assert control over *something* in your life. I think of it as "paying myself first" and it takes precedence over work, or paying bills, or tidying the house. I had started doing strength training twice a week a few months before my diagnosis, and I kept it up during treatment, going twice a week even during the chemo weeks. I did one session the morning after chemo, when I was still on steroids and feeling good, and then another session after the four bad days that followed. I never missed a workout during my five months of chemo. And now I've added back in a three-mile walk several times a week. I'm actually feeling strong and healthy and energized.

My life is a strange mixture of planning for a short future and planning for a long one. I treated myself to a new car during my treatment, but took a three-year lease instead of buying it, because the salesman said that if you die while you have a lease your spouse can give the car back with no repercussions. My ten-year life insurance policy coincidentally expired right when I went into remission, and I re-upped at the insane price you have to pay if you're not willing to go through a physical and disclose your illness. Yeah, I was betting on dying, but it was just an economic decision.

But at the same time that I'm planning for the next forty months, I'm planning for the next forty years. Because that scenario is equally likely. I'm dutifully applying my SPF moisturizer so I won't get skin cancer twenty years from now, I'm redecorating a couple of rooms in the house, and I'm planting new trees on our property.

How does this all fit into a book called *Think Positive, Live Happy*? One of the things that I learned from editing this book is the value of living in the moment. At the beginning of this cancer journey, I would be enjoying a "moment," whether it was hosting Christmas Eve, or watching a bird in our yard, or having dinner with our children, and then break down as I thought about what it would be like to *not* be around to do that again. I was sad for myself and for all the people in my life. Now, I'm strangely happy. I'm thoroughly *enjoying* all the "moments" right when they're occurring. I'm letting myself look forward to all the good things that are coming in the near-term, like vacations and another grandchild... and tomorrow's three-mile walk and the New York Times word puzzle that my husband and I will do tonight before we go to sleep.

It sounds defeatist, but we all die of something, and the older we get the more likely that is, so I've tried to reposition this whole mess as just creating a little more specificity for me than most people have. It will be this cancer, on the earlier side, or it will be something else way down the road, but in the meantime there are sixteen waking hours every day that I can fill with fun, purpose, and my favorite people.

— Amy Newmark —

A Splash of Perspective

*Living in the moment means letting go of the past and
not waiting for the future. It means living your life
consciously, aware that each moment
you breathe is a gift.*
~Oprah Winfrey

My presentation was horrible. I knew it before I heard "we'll be in touch" from the client. My boss wouldn't look me in the eye and the rest of my day was spent in relative silence — I was left alone, in reality. Finally, I left my air-conditioned office and of course, outside there was a heat wave; it was hot as hell and I was boiling in the three-piece suit I'd bought specifically for this big day. I was hot literally and figuratively as three buses passed, too full to stop and then the one that did stop should have kept going because the AC wasn't working.

I boarded the bus but was unable to stand it, so I squeezed my way off at the next stop. I would just walk the mile and a half to home. A country mile and a half it seemed as I passed bodegas, unleashed dogs, beggars, young girls in short shorts and young boys cat-calling. "Idiots," I thought to myself, annoyed further, as I continued my journey. I refused to take off my jacket, purposely maximizing my frustrations — when it rains let it pour was my philosophy.

A block from my building, I heard the water splashing and kids screaming so I knew the fire hydrant had been turned on.

"If I get wet…" I muttered, without even thinking about taking an alternate route. As I turned the corner, sure enough, there was a group of kids frolicking in the water. They were courteously on the lookout to stop the water from spraying on any pedestrians, so when they saw me in my suit they stopped the water and when they saw my mean look they even got quiet. The younger ones in bathing suits, the girls wearing shower caps and the boys with water guns all stared at me as I started to stride by.

Then I noticed a little one, no older than five, holding a water gun down by his side, eying me a little harder than the others. I eyed him back. Then his brother, who I'd seen around the neighborhood, nodded at him like he was saying, "I dare you." My eyes tightened a little further as I communicated my own "I dare you" to the five-year-old. Then his eyes darted, planning his escape route through the alley, and in that spilt second I knew I was going to get soaked.

And he got me, behind my ear, before he ran toward his exit. What probably only took a few seconds seemed like an eternity as I headed toward the alley to block his escape, but as I took my first step, his brother, the instigator, tossed me his water gun. It was either a bazooka, a water gusher, or a cannon, I didn't know, but as I caught it in one fell swoop, I was able to pull the trigger just as I met my "assassin" at the alley. He squirted back but his shooter was no match for my power, so instead he turned his water gun on a few other little kids who were stunned into stillness at what just happened.

Then, I too turned my bazooka on these kids and before long we were in all-out water warfare. Soon, there were water balloons hailing from upstairs windows and the whole block seemed to be involved. Needless to say, I was soaked and laughing like I'd never laughed before.

I couldn't remember my last water fight and if I did, it couldn't have been as fun as this one. One of our neighbors, an elderly Spanish lady, was selling flavored ices when she heard the commotion. She pushed her cart around the corner and later she told me that witnessing this water fight made her day. She invited us all over for some free mango ice. All of us grown-ups and kids.

It took a five-year-old to bring out the kid in me, put life in perspective, and help me realize that you may not be able to control disappointment but you can still let in the joy. And you can ruin a suit, too, and not really care!

—Marcus A. Nelson—

A Plague of Joy

Joy doesn't just happen. I have to pursue it.
~Elizabeth Myers

It was Friday at the end of a really, really long week. Mike and I were having friends over for dinner and a glass or two of wine — definitely two.

Just before I got home, Mike texted me to say that he had to stay late at work. I was now on my own to get everything ready for the night. Already running late myself, I could feel my frustration mounting as I drove to pick up Haydn and Michael from school. I rushed them into the car and informed them that we were making a few stops before heading home, and that they needed to help me tidy the house.

Both of them started whining immediately. I turned and pointed a threatening finger at them, giving them fair warning that I was not in the mood to listen. They crossed their arms and sulked. Michael even whispered under his breath, "This sucks!" For the next hour, I dragged the boys from one place to the next. The more I needed them to hurry, the more distracted and silly they became. I told them to cut it out, but they didn't seem to listen that day. My patience was wearing thin.

Just as we finished our last errand, the boys reminded me that we needed to stop at the pet store to pick up crickets for their bearded dragon lizards. "You promised," they said. And they were right. I had. But in the frenzy of the day, I'd completely forgotten. "Fine, but we need to be fast," I said, and we raced to the pet shop.

Fifteen minutes later, we were back in the car with some new passengers: one hundred live crickets in a clear plastic bag. I pulled into the driveway with only forty-five minutes left to unpack the car, clean the house, and set the table before my guests arrived. How would I make it?

I started barking orders at the boys like a drill sergeant, but they were focused on pouring the crickets from the plastic bag into the top of their little cricket-keeper thing.

My annoyance started to soar, and I yelled at them to hurry up, but to do so carefully.

I don't really know how it happened, but the next time I looked up, one hundred crickets were jumping all over my kitchen, chirping chaotically.

I screamed and scrambled up onto a chair to get away from them. My frustration exploded, and rage suddenly gripped my senses. I could feel myself about to start yelling in a way I rarely do.

But then the most amazing thing happened.

As I watched my two sweet boys try frantically to capture the crickets, it felt like

I could continue feeling annoyed and angry, or I could let go and enjoy this ridiculous moment.

time slowed down, and I saw the situation clearly for the first time. They were running around like lunatics, screaming with laughter.

It was pure joy, and it was an amazing thing to watch.

In that split second, I realized I had two choices. I could continue feeling annoyed and angry, or I could let go and enjoy this ridiculous moment for what it was.

I chose joy.

Laughing uncontrollably, I jumped off the chair and started chasing crickets with the boys. They were everywhere! Every time we tried to put a cricket into the keeper, another one would jump out. It was like a comedy routine. We squealed with excitement and pretty much had the time of our lives. The clock was still ticking… but we didn't care.

It took us about fifteen minutes to get all of the little guys into their box. Once we were done, my boys enthusiastically helped me scramble to get ready for the dinner. It became a game to see if we could make it in time. We were all in such a fabulous mood.

Mike got home with five minutes to spare. Anticipating the cold shoulder for leaving me to deal with everything myself, he was pleasantly surprised to hear about our crazy cricket adventure. Our guests arrived. We had a fabulous dinner party, and the boys helped me tell them all about our "peculiar plague problem." For weeks after, I could still hear chirping from some crickets that had evaded capture. It always made me giggle.

That moment is a constant reminder to me that I should never let frustration keep me from enjoying life. Things go wrong, and there's nothing we can do about that. But we do have the power to decide how we're going to react to things.

Next time you feel negativity bubble up inside, just chill, take a few deep breaths, and try to think of something that makes you happy. You'll find something if you try. Wouldn't you rather laugh than lose it? Choose joy.

— Heidi Allen —

Positive to the End

Your actions are your only true belongings.
~Allan Lokos

The glass bottle was half full of spare change. An oval piece of paper was taped to the front with five destinations written on it in colored marker: Washington, D.C., Alaska, London, Hawaii, and Italy.

The bottle was a bucket list of sorts, and I found it among my mother's possessions after she passed away in December.

My mom grew up poor and lived her life without any of the material trappings often associated with happiness. Yet, for my entire life, she stood as a role model of how to live a positive, happy life. She lived her last twenty years on Social Security and had no cash. Still, she squirreled away her pennies and dimes, believing to the end she might someday feel the sand of a Hawaiian beach between her toes or tour the Italian countryside.

I believe we could all use a role model to help us see the good in the world and keep a positive outlook in the face of adversity. I lost my role model, but not before she showed me with grace and determination what it meant to think positive.

For my mom, life was all about finding beauty in the little things. She rarely earned more than minimum wage in her lifetime. She lived paycheck to paycheck, often going without basic needs being met. It might have been easy to become bitter and disillusioned. Still, my mother remained a positive thinker.

As a child, there usually wasn't money to go out to eat or go shopping for extras. Instead, my mom would scrape together two dollars and send me to the convenience store. The order was always the same: a Coke, a Charleston Chew, and a pack of baseball cards.

We would sit on the porch and share the snack while I opened the baseball cards. She would talk to me about the players, asking which ones were the best or my favorites. It was simple, yet she turned poverty into positivity.

Without money to take vacations or even go on day trips, we would put a few dollars of gas into the car and drive around looking at houses on Sunday afternoons. The house we lived in was perpetually teetering on the edge of foreclosure, yet we would drive and dream, imagining living in one of the houses we saw. She had always wanted a log cabin. It would have been easy to bemoan what we didn't have, but instead she focused on what we might have someday.

Later, when I was deep into my career and my life as a husband and dad, my mom would call with words of encouragement when times got tough. Forget that she was poor, her health was failing, and she lived alone. She always had the words to make me smile, words that echoed a positive outlook that stood in stark contrast to her reality. I can't say I always appreciated her "glass half full" approach, but it taught me so much about how to face the many challenges life invariably throws at us.

When getting around on her own became impossible, my mom had to move to an assisted-living facility. For many people, that loss of freedom can break their spirit. While it was initially devastating, she quickly filled her empty glass back up.

I visited one day and found her busy knitting colorful mittens. She had seen a program on the local news about an organization that collected mittens for people in need. She used what little cash she had to buy yarn and knitted dozens of pairs of mittens over the coming weeks.

Living on just fifty dollars per month after her bills were paid, my mom managed to donate to a veterans' organization every year, knit mittens for the homeless shelter, and donate to an organization that provided cleft-palate surgeries in poor countries.

I once asked her why she was sending $250 to help a complete stranger when she could really use the money. Her answer: "I have everything I need here. That poor little kid, though..." Her voice trailed off, but the message resonates with me to this day. Even in the midst of living in a nursing home where she shared a room and had rapidly declining health, my mother saw herself as lucky.

She spent two of her last three birthdays in the hospital, taken both times by ambulance in the middle of the night. The third birthday was spent in quarantine with pneumonia in the nursing home. When I visited her in the hospital last year, she told me that she helped a woman at the home play her Bingo cards because she couldn't see very well. She was worried that no one would help her while she was in the hospital. She refused to see what she didn't have, instead focusing on others and what she did have. She was, in every sense of the phrase, a positive thinker. She was an inspiration, role model and fighter.

Digging through one of the boxes from the nursing home, I came across a small notebook. Inside, in her unmistakably neat handwriting, were the words "bucket list." As I sat and read the two-dozen entries that followed, it brought tears and a smile to my face simultaneously. Confined at the end of her life to a wheelchair, many of her wishes were astonishingly simple:

- Visit the farmers market.
- Go out to breakfast.
- Visit New Hampshire (where she was born).

As I read the items that were crossed out, I reflected on the good times we had. "See Kenny Rogers in concert one more time" was crossed off, as was, "Visit the beach," and, later in the book, "Have Matt make me swordfish."

She had no money, could no longer drive a car, had no job, and was confined to a wheelchair in a nursing home, yet in her final days, she remained the eternal optimist. The nurse who cared for her the night before she passed told me that when she stopped in, my mom told her, "I can't talk… I have to finish this cookbook I'm making for my granddaughter for Christmas."

Without money to buy fancy presents, she remained positive (and creative). She collected magazines from the waiting room and cut out recipes that she bound into a book for my daughter. Toward the back of her bucket list were three simple words: "Cook with Zoey." The partially finished cookbook was on her table when I went to say goodbye the next morning. She had passed away in her sleep.

She never got that log cabin. She never made it to Italy, London, Alaska, or Hawaii. Much of her bucket list remained to be done. But she never stopped believing, and that attitude of positive thinking was the greatest gift she could have given me.

— Matt Chandler —

Notice, Appreciate, Multiply

*Could we change our attitude, we should not only see
life differently, but life itself would come to be different.*
~Katherine Mansfield

One of my favorite movies is *Pollyanna*, the story of an orphan sent to live with her crotchety maiden aunt. I loved actress Hayley Mills' portrayal of Pollyanna, but what I loved in the movie even more was the Glad Game. Pollyanna's missionary father taught her to find something to be glad about in every situation. The point was to look at what was wrong, or perhaps not optimal, and find the silver lining.

The Glad Game starts with a negative and finds a positive. I felt that was how I lived. When dealing with adversity, I often said to my husband, "Aren't we lucky?" We always found a way through. I was, by nature, optimistic. I tried to see the best in any situation to the point that more than one person derisively called me "Pollyanna."

In my fifties, life took a lot of sudden twists and turns. My marriage ended, my child experienced life-threatening medical issues, I had breast cancer, and my mother died. There was not a great deal to be glad about. Life was challenging, almost bleak. For a long while, it was about getting through the next day. Sometimes, it was about getting through the next hour.

Once my son's and my health stabilized, and the divorce was final, I was faced with choosing how I wanted to live my life. In truth, I had no desire to look at the bad for even one more second.

I changed my thinking. Instead of focusing on the difficult things and trying to find something good in them, I focused on noticing the good already present in my life. I started small. When I woke up, if the sun was shining and cast beautiful shadows on the wall, I stopped and appreciated it. If I was walking down the street and found a penny, I appreciated that. If I was thinking I'd like to go out to lunch and a friend called and asked to do just that, I took a moment to appreciate that and be grateful for it.

While most of these "good" things were not connected to wealth or money, I began to feel quite rich. And the feeling was cumulative. The more I noticed the little things, and the more I appreciated the small gifts or pleasures placed in my path, the more there seemed to be. I began to share these occurrences — I called them "abundances" — with my friends. One friend in particular would often start our phone conversations by saying, "So tell me, what were your abundances today?"

I appreciated my friend's question because it made me aware of how many things I had to be grateful for that day. I began to write them down, to notice and appreciate the quantity, and to have them on hand in case I was having an off day where I felt a bit deprived or lacking. Rereading my notations would refresh my spirit. I decided to dedicate a journal to documenting my abundant life.

To make it fun, I chose a beautiful, sunny-yellow journal and treated myself to a set of good-quality markers. I used a two-page spread, opening the book flat, and sketched a small heart design across the crease. In the center, I wrote in the name of the month and the word "Gratitude." Each night of that month, I would sit down with my markers and my thoughts, and write down what I remembered from that day. I switched pens for each memory, making for a beautiful, colorful page. At the end of the month, I had perhaps forty or fifty notations. Rereading them gave me great joy.

The next month, I decided to carry my journal with me, noting the things I had to be grateful for as they occurred. This resulted in a much higher number of notes, perhaps double. The more I wrote, the more there seemed to be. My mindset switched from lack to abundance. I felt rich, blessed, successful, safe, and sheltered.

I have been keeping this abundance journal for several years now. Instead of a two-page spread, each month has expanded to four, or even six pages. I have begun to write smaller so there are more notations per page. My abundances have multiplied tenfold. My life is peaceful and joyful. The more I notice and appreciate my abundances, the more I receive. When I hit those bumps in the road that we all experience, I reach for my journal and read. And I can be glad again. It seems my inner Pollyanna is back.

— Jude Walsh —

My Basement

*Create a space in your life to relax, re-energize,
and reconnect with your sacred inner being.*
~Melanie Moushigian Koulouris

My basement makes me happy because it is my own personal space — a place for me to be creative. As a mom with a pre-teen daughter and a husband who works from home, I really appreciate it. However, my basement didn't always make me happy. In fact, when we first moved into this house, this basement made me feel downright depressed.

You see, I had always envisioned having a beautiful finished basement. I wanted a fun space down the stairs (away from real life!) that would be the perfect spot for us to entertain friends and family.

This finished basement of my dreams would be Pinterest-perfect. It would contain many wonderful attributes such as a high-end bar with rich, dark wood and cool pendant lights — maybe even a Tuscan-style wine cellar, complete with a panoramic view of a vineyard painted on one side.

It would also include a fun game area with foosball and air hockey and perhaps a ping pong table. And, of course, the icing on the cake would be the home theater replete with its own popcorn machine, snack bar, and posters of beloved movies tastefully adorning the walls. Plus, there would be a nice, comfortable carpet that warmed up the whole room while providing a cozy place for sleepovers.

Like I said, the house I'm living in now does have a basement.

Alas, it is not the basement with the wine cellar, home theater, popcorn machine, and cozy rug. Instead, this basement sports a gray tile floor, messy boxes of holiday decor and old books, a few pieces of ugly secondhand furniture, and a litter box.

Our basement remains half-finished and, in some areas, not finished at all. It looks as though someone attempted to finish the main room before we moved in. However, they did not do a very good job. The ceiling panels are crooked, and the can lights that were installed are always burning out. Plus, the two other rooms off the main room were not even part of the project, so they remain completely unfinished.

Unfortunately, we have not been able to afford the construction upgrades needed to turn this basement into the basement of anyone's dreams. "One day, we will," my husband promises. "Just be patient!" In the meantime, there it sits… ugly, a little too cold in the winter, and basically unused. That is, until I stopped waiting for my perfect basement to magically arrive and decided to turn this unattractive space into my own personal art cave.

Once I realized that my attitude toward our basement was simply a matter of changing my negative mindset, the rest was easy. First, you have to understand that nobody else comes down to the basement, since I am the one in charge of the laundry and the litter box. My daughter doesn't want to hang out in the basement, preferring her warm and comfy bedroom with its plethora of anime posters and stuffed cats.

So, one day when I was in the basement folding laundry, I suddenly realized that the peace and quiet was sort of… pleasant. There were no cartoons blasting in my ear and no news programs droning on with my husband talking back to them.

Not feeling particularly anxious to head back upstairs, I sat down at the old secondhand desk and pulled out a piece of printer paper. Then I started doodling. Before I knew it (with some guidance from an old picture book of cats), the doodle turned into a picture of a Siamese cat languishing in a garden. I liked the doodle. And I also liked the relaxing time I spent creating it.

The doodle inspired me to take a trip to the local Walmart for some acrylic paints, watercolors, paintbrushes, and glitter. Next thing

I knew, after spending more time down in the basement bundled in a nice thick sweater, I had transformed my doodle into an actual painting. Granted, the printer paper was a little flimsy, but that just inspired me to order some real art pads from Amazon.

I'm not a real artist by any account. The last time I spent so much time creating art was when my daughter was little, and that was only because I didn't need to worry that she would judge my drawings and find them lacking. She loved everything I drew, not caring that my shading wasn't right or the proportions were off. But I haven't really done anything artistic since that time, even though I always enjoyed drawing and painting when I was younger. I guess I never felt confident enough in my abilities.

When my daughter got a little older, she would still paint or make things out of clay with her friends, but I had stopped participating. Getting messy was for kids! Besides, I figured by that point my daughter would catch on that I wasn't very good. So instead, when I am upstairs, you will usually find me cleaning, doing dishes, watching Netflix, or sitting at the computer. However, it is important to note that there is no TV, kitchen sink, or computer down in the basement. There is only me and my art.

The basement has not grown better looking since those early days when it made me feel so depressed. There's no magic spell that's been cast, except for the magic of creativity, I suppose. For instance, the floor is still comprised of the same ugly gray tile that feels like a slab of ice in the winter.

We will replace this tile eventually with that nice, cozy carpet I talked about. However, I'm in no rush. After all, it's much easier to clean paint off a tile floor than it would be to scrub acrylics out of a rug. Besides, a rug might invite the rest of my family down, so I really don't mind the tile… for now.

Also, the furniture situation down here remains less than ideal. One might even call it "sparse." There is a total of one big, clunky desk with a scratched surface and one measly chair, both bought used. There is also a lounge chair purchased at a yard sale a few years back. However, the chair is so incredibly narrow and uncomfortable that nobody uses it... not even the cat!

Nonetheless, this less-than-perfect "lair" is all mine. My finished artwork sits on a shelf that snakes its way around the room. It is a colorful and always changing display of my burgeoning talent. I don't think any of my work is quite good enough to hang upstairs... yet. But for the basement, it's just fine. I can gaze at Purple Cat, Red Elephant, Surreal Deer, Magenta Tulips in Jar, Three Faceless Ballerinas, White Fox, and Love Birds Under Textured Sky any time I want.

Down here, I am the artist I always dreamed of being. Down here, I can make a mess on the scratched table and the tile floor. I spill glitter, and it doesn't matter. I can be creative without listening to the TV or my daughter and husband arguing about messy rooms or politics. Sometimes, our cat, Princess, slinks down to do her "business," but that's okay. I'm the one who cleans out the litter box, so it's just convenient that I'm already here anyway.

As women, we spend so much time worrying about making others happy that it's easy to forget what makes us happy. That's why it's nice, or should I say, essential, to have (as Virginia Woolf called it) "a room of one's own"—somewhere to explore our inner talents, meditate, exercise without feeling foolish, write our hearts out, or paint a picture of a girl in a green hat wearing a pink polka-dot dress, if we so desire.

In my case, that room is my basement. It may not look like paradise to anyone else. But really, paradise is what we make it. For me, it is a room with a cold, gray tile floor, burned-out lights, a few pieces of ugly furniture, a litter box, messy art supplies, and a never-ending display of creativity. I'll take it!

— Nancy Merczel —

7

The Light in the Produce Section

*The next message you need is always right
where you are.*
~Ram Dass

My son was often angry and disobedient. I suspected it was his way of handling his grief after his father passed away, or maybe it was just an eight-year-old-boy thing. Either way, it wasn't fun. I really thought I might have some sort of breakdown while solo parenting in this new, challenging phase.

So, like any near-the-brink-of-insanity mother would do, I took my tired, hungry and angry kids to the grocery store at about 5:30 p.m. The store was so busy that I had to yield to passing carts at every turn in between yelling, "No, we don't need that!" "Get over here!" and "Put that back!"

All of a sudden, my son spotted a little girl sitting in her mom's grocery cart. He recognized her from school, and he was so excited. We pushed the cart over to them, and my son said "hi" to his friend. It was clear to me that this little girl's family didn't speak English as a first language, but we didn't need language to communicate this time. They were as excited as my son was to see their daughter recognize someone from school. The little girl lit up with joy. She flapped her arms and smiled ear-to-ear. We all stood around giggling and smiling at each other because her joy was infectious!

Our interaction didn't last long, so I wasn't sure, but I suspected that she had special needs. It was hard to be certain because there really wasn't much talking… just smiles and laughter. So when we finally finished our shopping and drove off, I asked my son, "Is that girl in your class at school?"

"Yep!" he said.

"Does she sit near you?" I asked.

"No. She only comes into the classroom sometimes. She can't talk. She has to wear a helmet because she has really bad seizures sometimes. But she can sort of say 'hi' and 'bye,'" he said.

Then I totally lost it. Tears ran down my face because I was so proud of my boy for loving that little classmate of his. He was so excited to see her, and she was overjoyed about running into him. It was beyond beautiful. Every day when my son leaves for school, I give him a kiss and hug and say, "Have a great day… and show God's love!" And, boy, did he ever do that.

I bawled some more because my husband would've been so proud, too. My son has a tender heart, just like his daddy. He wasn't being nice to the girl from school because she has special needs. He wasn't showing her love and kindness because the teacher was watching. He was shining his light just because. All the darkness and burden I was feeling that day melted away in that moment.

That's what happens when we shine our light. Joy fills the room, and the darkness disappears.

—Jodi Whitsitt—

Opening the Door to Joy

A good laugh heals a lot of hurts.
~Madeleine L'Engle

My best friend swears I missed my calling as a stand-up comedian. I'm not sure about that, but I do know that humor has often helped to carry me through rough times.

I faced my biggest challenge yet when my beloved husband passed away last year. Humor was part of the fabric of our marriage, and every day I mourn our private jokes. Often, it took just one word to get us both laughing and recalling a silly event from our past.

John and I tended to laugh at life's adversities. When we traveled, we returned home with fun stories to savor and share. Friends commented that funny situations seemed to follow us around, waiting to spring on us. But I say it's all in the viewpoint, so why not put a humorous slant on life's absurdities?

> *It's all in the viewpoint, so why not put a humorous slant on life's absurdities?*

I remember laughing through some frustration during a tour in Europe. With each new hotel, we puzzled over how to turn on the shower, as well as how to flush the toilet. We'd giggle as we inspected the various knobs and handles — pushing, pulling, and twisting this way and that. We started a contest to see who could figure it out first. Once, I scanned the entire bathroom for the toilet flush. Then John said, "What's this?" He pointed to a big silver plate on the wall, about one foot tall and two feet wide.

I had thought that was just Spain's idea of modern art.

Recently, I ventured out on my first trip since John's passing with a good friend by my side and a sense of fun beginning to blossom again in my heart. We were headed to Las Vegas to see our favorite performer in concert.

Many people view airports as the pinnacle of all that is irritating, but with the right attitude, they can be good for a few laughs. As I posed in the security scanner with arms akimbo, an alarm sound pierced the air. What now? I'd skipped the underwire bra, having learned the hard way what havoc can be wreaked by the wrong undies. This time, a pat-down and visual scan revealed that my shirt sported just a little too much bling. "Let the fun begin," I quipped to Karen, as we strolled toward our gate. "Vegas is all about bling!"

After a smooth flight, we touched down and trundled ourselves and our luggage into a cab to endure a hair-raising ride. We adhered to my longstanding taxi mantra, "Just don't look."

Once checked in, we took the elevator up to our hotel rooms, key cards clutched in our hands. I wrestled with my key as Karen opened the door to her room and kicked her suitcase inside. I wasn't surprised when my door wouldn't budge.

In response to our phone call, a helpful young man soon appeared with a new key. I was poised to dart into my room, freshen up, and let the vacation commence. Not quite.

It turned out the door was actually broken. A special door-fixer had to be called in. I could have thrown a mini-fit; after all, I'd just gotten off a long flight, been tossed around in a taxi, and waited in a tedious check-in line. Instead, I rapped on Karen's door and informed her, deadpan, "Okay, the door is actually broken." She stared at me in disbelief, and we burst out laughing.

Once the door was restored to working order, the hotel manager paid me a visit. "Thank you so much for your patience," she said. "We're going to comp you $100 in food and beverage credit for this inconvenience." Who says keeping a sense of humor doesn't pay?

That evening, Karen and I had a fine time spending our credit, gleefully perusing each menu before choosing just the right restaurant for a splurge. The casino pulsed with activity, and tall stools afforded us a great viewpoint for people watching. I snapped a photo of Karen's burger, crowned with a fried egg and so tall it looked ready to topple over. It was over-the-top, just like the rest of this glittering city.

A feeling crept over me, a familiar, almost-forgotten emotion: happiness. Just as I started to feel guilty, I recalled my grief counselor's wise advice: "Don't stop your joy." I could miss John and still keep a light heart. In fact, I could honor him by continuing to face obstacles with humor and grace.

That evening in my room (with the door now working), I closed my eyes, envisioned John's smiling face, and shared the crazy highlights of my trip so far. I pictured him listening and laughing along with me.

— Kim Johnson McGuire —

9

A Stone's Throw

*Use your precious moments to live life fully every
single second of every single day.*
~Marcia Wieder

We had hiked just over a mile and a half. Our Golden
Retriever was dragging a little bit and needed a water break.
My wife grabbed her daypack and found the water bottle.
She poured some water into a beat-up bowl, and the dog
lapped it up quickly.

We settled onto an old tree trunk and rested our middle-aged
legs for a few minutes. The dog was tired but happy. She loves to hike
with us, and today was no exception. My wife was content as well.
She enjoys every opportunity to exercise, and hiking in the fall tops
her list of favorite things to do.

I had to be coaxed into the hike. My wife reminded me of how
we hiked when we first dated and said, "It can be like that!" I moaned
and groaned about wanting to watch football, but as the sun glistened
atop the colorful leaves on this Indian summer day, I was swayed to
join her. I also felt a twinge of guilt for not doing more of the things
we did when we were first dating.

As our hike progressed, I had to admit that the fresh fall air and
unexpected warmth helped make our time in the woods rather enjoyable.
I glanced over at some kids playing near a stream. Two boys and their
older sister chased each other around, and one of them exclaimed that
he had found some shells. This was a stream in Southeastern Ohio,

not the ocean, so both my wife and I looked at each other as if to say, "That kid has a vivid imagination." Within a minute, his sister was also holding up a shell. Sure enough, some shells had made their way to the edge of a stream in the middle of the woods in Ohio.

My wife loves shells almost as much as she loves hiking, so she jumped up and walked over to where the kids were playing. She grabbed a shell and held it up like a prize. I grabbed the dog's leash, and we walked over to join her. The dog jumped up and down and seemed to be telling my wife that the shell looked great. They both examined the shell closely as if they had found a gold nugget. My wife smiled as she picked up more shells.

I began looking around and saw a perfectly flat stone on the ground. In an instant, I recalled skipping stones near the lake where my grandfather took me fishing as a kid. I loved skipping stones! Watching a flat stone skip across the top of the water seven or eight times was like watching some sort of magic trick. I told my wife she could keep her shells; I had found a skipping stone. She gave me a puzzled look and then asked, "What's a skipping stone?" I walked over and showed her the flat, thin rock.

I said, "Watch this!" I flung the stone in a perfect motion so that it would hit the water just right and then skip along the top several times. She looked on in amazement and asked how I did that. To my surprise, my wife had never skipped stones. I gave her a quick lesson, and then she tried it. After just a few attempts, she was able to skip a stone like a pro. As she became more and more successful at skipping stones, her smile got bigger and bigger.

The dog looked on and was ready to chase each and every rock. I held her tightly so that she did not take a plunge into the muddy stream. A wet, dirty dog would ruin my wife's joy. For a few minutes, my wife and I took turns holding the dog and skipping stones. We had so much fun that we didn't notice the sun fading behind the trees. It was time to head back. We stood near the stream as we prepared to make the trek back to the car. For a couple of perfect minutes, I stood behind my wife and wrapped my arms around her waist. I could tell she was content and proud of her new skill. I was simply glad that I was there to share in it.

As a boy, I thought skipping a stone was magical. Now, as a middle-aged man sharing a moment with the woman I have loved for over twenty years, it was beyond magical. That's the beauty of life. The simple and unexpected moments are almost always the best ones, like a moment when you go hiking on a fall day and share something new with your spouse. Her joy of learning how to skip stones for the first time made me feel great, and it made me love her even more. We held hands as we hiked back, just like we did when we first dated. The dog led the way, wagging her tail with each step. The next time my wife wants to go hiking in the fall, I definitely won't want to skip it!

> *The simple and unexpected moments are almost always the best ones.*

— David Warren —

Count Your Blessings

10

A Change in Focus

We can only be said to be alive in those moments when
our hearts are conscious of our treasures.
~Thornton Wilder

The biggest mistake I made was the picture I'd created in my mind of how our retired life was going to go. My husband Wayne and I had worked hard through the years and did our financial-planning homework faithfully. We'd raised and educated our two daughters and were debt-free by the time he retired.

He'd enjoyed traveling the world for his job, and I'd assumed we'd travel once the daily office grind came to an end. All indications were that we were lucky in the health department with neither of us having any major issues.

When we'd talk of the golden years, we used to joke that we'd keep kicking until somewhere around age ninety or so. When it was time to go, we'd have one last piece of chocolate cake and then climb on his Harley-Davidson motorcycle for one final spin before aiming into the sunset for good.

It was a nice thought, but it was a no-go in the end.

My husband's intermittent odd behavior and memory lapses reached a point where we couldn't shrug them off. Extensive testing and an MRI finally put a name on it — frontotemporal lobe dementia with behavioral disturbance, commonly referred to as FTD — yet another wicked member of the dementia family of illnesses. The future of our retirement years evaporated with the words in the doctor's office. I was told he was only going to get worse as time passed.

It changed everything, including our relationship, daily conversations, and interactions with our kids and grandkids. Empathy, indifference, inability to remember from one moment to the next, and failing to follow personal hygiene habits that once were routine became the new normal.

We were no longer an "us." I was now his full-time caregiver and advocate, and he was a dementia patient with no future.

I kept him in our home for as long as I could, but two years after the formal diagnosis, his changes in behavior and his compulsive habits—like walking hour after hour, or eating or drinking just about anything in sight—required him to move to a facility where he could roam freely yet be kept safe.

I was a married woman living a single life in my early sixties. My husband lived six miles down the road behind locked doors.

It felt like some unseen giant picked up my life, tossed it inside a huge sphere and set it on a permanent tilt. Just when I thought I had figured out how we were going to adapt and adjust to this new change in life, the giant would give the sphere another violent spin.

> *I needed to change the way I looked back—with gratitude for what had been.*

The first year he was away, my days were dominated by sadness, loss, depression, and anger. I found solace in a journal because that's where I found release—and strength. On the lined pages, I could be honest with myself in trying to analyze how I was going to figure out my new life. At least, that was my hope.

Over time, I grew to realize that looking back on what *used to be* only made me feel worse. I needed to change the *way* I looked back—with gratitude for what had been.

Every night before I went to bed, I'd write down no fewer than three new things that I felt grateful for that day, such as:

- Going to sleep to the sound of rain
- Apple pancakes for breakfast

- Locating my lost pen
- My Easter decorations were up
- A movie, a cozy house and caramel corn
- Early morning bird chatter
- A twenty-minute nap
- My comfortable bed and pillows
- Coin-fed parking spots
- The checkbook balanced and the bills paid
- Took Wayne out for supper, and he remembered the words to a Beach Boys song

The point became clearer over time: I had a choice. I could focus on what I'd lost, or I could focus on what I still had.

My husband is never going to leave that care facility, but unlike so many afflicted with this horrendous disease, he is easy to redirect, and he is content and not violent. He still recognizes me. I can take him out for rides or a meal. He remembers the words to some of his favorite songs, and he still knows how to play the piano.

His illness has forced me to live in the moment.

I will never see Europe with him. We will never ride through the countryside on his Harley, and we can no longer share our stargazing porch nights like we used to.

But I have four grandchildren who love to play hide-and-seek with me. We color, read books, and sit at their little table and share ice cream. I have the friendship and love of two daughters, as well as two siblings whom I enjoy. And girlfriends, praise heaven! What would I do without my girlfriends? I have my health, a home, a yard to care for, and my writing life.

Clichéd sayings abound on the grief process, and they make grieving and loss sound like they should be easier to navigate than they are. But pages and pages of journaling and gratitude listing each evening reveal that, even in the face of a terminal disease, it is possible to find happiness.

— R'becca Groff —

Thanksgiving x 100

Gratitude turns what we have into enough, and more.
~Melody Beattie

Thanksgiving, to me, used to mean a long weekend, turkey and football. Now, however, it has become my favorite holiday because of a tradition at my church that has taught me to literally count my blessings.

For years, I had suffered from bouts of depression. One thing that fed the depression was an attitude of discontentment. I never seemed to be happy with my life, especially when I would compare it to someone else's. Everybody always appeared to be more successful than I was, and I would frequently feel I was not measuring up to either my own potential or the world's expectations.

Then, in 2008, I started attending Cherry Hills Church in Springfield, Illinois. Every year, they have an evening service on the Sunday before Thanksgiving. Two things happen every time — the food drive and The List.

The week before the Thanksgiving service, every chair in the church has a paper bag underneath it for people to take to a grocery store and fill with food items to be donated to local ministries. Then, at the evening Thanksgiving service, a team of volunteers places all the filled bags of food at the front of the church. The bags of food completely cover all of the steps up to the stage, which is more than fifty feet across. It is quite a sight!

Included in the church bulletin is a sheet with blanks numbered

1 to 100 on the front and back. At the top, it says, "Lord, I thank you for…" The first time I saw this at a Thanksgiving service, I wondered how I would ever be able to think of 100 things I was thankful for.

The pastor allowed a few minutes at the end of the service for us to start filling in our 100 blanks. He said we didn't have to necessarily complete it just then. Rather, this was an exercise to help us focus on gratitude. I looked at my blank list and was somewhat intimidated. I figured I could probably do ten or twelve, but 100?

Then I heard some kids next to me challenge each other to a race to see who could fill in all 100 the fastest. My competitive nature kicked in. I was not about to be shown up by a bunch of kids. So I started filling in blanks with anything I could think of—big things, little things, serious things and silly ones. I tried to think of any situation in my life where I had ever said, "Thank God for…" Something. Anything. To my own astonishment, I completely filled in the list in four minutes. Then I stuck it back in my bulletin and promptly forgot about it because the service was about to end. What I didn't know was that the real "service" was just beginning.

There were well over a thousand bags of food sitting at the altar, but every item in every one of those bags needed to be sorted and loaded on a truck. While we had been in the Worship Center hearing a message, singing songs, and filling in our lists, the same group of volunteers that had brought all the bags of food to the altar was setting up tables in the lobby for sorting. There were a dozen or so categories of food items, and two or three volunteers manned each table.

As soon as service was dismissed, many of the 600-plus people in attendance came forward to grab a bag of groceries, and the sorting began. The lobby at Cherry Hills became a roiling sea of humanity, bags, boxes, and cans. In just about an hour, thousands of food items were sorted, counted, boxed and loaded. By 8:30, anyone could have walked into the lobby unaware that anything had taken place there. What a night!

One day not long afterward, I was feeling particularly sorry for myself for no good reason. I found myself sinking into my familiar emotional chasm when I remembered the list.

I took it out and read through it. Obviously, I had filled it out in a rush, but now that I stopped to really think about the 100 entries on the list, my perspective began to change. I found myself laughing and crying at the same time. I started to realize that not only did I have a lot to be thankful for but that the things I had written on that list defined me as a person. They brought out my talents, hobbies, passions, faith, people who had a great impact on me, and so much more.

When one is straining to think of 100 things, the list contains some really random items. For example, #11 on my list was hot sauce. I love hot sauce. I put it on almost everything. But when I think about being thankful for it? Well, then I think back to the food drive that we did the night I made the list. That food was going to people who didn't have any food of their own on which to put hot sauce. People who didn't have a place to live. People who didn't have a job and would have loved to have a boss they couldn't get along with just to be able to have a paycheck to buy some of that food on which to put their hot sauce.

So, as it turns out, it's really not a stretch to think of 100 things to be thankful for. I carry my list with me every day in my planner. I do this so that wherever I am, if I am having a bad day, I can pull out my list, circle the next number, and take a few minutes to thank God for it.

Choosing to have an attitude of gratitude has made me more than happy. It has filled me with joy. We use those words interchangeably in our culture, but they mean something different. Happiness is a feeling that comes and goes, but joy is an attitude that can be cultivated. It's like gas in the tank of my soul. When I give thanks, I feel stronger because I know that there is a power greater than I am who provides me with everything on my list, and so much more.

And knowing that, I can be content and continue to choose joy.

— M. Scott Coffman —

12

Yogurt

When we focus on our gratitude, the tide of
disappointment goes out, and the tide of love rushes in.
~Kirstin Armstrong

It was a rough week. The price of oil skyrocketed as the temperature plummeted in Maine. We were looking at a high of eight degrees that week, and I had missed three days of work so my paycheck was going to be lower than normal. I was stressed, to say the least. I shopped strategically, looking for every possible way to cut pennies so I could buy groceries *and* keep the house warm.

My eight-year-old son didn't understand when I told him we were struggling that week. He wanted a special kind of yogurt, but I didn't have the extra three dollars to buy it for him. It was the kind of yogurt with a cartoon kid riding a skateboard on the front of the box, and a mere two spoonfuls in each cup. It was the kind of product that wastes a parent's money and makes me hate advertising.

I felt inadequate as a parent when those big eyes looked at me with confusion, as if to say, "It's just yogurt. What's the big deal?" So I found a way. I put something back and finagled as single mothers often do. He got his yogurt.

On the way back from the grocery store, I noticed a homeless man holding a sign by the side of the road. My heart hurt, and I tried not to look at him. I watched people dodge him on the street and walk by without even meeting his eyes. I looked at him closely then — bare hands clutching a piece of cardboard, snot frozen to his face, a ripped jacket. And there I was struggling because I had to buy oil—to heat my home.

My *home*!

I reached into my wallet where I had three clumps of money already folded and ready for rent, oil, and plowing. I had calculated what we needed to the penny.

I handed the man a five-dollar bill. He trembled as he took it.

"God bless you," he said with a smile. That's when I started to cry.

My son said from the back seat, "I thought you didn't have any money to spare, Mom."

I cried harder.

I told him that the man didn't have a home or food to eat. I said that he must be freezing, and so I felt like I could spare five dollars after all.

Then my son took his yogurt out of the bag in the back seat and handed it, along with his winter hat, to the gentleman outside his window.

"No, God bless you," he said in his small voice.

The man looked at me and smiled. I continued to cry while my son sat confused at the outburst of emotions.

The car behind me beeped.

On that day, my son performed an act that most adults wouldn't have done. He showed kindness and compassion. Even if it was just a matter of a few spoonfuls of yogurt, it was all he had, and he gave it to someone who needed it more than he wanted it.

He showed me that I am doing well as a mother. I'm raising him right. My son showed me that there are always blessings to count if we open our eyes, and that we always have the opportunity to be a blessing for someone else.

—Jamie Coombs—

13

Choosing Gratitude

There are blessings hidden in every trial in life, but you
have to be willing to open your heart to see them.
~Author Unknown

I'm not sure what my response would have been if someone had instructed me to write down everything I was grateful for after my husband died. One thing I've learned through personal experience and as a certified grief counselor is that no one wants to be told how to grieve. Yet, on the morning of March 29, 2012, forty-eight hours after my husband's death, that's exactly what I did. I sat at my kitchen table and began a tally that would fill three pages of my journal.

- My sisters rushing to my side when they heard the news
- My daughter Emily's inexplicable compulsion to hug her dad and proclaim her love every day for the previous three months — a compulsion that had concerned both of them, but now was a blessing
- A lapsed life-insurance policy that was reinstated just twenty-seven days before
- The five and a half years I'd cherished with David since his cancer, a period when our marriage was the best it had ever been
- Recent conversations I'd had with my husband about what he'd want me to do if he died before me — a topic we hadn't seriously discussed before, not even during his cancer fight

David had survived a heart attack and stent surgery, only to pass away sometime during the night three days after I brought him home from the hospital. As a writer, journaling seemed the appropriate method of working through my grief. After all, I'd written through my stint as a caregiver during my husband's cancer treatment, my mother's terminal cancer care and subsequent death in 2010, and my five-year-old grandson's cancer diagnosis a month later. It was no surprise that writing would be part of my healing, but gratitude? I vaguely recalled a Bible verse about giving "thanks in all circumstances," but looking for things to be grateful for seemed a stretch so soon after David's death. Yet it was surprisingly easy to come up with a long list:

- Doors that had so recently opened up to me — workshops and a weekly writing column that meant extra income
- The Christian radio station I'd begun listening to the month before, now playing songs that spoke directly to my wounded heart
- The last book David touched while in the hospital was about getting to heaven
- How often I'd recently caught David gazing at me, the transparency of his utter adoration flustering me with its intensity

It was easy to pinpoint when a distinct shift in our relationship had occurred. Bogged down with financial struggles and raising eight children, I'd lost sight of our marriage to the point that, at our twenty-fifth wedding anniversary party, I wondered if ours was even a partnership to be celebrated. Two years later, David was diagnosed with a cancer that had a fifty percent survival rate. Shocked into awareness of just how much he meant to me, and faced with the prospect of losing him, I made the conscious decision to put my husband first, to be the best caregiver I could be.

One day, after a long morning of radiation and chemotherapy, David collapsed on the couch in exhaustion. I knelt down in front of him, gently removed his socks and shoes, and began rubbing his feet. In twenty-seven years of marriage, I'd never touched that man's feet.

I looked up and saw tears in his eyes. From that pivotal moment, we were true partners in a newly revitalized marriage. From back rubs, to bringing each other cups of coffee, to putting the other's needs first, we'd actively searched for opportunities to serve each other. Yes, there was much I could be thankful for, even as I grieved the loss of such a special bond.

Choosing thankfulness that morning wasn't easy, but I'd had a good example in a husband who appreciated everything post-cancer. Despite suffering through six months of grueling treatment, he'd often take my hand in his and remark, "If it took cancer to get this kind of relationship, then I'm glad for it."

Instinctively, I'd chosen gratitude long before I would learn that science proved the physical and emotional benefits of practicing gratitude in a strengthened immune system, lower blood pressure, and a more positive outlook. I discovered that the word itself derives from the Latin *gratia*, meaning grace or graciousness. That makes sense. It was through grace that I could look back at my husband's bout with cancer, grateful for a renewed marriage that lasted another five and a half years. Grace meant falling to my knees at the side of the bed after experiencing his death, thanking God for bringing him into my life in the first place.

I once asked David if he dreaded those birthdays that ended in zero, as I always had. "Not at all. Think of the alternative," he answered. He was grateful to reach the age of sixty. He died the day before his next birthday.

It's been seven years since my husband's death. I've filled seven more journals in that time. Occasionally, I'll revisit that first one, marveling at how, even during those darkest days, I could find something to be thankful for. The attitude of gratitude has served me well. I end even the most mundane journal entries with a notation of something I can be thankful for. Sometimes, it's as simple as a smile from a stranger in the grocery store, the fresh smell of approaching rain, or the splash of bright yellow on a green lawn.

Recently, I've journaled about my fast-approaching birthday ending in zero — the same one that was my husband's last. I consider his broad smile and response to my question. Did he dread that birthday? On the contrary, he appreciated it. Just as I'll choose to be grateful for the milestone.

After all, think of the alternative.

—Mary Potter Kenyon—

14

When "Have To" Becomes "Get To"

*Having a baby is a life-changer. It gives you a whole
other perspective on why you wake up every day.*
~Taylor Hanson

I was utterly exhausted taking care of my first baby. The never-ending cycle of feeding, burping, changing, cuddling, and settling the baby down to sleep was relentless. While my baby napped, I might find time for a quick shower or a moment to unload the dishwasher. Perhaps I would have felt sorry for myself except that I knew how lucky I was to be working this hard.

When he was just a few days old, my son, who had been born healthy, suddenly developed a severe illness that sent him to the Neonatal Intensive Care Unit. One minute, the nurses in the maternity ward were helping me get him ready to go home; the next minute, he had a team of doctors trying to save him. Within a few hours, the crisis passed, but he remained in the hospital for observation for close to a week. We never knew why he got sick or why he got better.

That frightening experience was a reminder not to take anything for granted. It allowed me to remain positive even when motherhood was full of drudgery. So, when my baby's hungry cries woke me at 2:00 a.m., I reminded myself that I didn't *have to* drag myself out of bed to nurse him; instead, I was blessed with the opportunity to do so. When he suddenly spit up all over me, ruining my favorite blouse, I knew I was fortunate that this unexpectedly messy burp was my only concern. And when I had to change all his clothes only moments after getting him dressed, I recognized how lucky I was to have a healthy baby who could make a diaper overflow!

As my son grew older and his younger brother joined our family, I continued to remind myself that I didn't *have* to do some of the more boring or disagreeable parental tasks, but that I *got* to as the mother of two healthy, smart and happy boys. Picking lice and nits out of my younger son's hair? A yucky job for sure, but also the result of having a vigorous young athlete who shared a batting helmet with other boys on the baseball team. Getting out of the shower to find that my toddler had completely emptied all the books from the bookcase and removed dozens of CDs and DVDs from their plastic cases? Okay, picking up everything and putting it away was going to take me some time, but I understood that the need to explore and touch things was the delightful sign of an energetic child with loads of curiosity. Being jostled by the crowds at the mall as I shopped for a present for yet another birthday party? A small price to pay for having kids who thoroughly enjoyed strong bonds with their classmates and teammates.

Maintaining this positive attitude when my boys were little was made easier by the fact that I was often richly rewarded for my mothering efforts. A trip to the playground would result in fun and laughter. If I made a special dessert, I knew I could count on a kiss of thanks. When I read a favorite storybook at bedtime, I knew there would be an extra hearty goodnight hug.

> *I remembered that not everyone gets to do these things for their kids.*

But when the sullenness of the teenage years arrived, everything I did was wrong. It became harder to convince myself that doing another load of laundry was anything other than a thankless chore when it led to complaints that I was folding pants the wrong way. As dinnertime became a battleground, I began to resent the effort I put into cooking meals that were never really enjoyed by anyone at the table. I'll have to confess that there were moments when my bickering boys hardly felt like blessings to me.

And then I remembered that not everyone gets to do these things for their kids. My husband's mother, for example, was losing her fight with cancer when he was a teenager. I'm sure she was heartbroken at the thought that she would no longer be able to take care of her son, make sure he was fed nutritious meals, keep his bureau drawers stocked with clean socks, and see him grow into an adult. Remembering her struggle helps me appreciate how lucky I am that I am here. I am healthy and can still help the children I love so much.

By reframing those everyday chores as things I *get* to do, I remember that I am living the life I chose. And it's a wonderful life, at that.

— Victoria Otto Franzese —

Reach Out

*The unselfish effort to bring cheer to others will be the
beginning of a happier life for ourselves.*
~Helen Keller

One Saturday afternoon, tired of all the political news and discord, I disconnected from everything and everyone. I shut off the TV and computer, reached for my car keys and my camera, and set off to escape the divisiveness of the world.

Some people escape by shopping or going out for a run. Others bake or play piano or bridge. My go-to is photography. Framing things through a tiny viewfinder — intentionally seeking what is beautiful in this crazy world — has always managed to bring me peace.

That Saturday, I was enjoying a clear blue sky and the golden colors of fall in the Northeast. Just two blocks from my house, while cruising down a quiet street, I came upon a sight that I had to capture. There, in a slant of afternoon light, an old sugar maple was ablaze in color with that bluer than blue sky as a backdrop. There were even golden leaves arrayed all around it in the grass, and behind it were some contrasting evergreens and a white clapboard house with an idyllic, white picket fence. The sight took my breath away.

I hopped out of the car and started firing off pictures, hoping I was a capable enough photographer to do the scene justice.

I went straight home after that and downloaded the photos to my computer. That sugar maple looked as stunning on screen as it did through the viewfinder. I knew it would make a striking photo greeting card — and it would be a perfect image to share for Thanksgiving. I also thought that whoever lived in the shade of that sugar maple might appreciate the picture.

Two weeks later, after the photo greeting cards were printed, notes were written, and all the envelopes were addressed, sealed and ready to mail, I thought again of sending a card to the occupant of that sugar maple house. I didn't know who lived there, yet I'd been driving and walking by that property for fifty years, from my early childhood.

I wasn't sure if I should send a card to the occupants of that house. It seemed like an act of kindness, but would it somehow be misconstrued in this age of invasion of privacy? Would whoever lived at that address, after receiving my card, think that I had some ulterior motive or agenda? Would they think I was some sort of voyeur, casing their house like a stalker?

I vacillated. But then, on Thanksgiving morning — after I took stock of all the blessings in my life — I finally took the leap. I jotted a quick note inside one of the photo cards:

I live a few streets over in town and, one day when I was driving past your house this fall, your beautiful tree out front snagged my full attention. Something urged me to share a copy…. Wishing you a bright and beautiful Thanksgiving!

On my way out to celebrate the day, I stopped at that white clapboard house and slipped the photo card inside the mailbox.

Unless I drove by that house, I didn't give that card another thought… until six months later. In the spring, I received a response:

Just a few days after we received your card with the photo of our sugar maple tree, my husband of forty years passed away. Many years ago, the first fall we moved into this house, the leaves on that sugar maple looked spectacular — as spectacular as they appear on your card… I am in the process of making your photograph

*the centerpiece of a collage surrounded by photos of my husband
and other cherished remembrances of our lives here together...
Thank you for sharing the beautiful picture. I'll treasure it always!*

As I read that message, a shiver ran up my spine. I was never
so glad to have followed my instinct. It was such a gift to know that
my card held—and would continue to hold—special meaning and
significance for the occupant of that sugar maple house... but maybe
even more so for me.

—Kathleen Gerard—

My Gladitude Journal

Do not measure success by today's harvest.
Measure success by the seeds you plant today.
~Robert Louis Stevenson

A month after purchasing my gratitude journal, I marched into the kitchen and threw it in the trashcan. Writing in it every day felt like a silly addition to my already overwhelming to-do list. Besides, I had been keeping a "normal" journal for years. Why add another?

My friend and mentor urged me to give it another shot. He said that writing down a few things to be thankful for was different from free writing. For the next month, I found myself ending each day by staring at a blank page, wracking my brain for five things to write down. Sadly, after collecting more dust than words, that journal suffered the same fate as the first. Years would pass before "daily gratitudes" became a regular practice for me.

The value of a gratitude journal didn't resonate with me, but I did continue to write in an ordinary notebook. Jotting down thoughts and ideas was part of my daily ritual. It was a therapeutic way for me to decompress, a safe place where I could contemplate the day's events and let my dreams, fears and failures spill onto the page.

Along with journaling, consuming motivational material was a constant in my life. I bought dozens of personal-development books and listened to countless podcasts. The overall message from each author was the same: Set ambitious goals. Make a plan. Envision what life will be like once the goal is realized. Work your tail off.

I set goals, created vision boards, planned, and worked tirelessly. But my marathon-sized ambitions never seemed to manifest. The more I focused on the finish line, the more my inner critic told me it would be impossible to cross it. So, I'd give up. Then I'd read a new book, set more goals and start again.

My health goals were accompanied by diet and exercise, and I imagined myself a lean size 6. But when I looked in the mirror or stepped on the scale, I was discouraged. I pictured myself preparing meals in my newly remodeled kitchen, but doubted I'd ever have enough money to make it happen. I visualized authoring a book and seeing it on library shelves. But every time a manuscript was rejected I told myself writing was a waste of time. The coveted finish line had inched so far away that it was barely visible.

The read-practice-believe routine was exhausting and began to chip away at my self-confidence. Something was missing. What was I doing wrong? Recently, while organizing a cabinet, the answer came to me.

I came across the collection of journals I'd accumulated over the years. On a whim, I decided to flip through them. As I read, I realized these tattered notebooks were a roadmap of my past — a detailed narrative of my journey. Miles of blue ink flowed into hundreds of entries where I confessed my fears and captured fresh ideas. I wrote about new experiences and chronicled the events of everyday life. Each page-turn led me closer to the person I am today.

The more I read, the more I realized I was witnessing a transformation. Somewhere in those pages, I found the courage to pursue my dreams. I learned lessons, developed new skills and survived heartbreak with renewed strength. These daily scribbles were proof that I had been making progress all along, but had been so focused on the future I was unable to live in the moment. I hadn't been celebrating the little wins because I didn't recognize them.

My decision to dip into a stack of old journals taught me more than any self-help book ever has. Looking ahead to see how far I have to go can make the finish line seem unreachable. But enjoying the process and looking back to see how far I've come makes every small success feel more like a victory.

I still can't get into a pair of size 6 jeans, but I'm stronger, happier and fitter now than I've ever been. The old kitchen underwent a complete makeover. However, the new windows, fresh paint, updated appliances and modern flooring all came at different stages — over the course of six years. Although my book isn't published yet, I've rediscovered a love for the craft. And allowing myself to get lost in the practice of creating something new every day has given me a restored sense of purpose. Taking time to celebrate when my byline appears in a publication boosts my confidence and empowers me to keep writing.

> *I hadn't been celebrating the little wins.*

The gratitude journal found its way back into my life. This simple ritual that failed me in the past finally makes sense. But I prefer to call it a "gladitude journal." At day's end, it's where I reflect on what went right and acknowledge the little wins. It reminds me to give myself credit and slow down long enough to honor the process and recognize the progress. And if I see or experience something that makes me smile, I write that down, too.

Whether it's an essay on its way to an editor or a long walk with my dog, I'm learning nothing is too small to be celebrated. I still believe I can have it all, but I'm wise enough now to know I can't have it all at once.

— Ann Morrow —

17

The Day Courage Sat in the Barber's Chair

Above all, be the heroine of your life, not the victim.
~Nora Ephron

My husband Steve and I loved to navigate our small town of Grover Beach on foot. After breakfast on a Saturday morning, we'd decided to stop at Beach Barbers so Steve could get a haircut. The shop was crowded, but we found seats and passed the time listening to the chatter of other patrons and enjoying the old-fashioned furnishings and atmosphere.

An hour had passed when a handsome couple that I guessed to be in their mid-fifties came in. She was a bit pale, but otherwise they appeared to be in good health. They stood inside the door, so still they might have been mannequins. Then the man reached over and patted his companion on the shoulder. She stepped over to the closest barber, who happened to be Al, the owner.

The woman cleared her throat several times before she spoke. The chatter dropped a few decibels, and several customers looked up. A feeling of suspense seemed to settle over the shop. The other barbers stood still with their scissors and combs suspended a few inches from the heads of their clients. It was as though someone had pushed a pause button.

"I want you to shave my head," she said in a quavering voice. She swallowed a few times and continued, "You see, I have cancer. My doctor believes I can be cured with chemo and radiation. When I started treatment, nothing happened, but then my hair started to fall out."

By now I was holding my breath. I looked over at Steve, whose moist eyes mirrored my own. You could have heard the flutter of a butterfly's wings.

"I've decided I will get well. But I hate being sick. Every morning when I wake up and see handfuls of hair on my pillow, it reminds me I'm sick. I thought if I got my head shaved, I could feel eccentric and bold rather than sick."

The man who'd just sat down in Al's chair got up and stepped to the side with a gesture as graceful as a bullfighter sweeping his cape. Al lowered his chair and motioned for the woman to sit. He wrapped some tissue around her neck and draped her with a cape.

The other barbers finished with their clients. Instead of leaving after they paid, the clients found a seat or leaned against the wall. Al began clipping.

My scalp tingled as I imagined the little hair follicles hanging onto my head for dear life. I swiped at the tears I could no longer hold back.

The woman's partner stood close to the chair. His face revealed what looked like a mixture of love and fear of what lay ahead. I wondered if he had tried to talk her out of her decision, perhaps suggesting they make an appointment after hours so her shearing could be done in privacy. Why choose a barbershop instead of a beauty salon? Perhaps it was because a beauty shop is a place where women go with the expectation of a lovely hairdo.

This woman had no such expectation.

There was no sign of a wig, scarf, or hat. I shuddered in the face of my own discomfort and fear of ridicule. At the same time, I admired and celebrated her courage and determination.

Al, who'd kept her turned away from the mirror, whisked off the cape when he finished. She stood up and turned to face her image in the mirror.

She gave a small gasp and gently patted the tops and sides of her bald head. When she turned to face the other patrons, I thought I saw a tear glistening in her eye. Everyone stood and clapped.

Count Your Blessings | 59

"Now, it's my turn," her husband said, as he climbed into the chair and whisked off his baseball cap to reveal thick, curly hair. Soon, his salt-and-pepper hair mixed with hers on the floor.

"Anyone else want to join...?" Al looked at the woman expectantly.

"Marjorie and Vic," she said.

"Anyone else want to join Marjorie and Vic?" he asked.

A gentleman with a narrow fringe of hair walked toward Al's chair.

"Don't have much to lose," he said. "Boy, my wife will be sorry she sent me for a trim!"

Another round of applause followed as Marjorie and Vic exited the barbershop arm in arm.

—Judythe Guarnera—

18

Comparing Lists

I always say don't be scared. It's not that bad —
there's always something worse — and there is
definitely life after multiple sclerosis.
~Teri Garr

I was supervising a team of customer service representatives when one asked to speak to me privately. With tears in her eyes, she quietly confided, "The doctor thinks I may have MS."

Her despair at the possible diagnosis was one I recognized in myself eight years earlier. Now, mobility issues prevented me from hiding the disability multiple sclerosis had caused, and I understood her fear that she would wind up using a cane, too, or worse.

My first impulse was to reassure her that the disease is different in everyone. She couldn't assume she would have the same symptoms as I did, and I reminded her that although my diagnosis was just eight years earlier, we realized I had actually had MS for ten years before that. Even knowing I'd had the disease for quite a while, I sensed that still wasn't enough to quell her fear of what the future might hold.

That night, I told my husband my dilemma in not knowing what I might do to help her. And then the answer popped into my head. "I'll make a list!" I finally announced. I had had accomplishments since my diagnosis, and I wanted her to know that a full life was still possible, even if disability did occur.

I sat down at the table and began writing, but instead of simply itemizing positives (things I could still do), I decided to make comparisons to help gain perspective. What were my activities and accomplishments pre-diagnosis versus post-diagnosis? Since many of those listed in the pre-diagnosis column actually occurred when I had the disease but didn't know, it was a great comparison to my activities when I did know.

When I finished, I pushed back the chair and stared at the paper. Of course, there were the obvious things I could no longer do like run a marathon (as if I ever wanted to!), but there in front of me was proof that the disease had not affected the most important things in my life. What I expected to be devastating when first diagnosed wasn't at all.

I still traveled extensively with my family. I still participated in activities like making gingerbread creations with my husband for the annual Big Brothers Big Sisters of America fundraising event. I shopped 'til I dropped with the use of a mobility scooter when needed. I attended my sons' school and sporting events, and even had significant advancements in my career. And I volunteered… a lot.

MS had not taken my future, and now I had something truly encouraging to help the young woman. When I shared the comparison list with her, she was as surprised as I was. It's one thing to think you've done okay, and another to learn that you've done a whole lot better than okay. So, whenever I need perspective to change my attitude, making a list doesn't have to pop into my head; it's already a given.

—Vicki L. Julian—

Chapter 3

Give It a Try

19

From Dread to Dream

A professional writer is an amateur who didn't quit.
~Richard Bach

I trekked across campus with the June sun beating down on me. I sighed, feeling sorry for myself. Unfortunately, thanks to scheduling conflicts, I found myself devoting part of my summer vacation to "The Literature of Health and Healing." I was convinced I was in for a miserable couple of months.

At twenty-three, I had no idea that a summer class I dreaded would change my life and help me achieve dreams I didn't even know I had.

The class focused on literature centered around death, illness, and the idea that mortality is inescapable. We read stories, poems, and books that focused on heart-wrenching tragedy. We read *Tuesdays with Morrie* and talked about how horrific diseases could be lurking right around the corner. We watched the movie *Awakenings* and realized how simple pleasures that we overlook are the things life is built on. We read poem after poem from people who were dying, lonely, depressed, and abused. We read heavy works that made me feel guilty for complaining about attending a class for a few hours when so many others were carrying much heavier burdens.

A few weeks into the course, I realized that the class I had dreaded was changing my perspective. It was inspiring me to go after my dreams, set my priorities, and stop waiting for tomorrow to chase my goals. It helped me realize that the things I thought were so important weren't really what life was about. As I drove to campus one day, I reviewed my bucket list and realized that I wanted to see my name on the cover of a published book.

I'd always been a writer, scribbling stories and poems in journals as a child. I'd even started writing a chapter book in sixth grade. But the realities of adult life that slammed into me after high school coupled with a demanding course load of college classes had squelched my passion for writing. I had decided to focus my time and effort on things that would lead to success in the workplace. Publishing a book didn't seem to be a realistic, practical goal.

My class about death and illness made me realize that dreams are meant to be chased by the living. Thus, I went home, sat down, and started thinking about what story I would tell if I could. I stopped thinking about the safe, predictable path I could follow to success. Instead, I thought about what really inspired me and what I truly wanted to accomplish.

Recently, I'd followed several news stories about wrongful convictions. I realized I wanted to write about that topic and explore it more fully. A story unfolded in my mind. Motivated by the class that I had tried so hard to escape, I went out onto my parents' deck with a green notebook and started writing the first page of what would become my first novel.

Four years after I started scrawling in my green notebook, my manuscript was accepted by a small publisher. I remember shaking and crying when I received the e-mail, waking my husband up from a deep sleep to tell him the unbelievable news.

Even bigger dreams came true after that. I wrote more books, got picked up by one of the big five publishers, and even hit the *USA Today* bestsellers list.

Today, as an English teacher and a thriller author, it still amazes me how it almost never began at all. I can't even fathom how different things would be if I had spun on my heel and headed off to a summer of lounging instead of that summer literature class. Sometimes, the things we dread the most become the things that change us the best.

— Lindsay Detwiler —

20

The Now

Your life does not get better by chance;
it gets better by change.
~Jim Rohn

The idea of dating almost made me sick to my stomach. I didn't want to start over. I didn't want another failed first date. I didn't want another disappointment. I couldn't *take* another disappointment.

So I just told myself, *My life is fine. I don't need to date.*

It had been close to three years since my divorce. I'd been on a handful of dates over those three years, but I would always find the perfect reason to run.

One night, I decided I'd give it a real try. No excuses. No running. A real, solid try. I hopped online and began to swipe as if I were simply shopping for shoes.

No... no... yep... nope! Then, there he was: a cute blond with big, blue eyes. His smile lit up the page. *That's my guy...* Swipe.

We talked briefly. He asked me if I'd like to meet. I had promised myself "a real, solid try," so I said, "Yes."

As I drove to meet Mitch I planned my escape. I wondered if it was too late to cancel. I wondered if I could fake car trouble. I wondered if I could just have one drink and then leave, or would I have to stay for two?

I did the slowest walk of my life into the bar, fighting with myself the whole way.

Finally, I stood in front of him. I put on my best smile and tried to act like a normal person.

"Hi!" he said.

"Hi!" I said.

Immediately, I wanted to leave — not because I didn't like him, but because I did.

"So, how do you know Marco?" he said.

I had followed Marco's band for years. Come to find out, he had, too.

"I see you know Alison," he said.

"How do you know Alison?" I said.

Instant chemistry.

It didn't feel like a first date. Actually, it didn't feel like a date at all. It felt like two friends talking about music, bands, and mutual friends.

We realized we had known the same people and gone to the same places for five years and never met each other.

The more we talked, the more I laughed, and the more he looked directly into my eyes. That old, familiar feeling came rushing back. *Run!*

I didn't say a word. Not one word. But I thought to myself, *Get out of here! Now!*

Almost before I could finish my thought, Mitch pulled his chair close to mine, softly brushed the hair out of my face, looked directly into my eyes and said, "I'm not asking you for forever. I'm just asking you for tonight."

"Wait, what?" I said.

"I can feel your nerves. I can feel you. I'm not asking you for forever. Just for tonight. Can we do that?" he said.

I just stared at him. *How did he know what I was thinking?*

"Yeah, we can do that," I said.

I wanted to cry, but I smiled instead.

The rest of the night was a blur. We laughed. We talked. We danced. It felt as if I had known him my whole life.

It was my favorite first date.

That first date turned into six months. I often thought back to that first night. I was so fearful of getting into a new relationship. I did everything I could to avoid dating. I did everything I could to avoid getting hurt again. I distracted myself with work, friends, and family. Anything to not date. Anything to not get hurt.

I think of all the fun events, football games, holiday parties, and nights of dancing. I think of quiet nights at home falling asleep on the couch while watching a movie. The way he looked at me. The way I loved him.

None of that would have happened if I had run that first night.

Eventually, the relationship did end. My heart was broken. I could easily have avoided this pain. I could have walked away that first night. I could have gone on pretending life was fine. But something in his words, his eyes and his heart made me say, *Don't run. Not tonight. Don't run.*

As my tears fall, I think back to what a girlfriend asked me about my relationship with Mitch. "Knowing what you know now — knowing how it would all end — do you regret dating him?"

I looked at her and smiled. I felt the tears welling up in my eyes. I said, "No, I don't regret one minute."

> *If you worry about forever, you'll miss the now.*

Maybe we aren't meant to be forever. Maybe we were just meant to help each other grow or learn. Or maybe we were just meant to have an amazing, fun-filled six months together. I don't really know. But I know he was meant to be in my life. And I will never regret that.

If you worry about forever, you'll miss the now.

— Diana Lynn —

A Winning Smile

Because of your smile, you make life more beautiful.
~Thich Nhat Hanh

"**A**re you going to the audition?" someone asked my friend, Connie, as we came out of ballet class.

"What audition?" I asked.

"Oh, nothing," said Connie. "It's for *The Ed Sullivan Show*. You wouldn't be interested."

"Why not? I'd love to go!" I declared.

A couple of the girls smirked. Connie smiled at me kindly and said, "I don't think you are ready yet, Eva."

I felt slighted, but I thought maybe she was right. Connie and the others had been studying dance most of their lives and had already been in some shows. I was only a young novice hoping to get a job in show biz one day. Some day.

The Ed Sullivan Show was a big deal. It was an hour-long Sunday night variety show on CBS. It featured top-notch stars such as The Beatles and Elvis. This time, one of the performers was going to be Jimmy Durante. They were looking for six dancers to support him. Jimmy was close to the end of his career but still quite famous. Frank Sinatra, Jr. was also one of the performers in this episode.

After class, a few of us went for coffee. My classmates chatted about the audition that I was "not ready for." I listened to their animated discussions on the choreography and what to wear, and soon I realized I was not in their league as a dancer. I went home disillusioned.

But later that night, it bothered me. Who said I shouldn't go to the audition? I had a right to try. How would I ever know if I was good enough if I didn't try? What did I have to lose?

I had a hard time falling asleep. When I finally did, I had a dream. A voice was speaking through a loudspeaker; it sounded like Ed Sullivan talking about what a big show it was going to be, with his distinctive pronunciation: "A REALLY BIG SHOE! It's going to be a REALLY BIG SHOE." It was only a dream but when I woke up, my decision was made. I was going to the audition. I packed my dancing shoes, and put on my leotard and bright red lipstick. Red was my lucky color. As I looked at my reflection in the mirror, only one thing was missing. I put on a smile.

I took the subway into the city and walked to the rehearsal studio on Eighth Avenue. I climbed up the five flights and entered a huge studio filled with aspiring dancers. They all looked so confident. For a second, I questioned my decision to be there. What was I thinking?

Ordinarily, a show as prominent as *The Ed Sullivan Show* would not have open casting calls. Usually, one would need an agent to even find out about the audition. For whatever reason, this time any dancer could try out.

The choreographer and her associates were at a desk in another part of the room. I signed in and took my place nervously among the other dancers.

Connie and about five of my other friends were there. "What are you doing here?" one asked.

I said simply, "Well, I have nothing to lose by trying."

The look I got said, "Okay. Whatever."

The audition began with the dancers doing some basic steps that the choreographer's assistant demonstrated. Nothing difficult. The room was huge, but not large enough for all the dancers to try out at once, so we were broken up into groups.

I looked at my group of twelve lined up in front of the mirror. What made me think I had a chance? I looked again and got a good feeling. All the hopeful dancers had confident but serious expressions. I had a smile.

Most girls were preoccupied with getting the choreography right. I knew my dancing was not great, but I couldn't stop smiling because I found it comical that I was auditioning for a major TV show.

At first, the number of applicants was reduced to about half. Then the choreographer eliminated even more dancers. Then came the serious slashing. Some were asked to stand aside on the right and some on the left. It wasn't clear which side was reserved for the dancers who were being considered, but I was still with my friends so I thought it was a good sign.

When we had been divided into groups of six, the steps became more complex. I struggled, but kept smiling.

Then we were asked to do a *grand tour jeté en l'air*, individually. Roughly speaking, that French term means to stand on one leg, kick the other one up and out as close to a split as possible, and then do a turn in the air as you fly across the room. Hopefully, you'd land on both feet. We each had to do this several times, flying diagonally through the room. It was not an easy step, even for accomplished dancers, much less me.

I was impressed by the quality of these dancers. Each did the *tour jeté* beautifully. When it was my turn, to say I was nervous was an understatement. I took the preparatory step, and with that never-ending smile, I leaped up into the air, turned in mid-air and landed flat on my rear end!

The smile never left my face. Once it was determined that only my ego was hurt, my friends broke out laughing. The piano player stopped playing, and soon the whole room was filled with laughter.

When everything settled down, my friends were instructed to go to the right. When I was told to go to the left, their faces told it all. They felt sorry for me. I had tried my best, but I had ended up on the losing side.

I never stopped smiling as I picked up my belongings and prepared to leave. That's when the choreographer called out to me, "Where are you going? You've got the job if you want it."

Did I want it? I certainly did. I thought I had been eliminated!

My friends on the other side did not make it.

There were no *tour jetés* in the show. I made my first appearance on national TV as one of six young girls dancing around Mr. Durante and chanting, "Happy birthday, Jimmy! Happy birthday!" as he sang, "It's my nose's birthday, not mine."

I never stopped smiling, and I always landed on my feet.

In the words of Ed Sullivan, it was a really big SHOE.

Had I not believed I could do it, and had I not tried, I would have missed out on a thoroughly enjoyable experience.

It proved once again that a smile will get one further than a frown ever will.

— Eva Carter —

22

The Doctor Is In

All successful people have a goal. No one can get
anywhere unless he knows where he wants to go and
what he wants to be or do.
~Norman Vincent Peale

My grandma followed me into the living room to see what I was up to after I asked her for some double-sided tape. The day before, I had watched our new refrigerator being delivered, and now I was doing what any child would do with a huge cardboard box — turning it into something wonderful. In my case, it was Lucy's psychiatric help stand from the *Peanuts* comic strip.

Grandma looked fretfully at the large pair of scissors I had taken from the kitchen drawer as my determined little hands struggled to cut through the thick cardboard. "I'm going to help people, Grandma, and give them advice to solve their problems."

"Well, that's a very good thing to do. Can I help you with the scissors?"

Over the next few weeks, I readily dispensed advice to unsuspecting family members and friends from my makeshift therapy stand. Our Poodles, Rascal and Smokey, along with my grandma, made up the majority of my patient consultations.

My cardboard psychiatric advice stand fell apart pretty quickly after that, but the dream remained, although it went into hibernation for a while. When I graduated from high school, I won some scholarships but I still couldn't afford to go full-time to university. So I decided to work and take classes part-time instead.

Years passed, as did my grandma and my Poodles, but my dream didn't. From time to time, Lucy would pop up in my mind, giving me her sage and practical advice. "Snap out of it! You've got to stop all this silly worrying!" she advised sternly. "Go home and eat a jelly-bread sandwich folded over," she once quipped, reminding me not to over-dramatize a situation and just curl up with some comfort food until the storm was over. And once, when I was feeling particularly unsure of myself, there she was, advising, "If you really want to impress people, you need to show them you're a winner."

As I worked menial job after job, I always managed to set aside enough time and money to take college classes at night. Over time, the credits added up until I received my first college diploma.

Life continued, and so did my dream of becoming a psychologist. As my regular jobs improved, so did the amount of effort and funds I could spend on my university classes. Before I knew it, another college degree had been completed.

And so it went, taking class after class, enjoying each one along the way to a fuller, formal education.

After working at various universities for years and loving every aspect of education, my eighth and final degree was completed. I had realized my dream of becoming a psychologist.

Education is a lifelong process, and I managed to reach my goal over the years by taking one class at a time. My grandma would have been proud of the final result.

When I graduated, a friend — one of the few who knew of my inspiration from the comic strip — gave me a framed picture of Lucy hard at work in her makeshift office. I hung it on my office wall. Many people saw it and commented on how much they liked the iconic comic strip. But only Grandma and I knew the whole story.

— Donna L. Roberts —

23

Simple Courage

Success is not final, failure is not fatal:
it is the courage to continue that counts.
~Winston Churchill

Chaperoning a group of teens at our state's annual youth convention kept me busy, so I looked forward to free time one afternoon when we would all unwind by doing crafts. That's where I first noticed Jenny checking out the available projects. It was hard not to notice her. As she walked about the room with other teens, her limbs jerked unpredictably. Even when she tried to stand still, muscle spasms seized an arm and threw it into the air or wrenched her head to the side. Kids would glance up in surprise and then look away quickly. My heart ached to see how cerebral palsy affected her life.

Before long, Jenny settled on a wood-burning project and began gathering her supplies. Since I was never good at artistic endeavors, it didn't much matter which craft I chose, so I sat across from her. I picked up a thin plank of wood and penciled my last name on it with a little flower in the corner. That was the extent of my creative abilities. Meanwhile, Jenny sketched intently on her plaque. Soon, a handsome cardinal sat on a branch surrounded by dogwood blooms.

"Pretty," I said.

She smiled.

I picked up the hot, wood-burning tool to begin. How would Jenny complete her project without burning herself? She didn't. I

Give It a Try | 75

winced each time her spastic movements elicited another "Ouch!" But under Jenny's hands, a beautiful image took shape.

Dutifully searing my name into my piece of wood, I struck up a conversation. "What county are you from?"

"Pontotoc." Even her voice quivered from the effects of her disorder.

"That's not too far from us. What project area are you in?"

"Clothing."

"Oh, do you sew?" I marveled that she could control her hands enough to do such intricate work.

Her bright eyes looked straight into mine. "I sew some, but I'm here to compete in the clothing selection contest. We coordinate outfits from clothes we buy at the store. I'll model my outfit this evening at the general assembly."

Model? The night before, some of the youth had made rude noises and hurled insults at talent contest participants. She was going in front of that group? They would eat her alive!

I gave her my best encouraging smile. "I'll watch for you."

Later that day, I entered the auditorium with trepidation, remembering Jenny. After everyone sat down, the lights dimmed and the clothing selection contestants lined up onstage. I could pick out Jenny even at that distance. She stood in a model's pose just like all the other girls, but occasionally her head or arm twitched unbidden.

When it came time for Jenny to walk the "runway," I held my breath. The teens had clapped politely for the other contestants, but what would they do when Jenny lurched across the stage? A burned finger might be pleasant compared to this. I felt as nervous as if I were the one appearing in front of all those people with so little control over my body. Would I ever have found the courage to do it? I closed my eyes and prayed as my new friend took her first few steps in front of 600 kids.

For a moment, there was dead silence. Then the entire audience broke into thunderous applause. Tears streamed down my cheeks as I clapped, too.

Cerebral palsy may have controlled Jenny's movements, but it didn't control her life. With quiet courage, she demonstrated what she could accomplish with a positive attitude. Drawing, sewing, modeling? No problem. All she had to do was try. Whether her body cooperated or not, Jenny was determined to be happy doing the things she loved.

From that day on, I stopped thinking about what I couldn't do and focused on what I could. Following Jenny's example, I've walked a few runways I wouldn't normally have attempted and found happiness waiting at the end.

Sometimes, courage is putting one foot in front of the other.

— Tracy Crump —

24

Can't Is a Four-Letter Word

Never give up on what you really want to do.
The person with big dreams is more powerful
than the one with all the facts.
~H. Jackson Brown, Jr.

After twenty years of marriage, I suddenly found myself a divorced mother of two with a mortgage and a car payment. At the time, I was a waitress in a small, family-owned business. My husband had informed me that he'd never really wanted children, that they were my idea, and that he was leaving.

I had never dreamed that I would end up divorced. The biggest surprise after my divorce was the reaction of my church family. I had truly expected that the very people who had stood next to me singing, "I love you with the love of the Lord," would stand by me. Unfortunately, they did not. To them, divorce was an unpardonable sin. When I had stated that no one hated divorce more than I did, I was told that if I'd truly hated it, I wouldn't be getting divorced, as if I could somehow have stopped it. I'd never felt more alone in my life, but I forgave their ignorance.

I loved my children, and I did whatever it took to provide for them. I worked as many as three jobs, with little to no child support. One Easter week, I worked so many hours that I ended up in the hospital from exhaustion.

Not once did a bill go unpaid. Not once did my children go without anything they needed. The concept of failure was not in my vocabulary. To me, "can't" was a four-letter word.

A regular breakfast customer at my restaurant suggested that I apply for a job at the post office. They were hiring temporary help. What did I have to lose? I went to the human-resources department at our local post office and asked to apply. She told me they weren't hiring. When I told my friend the next day, he told me to go back, so I did. Again, I was told that they weren't hiring. A week later, I went back again. This time, she took my application.

I was hired for a temporary position as a "Casual," making $7.00 an hour and working an average of 59.5 hours a week. I was only allowed to work six months out of a calendar year in any given position. It seemed ridiculous to give up my waitress jobs for a temporary position, but I knew in my heart that it was the right thing to do. I worked harder than I'd ever worked in my life. I worked six months as a carrier in every kind of weather. Then I worked six months inside as a clerk. There was no promise of a career position, but I believed I would get one.

It was difficult managing work and the kids' sports schedules. I hated missing soccer and volleyball games. The hardest thing was when I missed my son's eighth-grade graduation. It was in the afternoon, and I couldn't get off work. Believe me, I tried.

After a couple of years, I began to ask how I could get a permanent position. I was told who to talk to at the main office, and I made an appointment. I sat in his office explaining why I was there, and he listened politely. When I was finished, he laughed and said, "I'm sorry, but Casuals don't get hired for career positions." Something happened to me at that point. I became more determined than ever to prove him wrong.

Shortly after my visit to the main office, it was announced in the local paper that tests were going to be given in our city for career positions at the post office. This was my chance to get a real job. I went to a bookstore and ordered the practice test manual for clerk/carrier positions. For the next six weeks, I took timed practice tests every spare second I had. I even took a memorization class offered at a local venue. I wasn't about to give up.

The day finally came for the tests, and hundreds of people showed up to take them. It was now or never. After the tests, we had to wait for what felt like an eternity to learn our score. When mine came in the mail, I was afraid to open it. I'd gotten a 91.5... success.

After I'd gotten my uniforms and completed my ninety-day probationary period, the man who told me I'd never get a career position came into our office. When he saw me casing mail, he stopped and said, "Well, I'll be. You actually did it."

I just smiled and said, "'Can't' isn't in my vocabulary. Never tell a woman she can't do something."

Last year, I retired from the postal service after a twenty-two-year career as a letter carrier. My children are both married, and I have five beautiful grandsons. My children saw me refuse to give up and I believe it made them who they are today. And the friend who suggested I apply at the post office? We're married and enjoying retired life together. Nothing can stop us when we refuse to give up on ourselves.

— Brenda Beattie —

25

Yes, I Will

Spirit has fifty times the strength and staying power
of brawn and muscle.
~Mark Twain

I stared up at the ascent from the trailhead. I had a lot riding on this hike. Just one year before, I had vowed to hike to the summit of Heart Mountain after my husband and father declared that I'd "never make it."

What they said hadn't come from a place of discouragement, but from concern for my safety. I had become sedentary and gained a lot of weight. I was sad and angry at myself for letting my life become so narrow.

I had always enjoyed hiking and being in the mountains, so I was determined not to let anything, mentally or physically, stop me from hiking to the top of a mountain I had admired since I was a kid. I wanted to get back a piece of myself I had lost.

Now I was with a large group, all family, and I was determined to make it to the top. My cousin and her kids started off at a rapid pace. My husband and I lagged behind a bit, with my father and uncle behind us.

"You don't have to stick with me," I told my husband.

"Are you sure?" he asked. He knew how much this hike meant to me, and I had made him promise not to let me quit.

I nodded. "I need to go at my own pace, and right now I'm trying to keep up with you. Dad is still behind me. I'm not alone."

I knew my husband would treat the hike like he did every goal. He would plow through until it was finished. My legs felt strong, but I couldn't keep up with him.

He gave me another unsure look. "I said I would help you."

"Well," I paused to catch my breath, "I think it will help me more to know I'm not holding you back."

I could tell he was torn, but he honored my wishes and continued at his own pace, soon catching up with my cousin and her kids.

The foothills were harder than I thought they'd be. With the lack of trees, it was hot, even though it was early in the morning. I found myself getting dizzy.

You're about to have heatstroke, and you haven't even made it to the tree line. You better quit now, my brain said. *You'll never make it to the top.*

I stopped, drank some water, splashed my face and then started walking again. *Yes, I will,* said my heart.

I could no longer see my husband, cousin, and her two kids, but I told myself to take more breaks. As strong as my legs felt, I was still feeling the altitude and becoming breathless.

If you keep resting every five steps, you'll never make it, my brain snapped.

Yes, I will, my heart said back, continuing up the trail.

Soon, my father and uncle caught up with me. My dad looked at me and smiled. "Tough hike, huh?"

I nodded. "Yeah, but I got this."

His smile grew. "I know you do."

I continued to hike with my father and uncle, thankful for the frequent stops my uncle made to take pictures. Even so, I found myself falling behind.

"Please, go at your own pace," I encouraged them. "I'll be all right."

"This pace is working just fine for us," they countered.

They're afraid you're going to hurt yourself. You will. You're never going to make it to the top.

"Yes, I will," I whispered as I trudged forward.

We continued to hike up the foothills, and I let out a sigh of relief when we made it to the tree line. We rested in the shade for a moment, taking pictures with the "Heart Mountain Trail" sign and then continued up the trail. I was feeling much better now that we were walking in the shade, and my confidence grew.

We reached the information kiosk and studied it, trying to see how much farther we had to hike. I took out my phone to snap some pictures and was surprised to see a text from my husband. "We aren't even at the top, and the view is insane. Keep going."

I smiled and texted him back, letting him know we were at the kiosk.

"I think we have just over a mile to go," said my father. "But it's going to be all uphill, so it'll feel like more."

You barely made it up the foothills. Turn back now, my brain pleaded.

I pulled on my backpack. "Let's get started then."

My dad wasn't lying. I had thought the foothills were steep, but they paled in comparison to the switchbacks we were now facing.

This is too hard, said my brain. *Just turn around now and try again next year after you've better prepared yourself. You'll never make it.*

"Yes, I will," I muttered as Uncle Bill stopped to take a picture.

I stared at the view. My husband had been right; it was amazing.

This is good enough. If you keep going, you won't be able to make it back down. You're too fat.

I was close to tears. The summit seemed so far away. Everything hurt, and I felt way out of my league. *You'll never make it.*

I forced my sore feet to walk and started up the trail. "Yes, I will."

As we neared the top, the switchbacks became shorter and steeper. I found myself grabbing onto trees to steady myself as I fought for breath. *Stop now, or they will be carrying you down the mountain on a stretcher. You can't do this.*

"Yes, I can," I said loudly, causing my dad to turn and look at me. I gave him a halfhearted wave, praying he wouldn't see my tears and make me stop.

I continued to repeat, *Yes, I will,* in my head with every step, too tired to say the words out loud, and refusing to let any more negative thoughts infiltrate my mind. My tears flowed freely as I pushed myself beyond exhaustion.

Yes, I will. Yes, I will. Yes, I will.

I only allowed myself to look a few feet ahead, concentrating only on what was immediately before me. I continued my mantra with every painful step.

Yes, I will. Yes, I will. Yes, I will.

When I heard cheers from my husband, cousin, and her kids, I finally gave myself permission to look up. I had made it to the summit. My tears of exhaustion were replaced with tears of joy and relief.

I scrambled to the very top and sat down to take in the view at 8,123 feet. I tried to organize my thoughts, but all I could think was, *Yes, I did.*

—Jennifer McMurrain—

26

Seeing with Your Heart

The purpose of life is to contribute in some way
to making things better.
~Robert F. Kennedy

It was a beautiful Southern California morning, complete with blue sky, a cool breeze and warm sunlight. I walked through the parking lot of the shopping plaza thinking of little else than my rendezvous with a pecan roll at the local bakery. As I strolled in front of the grocery store adjacent to the bakeshop, I noticed a young woman standing next to the store entrance with bags of groceries neatly stacked. As is my practice with strangers, I made eye contact with her and said with a smile, "Hello, there! And how are you today?"

She smiled back and responded with a Southern accent, "I'm fine, sir. How are you?"

"I'm doing well, thank you!"

I had only taken a few steps past her when I heard her say, "Thank you for seeing me!"

Her words brought me to a stop. Still smiling, I turned around and walked over to her, extending my hand. "My name's Mark. What's yours?"

For the next twenty minutes, I listened with rapt attention to Dominique share her story. She had grown up in Louisiana where her mother and sisters still lived. Three years ago, a family tragedy prompted her to make the move to California, where without contacts or the promise of employment, she had managed to create a life of purpose and fulfillment. She spoke with an easy Southern charm and a smile that radiated joy.

A car pulled up to the curb. Dominique introduced me to the driver, a friend of hers. I helped her load the groceries into the back seat. She thanked me and opened the front passenger-side door. "My daddy used to say that a person will remember how you made them feel long after they've forgotten what you said. I know I'll remember this for a long time." I smiled, knowing I would as well. The car drove away, but I stood there for a moment longer before stepping inside the bakery.

Sipping my coffee, with the remnants of a pecan roll on my plate, I looked around the bakery at the people there. I nodded to the regulars sitting at their favorite tables, some reading the daily newspaper, others on their laptops. Business types hurried to the counter to pick up the orders they had phoned in. I smiled while thinking about what I had just experienced with Dominique — two strangers who had made a connection based on nothing more than shared humanity.

Every person has a story to tell if we're willing to take the time to listen. Greeting a stranger with a smile and a kind word is a very small thing to do and yet can have a profound effect on both people. One of my favorite quotes is from Mother Teresa: "Not all of us can do great things, but we can do small things with great love." I have found that the benefit of doing these small things not only helps me maintain a positive outlook on life, but may even sow a few seeds of hope for someone else.

Perhaps I'm ascribing too much significance to the potential of what a simple "hello" between two strangers can do. Certainly, not all of my encounters are as dramatic as the one I shared with Dominique. And yet, I cannot shy away from doing it simply because I don't know how the other person might react. I have done this hundreds of times over the past few years, and it has never been met with anything other than a positive response.

When I share with others what I do and encourage them to give it a try, I'm usually met with comments like, "Well, that's easy for you,

Mark. You're an outgoing person." At that point, I assure them that I am anything but outgoing. Yes, it has become easier over the years, but I still have to make a conscious effort to do it.

When somebody steps up beside me at the self-serve coffee for a refill, rather than turn to them and say, "Hello! How are you doing today?" my natural inclination is to remain silent and mind my own business.

Dominique's words, "Thank you for seeing me," reminded me of a conversation I had with a friend just a week prior. He and I were sharing our perceptions on how technology is redefining human relationships. Social media is creating a society where we are becoming more connected, but less relational — a society where we can all be alone… together. We are in danger of losing the ability to have real conversations.

> *"Thank you for seeing me!"*

Don't get me wrong. I always enjoy reading a text from my wife or daughter that says, "Thinking of you. Love you." I'm on Facebook and find it useful to keep tabs on what's going on with my friends. (I especially appreciate the birthday notifications.) But no number of texts, tweets or Facebook posts will ever amount to having a *real* conversation with another person. A person can be inundated with electronic communication and still feel alone. People have a need to be seen. A need to be heard. A need to be treated as if they matter. Because they do.

One particular restaurant chain understands this. New employees are required to watch a short, three-minute customer-training video that captures a few minutes of activity inside one of their restaurants. A simple, instrumental soundtrack with captions appears whenever the camera focuses on an actor portraying either a customer or staff member. Each caption gives a brief description of one aspect of that person's life at that moment before moving on to the next person.

The snippets of information cover the spectrum, from joyful and celebratory to somber and even heart wrenching. One caption for an older male customer reads: "After years of battling cancer, he is finally free of the disease." Another one for a female staff member reads: "Worked hard through high school, was accepted to the college of her dreams." Still another for an elderly woman sitting by herself in a booth reads: "Husband died one month ago. Today would have been their fiftieth anniversary."

It doesn't take much to brighten the day of a stranger. To smile. To offer a friendly greeting. To engage in a brief conversation. To see someone. And it makes me feel so good.

So don't be surprised if one day a bespectacled, white-haired man walks up to you smiling and says, "Hello, there! And how are you doing today?" It might just be me!

— Mark Mason —

27

Just Start

There is something magical about running;
after a certain distance, it transcends the body.
Then a bit farther, it transcends the mind.
~Kristin Armstrong

I was standing in my family room in my running clothes, struggling with an armband that was supposed to hold my iPhone. "Wouldn't it be amazing if we could pay someone to exercise for us, and the calories would still magically disappear from our bodies?" I said.

My husband looked at me as if I were nuts.

"That would be cheating."

"Yes and no," I replied. "We'd still be paying for a legitimate service, but we wouldn't have to suffer the hard work of doing it ourselves, or the consequences."

"Like losing weight and being healthy?"

"Well, yeah, now that you mention it...."

To me, running was the worst thing in the world. Running was for athletes or people who liked to hurt themselves. Running was for anyone but me.

"Hon," he said, "that's how you and I both got into this mess."

I nodded, fiddled with my armband again and gave up. It would be annoying regardless of how the phone sat on my arm. I needed it to listen to music, to distract myself from how much this was going to hurt.

I also needed it so I could hear the computer voice of my mile tracker telling me how much closer I would be to dying with every passing mile.

There is some exaggeration in this description, but not much. I wasn't getting any younger. And the pounds weren't exactly disappearing as I ate what I wanted and hoped for the best. Said pounds were slowly creeping to my thighs and backside. Actually, they were creeping everywhere. As my doctor put it, "I think it may be time to put some exercise into your schedule."

My only hope for combating age would be with exercise. So here I was about to embark on the very thing I disliked.

"Hon," my husband said again, interrupting my thoughts, "it really won't be so bad. You just have to get started."

I smirked at him. "Right," I said as he continued to eat breakfast and relaxed deeper into the soft folds of the leather sofa. *His time will come,* I thought. *His time will come.*

Meanwhile, my time was right in front of my nose. I had to just do it… and try to make it back alive. "If you don't hear from me in a half-hour, come look for me. I could be on the side of the road… dead."

My husband didn't even look at me. Instead, he took a sip of his coffee while watching the weather forecast and said, "You'll do great!"

It was dark and cold outside but I wasn't going to turn back. I needed to run for my health. I needed to run for my family's health. I needed to run so I could get back to drinking a nice hot cup of coffee.

I fired up the music and my running tracker, and began to run.

The air was obscenely crisp, and I could hear my thighs squishing together as I lumbered along. But in a matter of minutes the air became less crisp and I found a steady rhythm. The music was loud and it was working. I was running… I was actually doing it!

I replayed my husband's words as I smelled the morning air, thick with apple blossoms. "You just have to get started." By golly, the man was right. And not only was he right, but the concept was applicable to nearly everything around me.

Getting started was the sticking point of all the good things in life. I even said those words to my kids when they didn't want to do their homework. The sooner they started, the sooner it would be over. And all they had to do to get there was to start!

But it took me taking my own advice—and my husband's reminding—that this was true for me, too. From starting a diet to a new running program—heck, it was how I got out of bed every day. I just had to start!

I did make it home that morning. I didn't die, and my husband didn't find me lying on the side of the road. Years later, I'm still running and I still don't like it. My lungs still scream for mercy and my legs get a workout

> *Getting started was the sticking point of all the good things in life.*

that shouldn't even be possible with this many years under my belt, but they do.

I wasn't made for running, but I became a person made to run.

Something good comes from challenges if we're willing to look at them from an alternate point of view. For me, this view involves feet hitting the pavement and watching blind corners in the early morning darkness so I don't trip and fall on my face.

Running changed my health, and it changed every facet of my life. I don't have to like it, but getting up early and starting my day doing something that isn't easy makes me feel like I've accomplished something huge.

Starting may be the hardest part, but starting is also the way to achieving everything we want.

And that is something I can run circles around any day.

—Heather Spiva—

Chapter 4

The Power of Attitude

28

A New Way of Thinking Big

Each time we face our fear, we gain strength,
courage, and confidence in the doing.
~Theodore Roosevelt

If anyone had listened in on my thoughts during the first few weeks of my community college Introduction to Business class, they would have heard, *What if my answer is wrong? I'll look like such an idiot. The teacher will hate me. My classmates will hate me. I'll end up wasting everybody's time. I'd better not mess this up.*

Add in a bit of nervous knee knocking and the intense desire to hide — or, at the very least, to start nibbling my fingernails down to the quick — and they'd have the entire picture.

You see, my professor was a retired criminal lawyer, and he had a unique way of going over the answers to our class's weekly quizzes. For each question, he would call on a random student and ask for their answer. Then he would proceed to grill the student mercilessly, forcing him or her to defend that answer — after which he'd ask the class to vote on whether they agreed, or whether they believed that the hapless student was "full of sh*t." If the latter, a new student was picked to give a different answer, and the whole process would begin again.

It was certainly a memorable way to review, and if I'd been a more experienced student, it probably wouldn't have thrown me. But I was just a freshman, and quiz-review days terrified me. I'd spend the entire review shrinking in my seat, praying that I wouldn't be called on.

One of my other professors saved me. In my anatomy class, we watched a TED Talk by Dr. Amy Cuddy, a social psychologist who had studied how body language affects self-confidence. Dr. Cuddy explained that humans could choose to take either "high power" or "low power" positions with their bodies. "High power" positions involve taking up as much space as possible — standing up straight, squaring your shoulders, and moving your arms and legs away from your trunk so that you look as big as you possibly can. "Low power" poses, in contrast, involve making yourself look small: tucking your head and rounding your shoulders, and keeping your arms and legs crossed and held close.

Not surprisingly, people tend to see others who habitually adopt high power poses as natural leaders, and are more willing to hire them for jobs and otherwise give them their trust. But the truly revolutionary portion of Dr. Cuddy's research was not the effect of high-powered body language on others; it was the effect it had on the person taking the poses. She found that spending just two minutes standing in a high power pose measurably increased a person's feelings of power and self-confidence. And she wanted all of her viewers to try it out for themselves.

"Before you go into the next stressful evaluative situation, for two minutes, try doing this," she encouraged.

So I did.

I arrived ten minutes early to class on the next quiz-review day, just as I always had. However, instead of hunching over my book studying quietly while I waited for class to begin, I tried something new. I sat up straight and spread my feet out wide underneath the table. I spread out my books and notebooks, too, using the entire surface of my desk. When my classmates started trickling in, I smiled at them and said, "Good morning," instead of hiding behind my phone. And when our teacher arrived and asked if anyone had any questions about the material before we began our quiz review, I actually raised my hand — not with the tiny, elbow-on-table-and-hand-at-chest-level gesture I usually made, but by throwing my arm up straight and high.

"I am big," I told myself. "I am strong. It is all right to be seen and take up space."

The effect of this was astounding.

My professor answered my question calmly and politely, as if he were talking to a colleague. There was none of the belittling language he sometimes used. But even more important was the way my inner dialogue had changed. When the review started, instead of thinking, *Oh gosh, oh gosh, oh gosh, what if I get this answer wrong?* I had a revolutionary new thought instead: *Well, so what if I am wrong?* A wonderful feeling of calm descended over me. Suddenly, I realized that the important thing was simply that I was participating. I didn't need to be right. I just needed to engage fully in the class and learn, like everyone else.

Now, this was an attitude many people, including my parents and my best friend, had often tried to communicate to me before. It had never really sunk in. But something about taking the "high power" pose made the same thoughts come, not from someone talking outside of me, but from the inside of my very own brain. And the feeling of peace that came with it was incredible.

Eventually, I earned an A in that class, but the real success was in finding that sense of peace. Today, every time I need to make a presentation or take a test, I spend a few minutes "thinking big" — giving myself permission to take up space and be seen, to stand up tall and strong. It never fails to calm me down and help me to know in my bones that it really is okay just to be present and do my best. And when I do, my best always turns out to be pretty darn good.

— Kerrie R. Barney —

29

Biking to Life

Encourage, lift and strengthen one another. For the
positive energy spread to one will be felt by us all.
For we are connected, one and all.
~Deborah Day

I was fifty-three — a healthy, athletic, vegetarian, non-smoking daily runner. How could I have breast cancer? Nobody else in my family had ever had it.

I barely had time to process the news from my doctor, what with all the appointments, X-rays, and consultations. After several weeks, we had a plan. The cancer was very small. I would have a lumpectomy with radiation — to make sure nothing was left behind. I was going to the University of Michigan Rogel Cancer Center, a premier medical center. I was in good hands, and the treatment was straightforward. In a few months, it would all be behind me. I was one of the lucky ones — stage 1 cancer, great surgeons, early detection, a supportive husband and wonderful friends, including the seven girlfriends I ran with every morning.

After the lumpectomy, my doctor gave me a thumbs-up. Everything went well. She felt sure the surgery had gotten beyond the borders of my cancer, and the radiation would be just an insurance policy. Then, five days later, I got the phone call.

The cancer had spread. My doctor had biopsied one of my lymph nodes, and it was cancerous. I put down the phone and cried. All my natural optimism drained away. This meant more surgeries and chemotherapy. All those upbeat proclamations from my doctors were no longer true. I really might die.

I had more biopsies and surgeries to remove lymph nodes. Then I spent an entire long summer and fall in chemotherapy. By the time it was over, I looked like a bald, skinny chicken heading for the chopping block. My running girlfriends, who had been bringing me chicken soup for months, switched to chocolate-chip cookies and cheesecake in an effort to fatten me up so I could get back on the running trail. But I was so wiped out that I spent most days in a huge leather chair reading books on overcoming cancer. And I still had radiation to go through.

I didn't want to make the long round trip to the University of Michigan for radiation every day for six and a half weeks, so I found a hospital only eight miles away from home.

"You don't need to drive me," I told my husband Paul. "It's close enough that I can drive myself."

He crossed his arms and looked at me for a long minute. "It's close enough that you could bike it."

"Huh?" I could barely muster the energy to walk to the mailbox.

"You can do it," he said. He pulled out a map and a highlighter and drew a route from our subdivision, down side streets and other neighborhoods, through a little woods and finally to a long, wide sidewalk that ended up across the street from the entrance to Henry Ford Hospital radiation center.

"I'll bike with you the first time," he said.

I was exhausted, but I was also tired of feeling like a punching bag. Suddenly, I wanted to do this, to prove that I still had some control, even if it was only choosing how I got to the hospital every day.

That first morning was a slog. Paul led the way, and I pedaled behind slowly. It was the very end of August, hot and dry. Little kids running through sprinklers, people washing their cars and other bikers waved at us. I felt a little confused, like I didn't belong out there in the world with the rest of the people. Could I really bike eight miles? And then turn around and bike eight miles back home? I hadn't done anything physical for months. But this bike ride on this day had become an answer to all that I had been through — the beginning of my journey back to myself. After my radiation, I came home and collapsed in the leather chair for the rest of the day. I felt like I had climbed Mt. Everest.

Paul biked with me the next couple days just to make sure I knew the route, and then he had to get back to work. "You can do it. You know you can."

I nodded, put on my bike helmet and went outside. There, next to my bike, was Anita — blond, fit and smiling. She was straddling her bike. "You ready?" She laughed at my expression. "If you can't run with me, I'll bike with you."

And that's how it began. Anita biked the eight miles with me that day. She sat in the waiting room during my radiation treatment, and she biked the eight miles home with me. The next morning, Nelle was waiting outside. And then Jan. I had known my girlfriends for years. We had run together and raised our kids together, through thick and thin. Who knew that what I thought was a "thin" would turn out to be such a "thick"?

With my girlfriends beside me, I looked forward to that bike ride every day. We told jokes, chewed bubblegum, and sang old pep-rally songs. We complained about the heat, and then we complained about the cold when autumn arrived. Anyone seeing us laughing and chatting away never would have guessed our destination. I didn't care what the weather was like anymore — I was on a mission, and I was getting stronger. I would never drive to radiation. It could rain — and it did. Still we biked. The temperatures dropped into the low thirties. Jan and I put on long underwear under our sweats — and biked away.

Our cheerful chatter as we burst into the cancer ward morning after morning attracted attention. The nurses watched us through the glass doors as we dragged our bikes into the anteroom. They cheered our fortitude when we peeled off dripping rain gear. My doctor, who knew of my "mission," asked me every morning if I was still biking. One rainy morning when I biked through a muddy patch, my tire slipped, and I went down, slicing my knee. The crowd in the waiting room parted for us as I limped in, torn and bloodied, and I was taken immediately to the doctor. Even with injuries, even through the rain and the cold, Doctor Gable never told me not to bike. She said, "Keep it up. You'll be stronger when this is over."

And, one day, it was over. Anita and I biked the last eight miles to the hospital one cold day in October. The nurses cheered as we entered. Doctor Gable appeared in the waiting room. She held out her arms, and I walked into them. "You did it."

Yes, I did it. But it was Anita, too, and all my friends. It was Paul and Dr. Gable. It was the sun and the rain and the woods and all the people we biked past every day. What a gift it was to be alive.

— Ingrid Tomey —

30

Playing All the Angles

Turn your obstacles into opportunities
and your problems into possibilities.
~Roy T. Bennett, The Light in the Heart

"Yes! Yes! I did it, I did it!" I shouted as I jumped up and down in exhilaration. Okay, maybe I was a little more exuberant than the occasion called for. I had just beaten my wife at pool, banking a shot off the bumper and knocking in the eight ball in the game room of our building. From my reaction, you would have thought I took down Minnesota Fats in a winner-take-all billiards match.

Before we moved in, pool was not my game of choice. I had played at times growing up, but I wasn't very good at it and never developed a fondness for the game. However, we had vowed to use the amenities in our new residence, and thus we were shooting pool. My wife and I played once a week, and we usually found the table unoccupied. It seemed like our private game room, and I even found myself playing games against myself on my days off.

As time went by, I started to improve. I also enjoyed playing more than I ever had in the past. I felt confident enough in my game to say that I was not bad. I wasn't running down to any pool parlors to hustle the locals, but I had a newfound appreciation of the game.

One Sunday night I had a breakthrough. I suddenly started to visualize things on the table that I didn't know were there or even existed before. As a novice, I had only seen the obvious shots in front of me. But now I started to see all kinds of options that were previously missing. Maybe they were hidden by other balls impeding their path, or I would need to have taken advanced calculus to figure out the angles to make it work, but a whole new world of possibilities opened up for me.

What I didn't realize until that day was how shooting pool imitated life.

It didn't all come to fruition that night. As part of my effort to improve during the previous months, I practiced different shots just to see what happened. If there was a gimme available or a shot that required more skill, I opted for the tougher option. It was easy to take the path of least resistance, but it was much more rewarding when I accomplished something I had thought was out of my reach. I figured the easy alternative would still be there, and I could learn how the ball bounces, so to speak, when going out of my comfort zone.

I was amazed by my discovery. I didn't just see balls on a table. I saw answers to life's questions by seeing what wasn't always visible to the naked eye. Some would say I was "thinking outside the box," but I think the term has become a cliché. I learned to look beyond the obvious and open my mind to different ideas and solutions than I previously thought possible.

> *I give myself the chance to make decisions that will give me the outcome I want.*

Now I don't just accept what's in front of me. I give myself the chance to make decisions that will give me the outcome I want. I look at things from every angle; I play every angle.

When I play pool, I examine every option before I commit to a shot. I want to make sure I have left nothing to chance. I ask myself: Is there a better opportunity somewhere else on the table?

It's amazing how pool mirrors life. You can set yourself up for your next shot if you execute properly. In the game of life, every adventure or step along the way creates a pathway to your destination.

The answers are there if you search them out. You have to put in the work. Getting better at pool or at life takes practice. As I was getting better at pool, I got cocky and tried to jump steps ahead before

I was ready. When I didn't give a shot the time it deserved, I failed. I saw the folly of my ways and recommitted to staying consistent and sticking to the plan.

When I look at the table now, I know what to look for. The answers aren't always there, but I keep searching to find them, whether it's experimenting with a shot to see what happens or setting myself up for the next opportunity before me.

Having spent my life in sales, I've learned the wisdom of this saying: "Until you get your first 'no,' the process hasn't even started." I can choose to see a situation as hopeless, or I can visualize the possibilities, whether it's on the pool table or in my life.

That breakthrough changed my life. One minute, I saw the same table I had looked at countless times before; the next, a totally new vision popped up out of nowhere. Now I rack them up, break, and watch the balls scatter. And not just when I'm playing pool.

— Darrell Horwitz —

31

I'm Wonderful!

The habit of being happy enables one to be freed,
or largely freed, from the domination
of outward conditions.
~Robert Louis Stevenson

When I was a young mother, I decided to venture into the workforce. I needed a job that would allow me to be home with my children when they needed me most. Tupperware home parties were the answer for many of us during the 1960s and 1970s. I was fortunate to have an incredible trainer who not only developed in me a positive mindset, but also left me with a winning outlook on life.

I can still hear her first words in our training class: "Hi, class. How are you?" The answers varied around the room — fine, okay, scared, etc. But her next words have stayed with me forever: "That is a polite question. No one but your mother really cares about an honest answer!" From then on, when asked how we felt, we all said, "Wonderful!"

I made "wonderful" part of my everyday language. One morning when I went out to get the newspaper, my neighbor said, "Hi, how are you?"

I replied, "Wonderful. How are you?"

She said, "Are you always wonderful? Don't you ever have a bad day?"

"Sure, I do," I said, "but if I told you all my problems, it wouldn't make either of us feel better. Plus, saying 'wonderful' keeps me thinking and feeling that way."

Feeling "wonderful" is a choice every day. It's certainly easier to give in to the pressures of life, to let negativity invade our minds and souls. However, saying "I'm wonderful" at least once a day can become a habit that will change your life and the lives of those around you.

> *Feeling "wonderful" is a choice every day.*

Several years into my Tupperware career, my trainer (now mentor) asked that I start teaching her classes. I was excited every day to teach all the life-changing lessons I had learned. Of course, every class began with "I'm wonderful." My new attendees were aspiring Tupperware managers. They had heard and hopefully said, "I'm wonderful," many times by now. After my class, one of my students approached me and said, "You always say you're wonderful, but you can't be wonderful all the time."

I looked at her and responded, "My grandmother is dying! I have three teenage daughters who are a handful! I'm going through a divorce! I may have to sell my home! And I have a yeast infection! Does that make you feel better?"

She said an immediate "No," and I said, "Well, it doesn't make me feel better either! So, I'm wonderful."

Everyone has their own problems and daily issues. We can choose to share them with the world and all feel bad together, or we can simply say "wonderful" and change the dynamic!

— Kristine Byron —

32

How I Rebuilt My Life Using the Joy Test

Change your thoughts, and you change your world.
~Norman Vincent Peale

I knew I'd made it when I drove to my former house to pick up the kids and felt, well, nothing. Those ugly pangs I'd felt driving up into that stylishly hip enclave each week for the past two years? Gone. The lurch of emotion I'd felt when their dad came to the door to wave hello? Also gone.

Instead, I felt peace. I looked at the beautiful landscaping I'd overseen, the terraced river rocks and weeping cherry trees. I looked at the car of my ex's new partner parked out front and thought, *It all worked out.*

I was deeply proud of that feeling because I had never worked so hard at happiness in my life.

I had known, when I decided to leave two years prior, that I had a lot of work ahead of me. I had made the decision one cold Monday morning — the same week I lost my lucrative law job and just a few months after my mother's sudden death. I'd been waiting for the right moment, and that was it.

I knew I had the moxie to rebuild the external parts of life, like a house and job. But I didn't know if I could do the really hard part: move past the anger and hurt that had marred much of our eighteen-year marriage. I didn't know if I could fully mend my internal life.

My mother never fully recovered from her own unhappy forty-three-year marriage or from my dad's decision to leave her at age seventy. She made a brave effort after he left, but she also cut his picture out of every photo album, filled spiral notebooks with rage at the "SCOM" (self-centered old man), and recounted each point in her life when she knew she should have left but didn't. Although she found peace and forgiveness during the very last month of her life, neither that nor dementia erased the decades of pain she had endured. Anger kills.

I wasn't exactly sure how to go about reshaping my internal life, so I just felt my way. Looking back, here's how I did it:

1. Ban anything that doesn't bring joy.
2. Actively seek joy.
3. Work at gratitude in general.
4. Work at gratitude toward my ex.
5. Repeat steps 1–4, as needed.
6. Presto! End up at forgiveness.

If I had read a list like that two years earlier, when I was scared and alone, waiting for my real estate agent to show me yet another so-so house, I would have tossed it in the trash. I didn't have the list back then, but as I felt my way along, the strategy developed.

Those first few months, I used the Joy Test for everything. I'd only let people or things into my new life that brought joy. How would I know? I'd sit still and focus on that inner voice, the one I had ignored for so many years as I sought status and stability instead of true happiness.

I used the Joy Test to buy my first house. I was unemployed, and it was the bottom of winter, so I did not have a lot of options. Still, I eventually picked a sweet little house that felt relaxing the minute I walked in. It was not fancy, but it felt like home.

I furnished that house the same way. I brought next to nothing from my marital house. I wanted to start over. My rule was that if I didn't love it, I didn't buy it. Canopy bed with gauzy curtains so I could pretend I lived in a hacienda? Yes! Stuffy dining-room set that I would rarely use and would remind me how much I disliked dinner parties? Nope.

It was the same thing with my job search. I kept interviewing until I found a great fit. At times, it was humiliating to watch the cars leave my block every morning while mine sat with nowhere to go but yoga class or the grocery store. I told myself I was on "sabbatical" and I was lucky to have such a low-key life.

I only invited people over whom I trusted. People make a lot of offhand comments about divorce, not understanding it's something that no woman wishes on herself and no mother wishes on her children. Those gossipmongers who were eager to tell me about my ex's new girlfriends? Bye. The friend who also lost her job and marriage at the same time and sat with me on my pretty porch every morning? I will love her forever.

Since I am not passive about anything, I also decided to seek out Joy actively. I thought about the things that made me truly happy and did them. I joined a friend in New Orleans for Jazz Fest and spent the weekend in her wake, buoyed by her infectious spirit, rakish fedora and easy laugh. I celebrated a friend's birthday in Spain, reveling in the beauty of the place and of women's friendships. I grew my hair longer and started wearing skirts. I became a competitive, open-water swimmer. I never looked, or felt, better.

I decided to date, but only if it included dancing. Dancing has been a source of joy for me since I started sneaking into nightclubs at age fourteen, and I wanted to be with a man who understood that. I was lucky to find him on my first try. Like me, he was newly separated and heartbroken. Like me, dancing had been the center of his young life and was still a part of his mature one. We met, clicked, and started dancing it all out together. We signed up for ballroom dance lessons because the dancing—and relationships—that had defined our youths were over. We were both eager to grow, as dancers and partners.

But joy alone is not enough. My ultimate goal was forgiveness. I played that India Arie song, "Heart of the Matter," again and again until I stopped crying when she sang, "It's about forgiveness, forgiveness, even if, even if you don't love me anymore." I understood that my ex did not love me anymore. I also understood that it was okay, and I had to forgive him. And myself.

I was not exactly sure how to make that happen, so I practiced simple gratitude. I was grateful that my fancy law job had given me a severance package, and my mother's untimely death had given me a modest inheritance. It was not lost on me that I enjoyed a life of health and privilege. I made sure that pro bono legal work and donating to charity were part of my rebuild. Every night, I also made sure to hug myself in my beautiful canopy bed, in my peaceful little house, and give thanks for all that I had.

I also made myself think nice things about my ex. I did not do this willingly. I did it in part because it seemed that whenever I let myself think really dark, vengeful thoughts, something bad would happen. I'd drop a plate. I'd stub a toe. I would remember my mother's notebooks and understand that my heart wanted to be light, not dark. "Forgiveness is a gift you give yourself." I'd read that line and felt its truth.

I made a list. We had both supported each other's post-grad education and career over the years. He had never cheated, and I saw how deeply that particular betrayal cut into women's souls.

I forced myself to say nice things about him, especially to the kids. Sometimes, I had to spit out the words, but I made myself do it. "Well, Dad is good at that." "I got that idea from Dad."

Eventually, the gratitude became easier. I'd see the pleasure (and surprise) on the children's faces when I said good things about their father, especially when I actually meant them. The day I told my daughter that I would be happy, truly happy, when my ex remarried, I realized I meant it. So did she. She gave me a big hug.

Now when I drop off the kids, I am happy to see the signs of blossoming in their life with him. Most of all, I am happy to drive back to the rich life that I built, piece by piece, joy by joy.

The work of happiness paid off.

— Joyce Lombardi —

33

Happiness Is an Inside Job

Life is 10% what happens to me and 90%
how I react to it.
~John C. Maxwell

A t my first Lions Club meeting I found myself sitting next to the happiest person I have ever known. In his late eighties, Lion Ken was a soft-spoken man with a weathered face and an impish smile. Over the next few years, I would learn about his sixty-six years of perfect meeting attendance and service.

As Ken entered his nineties, it became increasingly difficult for him to drive, so I volunteered to pick him up so he could continue to attend his beloved Lions meetings and service events. I soon cherished our weekly drives together as Ken began to share nuggets of his life with me. Over the next seven years, he thoughtfully unfolded his life story, layer by often-painful layer.

Growing up as an only child, Ken's family had little money, yet he was determined to attend college. By joining the Army ROTC, he could realize his dream to become a dentist. The year was 1942. As America found itself in World War II, Ken found himself crouched down in a landing craft crashing through the waves toward Omaha Beach. An incoming shell burst into his craft and he was wounded. He managed to scramble to safety on the beach. He would receive a Purple Heart. Shortly after, he volunteered to lead a night mission to break a Nazi stronghold. He would be awarded the Bronze Star for bravery.

Ken was among the first American troops to liberate Paris. He was appointed the Commandant for Paris and was responsible for the anti-aircraft positions protecting the Eiffel Tower, the Louvre, the Arc de Triomphe, Notre Dame Cathedral and numerous historic bridges. Decades later, he was knighted by the President of France in recognition of his efforts to preserve those historical French treasures.

Ken also fought through the horrific Battle of the Bulge. Full of hope and anticipating the end of World War II, Ken advanced into Germany, only to come face-to-face with the atrocities of the concentration camps.

Sharing these painful stories, Ken always found a way to end each car-ride vignette by sharing a positive human story of hope, whether it was about a soldier or a war-torn family that was helped. Ken would challenge me to maintain my perspective and focus. When I would say, "I have to go to work," Ken reminded me to re-frame my mind to say instead, "I *get* to go to work." It is a seemingly small change that reminds me I have the incredible power of choice and gratitude in my life, including the choice to live a life full of happiness.

Over the years, I made my pilgrimage on Saturday mornings to Ken's nursing home for coffee, donuts and conversation. One Saturday after grabbing my donut and coffee, I went to the regular table where Ken and I would visit. Ken was not there. As I stood scanning the room of seniors, a nurse approached me and shared the news. "Ken's just suffered a terrible stroke and has been rushed to the hospital." My heart sank. I will never forget walking down the long hallway of the rehabilitation facility at the University of Minnesota Medical Center. I would glance into each room to see those going through rehab as a result of stroke or brain injury. It struck me how young most of these patients were. Many were just kids.

As I approached Ken's room at the end of the hallway, I wondered, "How does this affect a ninety-five-year-old?" I expected the worst. As I entered the room, I saw a frail Ken sitting in a wheelchair. He glanced up slowly and recognized me. Quickly, he flashed his distinctive impish smile, but this time it was only half of his usual happy smile. The other half was unresponsive due to the stroke. After greeting and hugging each other, Ken proclaimed with glee, "Look, this side works!" He waved his good arm and leg.

I have often thought of that moment and wondered, *Would I have reacted in such a positive way?* That day, I learned a valuable lesson from Ken: Do not waste time worrying about what you do not have. Instead, use your energy to celebrate those things that you *do* have. Happiness is not conditional. Stop waiting for other things to make you happy. Choose to find your happiness in the present. Ken taught me that true happiness is an "inside job" and only realized when we can be happy alone within ourselves.

Ken fully recovered from his stroke, and I was able to enjoy more time with him until he passed at ninety-seven. Lion Ken taught me much about happiness. He would tell me, "Few things in life are fatal. It is certain that life will throw lemons at us, but it is up to us what we choose to do with them." I am so blessed to have been a part of his life and to hear his personal stories. Ken had become my best friend, and by the way, he was also my dad!

— Tom Guetzke —

34

Right Turn Only

To bring anything into your life,
imagine that it's already there.
~Richard Bach

I was engaged in my daily job search, and the ad just seemed to pop out at me. The job was within walking distance of my home, and it was the last day to apply. I wondered how I'd missed it before.

"I want that job," I whispered to myself, and then, trying to muster up some confidence, "That job has my name on it."

Anyone who has been out of work for a lengthy period of time knows how badly job loss can affect one's self-esteem. One moment, I was an asset to the company; the next moment, thanks to internal restructuring, I was deemed surplus. It was quite a shock. I began to question my abilities and myself.

But now, for this perfect job, I pulled up my résumé and composed what I hoped was the perfect application. As I pushed Send, I closed my eyes and told myself with every ounce of certainty I had, "I've got this job."

I started thinking about the job as if it were already mine. I pictured myself walking to and from the office building that was just one right turn away. It was a happy feeling. Being so close to home, the weather wasn't a concern, so I imagined variations of the same scene during different seasons.

A couple of days later, I received an e-mail inviting me to an interview. I was absolutely delighted! I selected what I would wear and began to envision how the interview would go. As I ran everything through my mind, I could feel my confidence build.

"I know this is my job." I spoke the words to my reflection in the mirror the day of my interview. I'd be lying if I said I didn't feel a bit nervous, but I knew that I was going to put my best foot forward and make a great impression.

It was a gorgeous summer day, and the sunshine seemed to energize me. I entered the office building and took the elevator to reception. I could clearly see myself doing this every day.

I was led into a conference room where the human resources and department managers greeted me. They had my résumé in front of them and took notes as I answered their questions.

"And when would you be able to start?" asked the department manager.

"I can start immediately," I replied, hoping they could hear my interest. A look passed between them, and I crossed my fingers. *Pick me!*

What I had seen of the office appealed to me, and I could already picture myself sitting at my desk. A sense of belonging filled me. When the interview was finished, I realized the time had passed quickly.

"We'll be in touch," said the HR manager as she escorted me back to the reception area.

"Thank you." I smiled before entering the elevator. The heavy doors slid to a close. Now it was time to play the waiting game.

I filled my mind with thoughts of success. It wasn't always easy to squelch the doubt that tried to creep in, but I did my best. I found the easiest thing to do was to continue to imagine already working at the company.

The next day, I discovered the company's human-resources department was in the process of checking my references, and I knew the wheels were in motion. By the end of the week, the desired call arrived, and my dream became reality. I accepted the job, and my heart leapt with joy.

The moment the alarm rang that first morning, I realized how wonderful it was to have time on my side. I didn't have to rush because

I didn't have to worry about traffic. By the time I was ready to leave home, I was relaxed and eager to begin my day. The sun was a brilliant beacon in the sky. As I walked, a familiar feeling rose inside me. I'd taken this walk to work many times in my mind, but now it was real!

—S.K. Naus—

35

Think Like a Winner

The key is not the will to win... everybody has that.
It is the will to prepare to win that is important.
~Bobby Knight

"I don't know why I buy raffle tickets. I never win anything!" If it hadn't been a friend saying this, I would never have gently suggested this might be the reason she never won. At almost every charity event, I overhear someone say those exact words. I have always believed if you *think* you're a winner, you *will* be.

Had that moment with my friend not happened the other night, I would not have thought about the day in late 1979 when our phone rang with amazing news.

That summer I had been thumbing through magazines and, just for fun, filled out three contest entry forms: one for cat food, one for a free trip for two to Hawaii, and one called "Join the Pepsi Generation."

In September, the cat food company sent me a check for fifty dollars. A week later, a Polaroid camera arrived from the airline that was running the travel contest; I didn't win the trip to Hawaii, but I did get the camera. And then I received a bike outfit from Pepsi because they had asked for my favorite sport on the entry form.

A few months after I did so well in those three contests, I spotted an interesting class that was being offered at Everywoman's Village, which was near our home in the San Fernando Valley. The brochure said, "Learn the art and skill of winning contests and sweepstakes." I drove over to Everywoman's Village and signed up.

Much of the fun of taking these classes was playing a guessing game with my husband. Whenever I signed up for a new class, he had to guess the subject in twenty questions, and he always nailed it. But with this latest one, I was gleeful when he got to the twentieth question without even getting close.

After describing the class, he scoffed and said, "Yeah, right. You really think there is a skill to this?" Not one to resist a challenge, I got huffy and predicted I would win something in excess of $5,000 by the end of the year. It's not that I was disgustingly confident, but I had always believed in positive thinking. And if there were some clever tools, then I intended to find out and throw my energy into this new challenge.

The teacher told us about her many "winnings" and suggested we all subscribe to a contest newsletter. Rule #1, she emphasized, was to follow the rules—exactly! If a company required entrants to send their information on a 3"x5" card in a #10 envelope, that's what one had to do. If they specified block letters, don't write in lower case. We also learned that the major prize might be a free trip to Hawaii, but the sponsor often gave away a multitude of lesser prizes—thus the Polaroid camera I got from the airline.

We were all surprised to learn that you were never required to purchase a product in order to enter a contest. We also learned the difference between a contest and a sweepstakes. A contest required only name, address, phone number and little else, while a sweepstakes might require a brief essay on why one liked a particular product.

At the end of the four weeks, the teacher reminded us of her motto: the "3 Ps"—Patience, Persistence, and Postage.

I suggested she include Positive Thinking.

I stocked up on #10 envelopes, 3"x5" cards and postage stamps. As the weeks went by and my husband saw me putting stamps on envelopes, he resisted saying anything negative.

Soon, our mail became quite interesting. We received an almost constant stream of stuff: seven Polaroid cameras, assorted T-shirts, flowers, exercise balls, potted plants, costume jewelry, books, wallets....

It was a weird but interesting mixture of "sub prizes." We gave most of them to our amazed friends.

And then, in late November, it happened — a phone call informing me I had won a fully loaded Ford Escort station wagon! It was so much fun to call my husband at his office. "Hi, honey. Sorry to bother you at work, but do you remember a prediction I made last February when I took that class in contesting?"

There was dead silence on his end until he said hesitantly, "Don't tell me you won something big."

"Yep," I said, milking the moment, and then I told him about our new car — worth more than the $5,000 I had predicted.

So, was it a large national company that awarded me the car? Nope. It was a promotion by a local newspaper. They required only a postcard with my name, address, and phone number. That was it — but I had carefully read the rules. They had specified "One postcard per family" so, of course, I followed that simple rule. When I went to the newspaper to collect my prize, they made a big deal of interviewing and photographing me for an article. I could not resist asking if there were people who did not follow the rules. I admit to feeling a bit smug when they said they had carefully gone through the entries and discarded the ones from people who had sent in more than one per family. Little did those people know that every single one of their postcards had been tossed into the round file.

The other night at a charity event, I won a nice bottle of wine and gave it to my friend, saying: "Here, enjoy! Consider it a reminder of the power of positive thinking!"

— Bobbie Jensen Lippman —

36

I Woke Up this Morning

A cloudy day is no match for a sunny disposition.
~William Arthur Ward

One of the few benefits of receiving weekly chemotherapy is free valet parking. As I got out of my car awaiting my twenty-fifth treatment, I gave my keys to a man who seemed old enough for Medicare. "Have a good day, my man," I said.

He grasped my hand and replied, "Son, I'm having a good day. I woke up this morning."

I thought about this man and his greeting for the next four hours, waiting for the last drop of the Abraxane drug to enter my bloodstream. Yes, I woke up this morning, and today is a good day! I woke up this morning next to my beautiful and faithful wife — the one who refused to believe that I was going to die, even though the doctors told us that I had inoperable stage IV pancreatic cancer.

At the time, my prognosis was measured in months — not years. After I learned that I had terminal cancer, I visited many medical centers, doctors and specialists. Quickly, I found that I did not qualify for surgery — the only cure for pancreatic cancer — or any clinical trial. Ironically, I received the best advice from a podiatrist, who told me, "Don't dwell on your illness. When you do that, you are only hurting the people you love. Stay positive." He was right, demonstrating that he knew as much about people's heads and hearts as he did about their feet.

I could tell by the expression on their faces when we talked about my illness. They were feeling the pain more than I was.

"I woke up this morning." I did, and I'm grateful for my family has always sustained me. My wife laughs at my bad jokes and rubs my feet when my toes are numb from the chemo and radiation. I am surrounded by my grown children who have become wonderful parents to the grandchildren I love and cherish. My son sends me articles about the latest medical research while my daughter makes me "secret salsa" and shares the latest cancer-fighting recipes. My granddaughter lovingly pats my bald head while my grandson tells me, "Pop, you live fearless. Do you still have cancer?"

I woke up this morning and thought about how I'm healthy enough to continue working, with few side effects from my treatment. I teach talented students who have dreams that inspire me. I have friends who support me and cheer me on. One special friend calls me every Sunday night at seven just to check in. Initially, I told him that he didn't need to call so often. But he insisted, and now I look forward to those conversations every week. I am more than a little superstitious that these calls are bringing me good luck!

I woke up this morning, living *with* this cancer. I am not "battling" cancer, for to do so would be a fight with myself. I am learning what it means to love deeply without conditions. And how to receive the love of family and friends in a way I had never experienced before. Thinking about imminent death has shown me that I am living the life I am meant to live. And that death is not about me but the people I'll leave behind. What can I give them that will live on? It cannot be found in things or treasures. It is, quite simply, love — a love that they can hold on to and treasure and pass on to others.

I woke up this morning knowing that each day is a good day no matter the challenge or unknown future. Each day is a gift. The question is how we can use this precious time to help others — the way that the elderly valet-parking attendant helped me that day with his simple and sincere words.

I woke up this morning, thankful that I am receiving the best possible treatment at a world-class cancer center. After my fifty-fifth chemotherapy treatment more than two years ago, my cancer is stable.

The Power of Attitude |

Less than one percent of patients with stage IV cancer survive after five years. My doctors have no medical explanation for my good fortune. In fact, my oncologist asked me recently, "What do you tell people when they ask you how you are doing?"

I tell them simply, "I feel great, and I am grateful for each day."

I have been able to stretch my initial prognosis of five months to five years. As I write this, I am planning the ninth vacation trip with my children and grandchildren since my diagnosis.

I woke up this morning, excited, because each day is a miracle in the making.

—Frederick Loomis—

Darkness & Light

Through darkness diamonds spread their richest light.
~John Webster

My boys giggled and splashed in the crowded pool, taking refuge from the bright August sun. Their latest pool games involved squirters and cannonballs. The carefree vibrant scene was a stark contrast to the dark and crippling words echoing through my cell phone.

"The CT scan showed a mass on your father's pancreas," my mom said as she struggled to get out the words. My tall, strong fifty-nine-year-old father had suddenly started losing one to two pounds per day. Of all the possible causes I'd read about, this was the worst imaginable scenario. The deadliest of all major cancers, the pancreatic-cancer prognosis was horribly grim. Most patients don't live a year beyond diagnosis, with many taken in just three to six months.

After marrying young and working hard their entire lives, my parents were looking forward to retiring, traveling and spending time with their grandchildren: my sons, Kyle and Tyler, ages eight and four, and my brother's daughters, Kaitlyn and Audrey, ages nine and six.

It was a devastating diagnosis.

The first oncology appointment was on my boys' first day of school. Second grade and preschool were to be exciting school years that their beloved Pop wanted so desperately to see. Every year on each grandchild's birthday, he'd make a video highlight reel of the past year, and he was already hard at work planning a baseball theme. My dad and my boys shared a passion for baseball. Kyle earned a spot on the travel baseball team and would be starting in the spring. Tyler knew all the names and stats of Pop's beloved Philadelphia Phillies.

My dad asked his oncologist if he would make it to Christmas. After reviewing the scans showing an inoperable tumor, the doctor pursed his lips and said with deeply apologetic eyes, "I'm sorry, Fred. Probably not."

Since my mom was a teacher, with limited time off, I often accompanied my dad to chemotherapy. My brother, Mark, met us during his lunch break. We marveled as Dad sat there, hooked up to the IVs, chatting with the nurses. As a college professor, my dad loved hearing about their educational backgrounds, and they adored his pleasant demeanor. He made it easy to forget the grave reason we were there.

After the initial infusion at the hospital, he remained on chemotherapy for forty-eight hours in the form of a backpack with tubes hooked up to his chest port. We'd visit him at home, armed with movies and board games so he could relax. But before long, we'd find him in the driveway with the kids, pitching and chasing fly balls while wearing his chemo backpack!

During one infusion at the hospital, he decided that instead of fearing the Christmas holiday he might not live to see, he would plan to celebrate it in the biggest way possible. Forty years prior, during Christmas week, my parents had honeymooned in Disney World. In honor of this anniversary, he wanted to take all of us there to celebrate Christmas. Traveling posed health risks to his immune-compromised body. I planned cautiously, packed secretly, and hoped. Knowing it was possible the trip wouldn't happen, we all agreed not to tell the kids until we were sure. Days before Christmas they awoke thinking it was an ordinary school day. Instead, we all met at my parents' house for the ultimate Christmas surprise.

Joyfully, my dad told his grandchildren that their suitcases were in the car and we were heading to the airport.

A family friend and former Disney employee arranged to have our room at the Pop Century Resort decorated with anniversary greetings and instructed us to view the parade in a particular spot.

We rode rides and laughed with Disney characters in the beautiful Florida sun. My dad had no hair and limited energy, but he wore a Disney button that declared proudly, "I'm Celebrating LIFE." The brightly lit park sparkled as pretend snow fell, and the kids danced around us, catching snowflakes on their tongues. At last, Santa concluded the parade in a spectacular sleigh. As he rode by, he shouted for the entire crowd to hear, "I want to wish a very special Merry Christmas to the very special Loomis family" as he called each one of us by name. It was a magical memory from a most magical trip.

But the magic didn't end there.

My dad survived six months post-diagnosis to celebrate his sixtieth birthday. We planned a surprise baseball-themed party and gathered friends from his childhood, college and career. Extended family traveled from around the country to be there. We told him to arrive in costume for "a baseball team fundraiser." Dressed head to toe in his favorite Phillies pinstripe uniform, my dad was surprised by "Fred's Fans" wearing baseball gear for an evening of his favorite ballpark food. At the end of the night, he stood up to quote baseball legend Lou Gehrig. He said that he might have been given a "bad break... Yet today I consider myself the luckiest man on the face of this earth."

But we were the lucky ones because he continued to choose happiness.

That spring, he attended every one of Kyle's baseball games with his chemo backpack. I thought it was going to disconnect when he jumped out of his seat to cheer as Kyle hit a walk-off single to win the district championship game!

The following year, he planned a Thanksgiving feast at Disney's Animal Kingdom Lodge to celebrate all that we had to be grateful for. The next trip was to an indoor waterpark for his sixty-second birthday, where he and all four grandchildren boarded raft after raft, screaming while soaring down the thrilling tube slides. The following year, we all shared a house in Ocean City, New Jersey, a favorite childhood destination. He'd start each morning with a bike ride down the boardwalk, each afternoon splashing in the waves with the kids, and each night on the boardwalk with ice-cream cones and laughter.

Despite fifty-five chemo treatments and five weeks of daily radiation over the course of two-and-a-half years, the pancreatic tumor never shrank, and it spread to his liver. He was diagnosed with stage 4 metastatic pancreatic cancer, and the five best cancer hospitals on the East Coast all deemed his tumor inoperable. When the chemo side effects became severe, he made the difficult decision to stop treatment and choose quality of time over quantity.

And he planned another trip to Disney World. I sat beside him as we rode Snow White's mine train, and he sang "Hi ho, hi ho" along with the dwarves as we soared through the tunnels with our hands in the air. We returned to ride Space Mountain at midnight just like we had when I was a child. Most nights, he and I were the last adults still standing with the kids as the parks closed with spectacular fireworks.

It has now been an unbelievable five years since my dad's diagnosis. Miraculously, he has been off treatment for the last two-and-a-half of them. His journey is known by many in the cancer community as a rare story of hope in a sea of heartbreaking ones. But it's his incredibly positive attitude from the very beginning that continues to inspire everyone he meets.

This year, Tyler Frederick (named for my dad), now in second grade, started his first year of travel baseball, and Kyle, a sixth grader, began his last. My dad cheered wildly as Ty pitched his first game and Kyle made his "major league" plays. Kyle's season will culminate this summer with the ultimate baseball experience at Cooperstown Dreams Park in New York. My dad most certainly plans to be there, and I no longer doubt that he will be. He and my mom have both retired and are busier than ever. The cancer remains. He still has scans every three months, and we never know what they will show. No doctor can medically explain how he is still living.

His latest big idea is for us all to go on a Disney cruise to Alaska, a dream destination of my mom's. I'm sitting by the pool reading the list of excursions and watching the four kids — now eight, ten, twelve and thirteen — splashing in the bright sun with my dad. The pool games still involve squirters and cannonballs. I think about the devastating diagnosis that he didn't let devastate us. In his very darkest time, he has chosen to live in the light.

—Jennifer Loomis Kennedy—

The Words That Changed My Life

38

On Roses and Life

Change always comes bearing gifts.
~Price Pritchett

I looked at the brochure for Ballston Spa High School. "I don't want to go to this school," I said. "In fact, I don't even want to be here. Can't we just go home to New Jersey? I hate it here. I have no friends, I have nothing to do, and I hate it."

My mom and dad exchanged glances. It had been a week since we moved to New York. Sighing, my mom turned to me from the front seat of the car. "Can't you try to look at the bright side? You used to love Saratoga when we came here on vacation."

"It's different living here. I want to go home. I don't have any friends here."

The car was silent for a moment. I watched the Pilot swivel into the shady path leading to Yaddo Gardens, and I worked to hold back my tears.

"We're here!" my dad said, attempting enthusiasm.

We unloaded the car — baguettes, fresh tomatoes, mangoes, iced tea, everything for a perfect picnic — but it was soured by my imperfect mood.

We laid out the blanket, looking at the gardens that were just starting to bloom. A number of people vested in green shirts and garden gloves bent over the bushes, hard at work.

As we watched the workers, we wound up in conversation with a particularly chatty woman, Vera, who told us more about the history of Yaddo Gardens and the volunteers.

"We work every Tuesday, Thursday, and Saturday morning," Vera said with a smile.

"Hey," my dad nudged me, "maybe you should work here!"

I started to roll my eyes, but my dad, ever the talker, brought up the idea to Vera. Before I knew it, I was there bright and early on a Tuesday morning.

Entering my assigned garden, my hands struggled to carry a bucket, gloves, potato rake, petal rake, strainer, and knee protector. Vera introduced me to John, the head gardener of quadrant four. I was impressed by John's spryness and energy; he was still hiking mountains at eighty-one. He bounded around the garden with ease, clipping, raking and pruning with more deftness than I could ever muster.

"Dana, come here!" he called across the garden. He cupped a peppermint-striped flower in his hands, still on the vine, and showed it to me. "You see this flower?"

I nodded.

"Looks alive, but…" He brushed his finger on top of it. I watched the petals swirl and twirl down like rain. "It's actually dead. This, on the other hand…" He pointed to a bush that looked stick-like and flowerless. "This one will bloom in a few days. Just wait."

I smiled and returned to my task.

It was like that over the next several months. I'd come to the gardens on a Tuesday, Thursday, or Saturday, and John would always be there, smiling and ready to teach me a new lesson about roses and life.

I learned the secret to sinfully sweet rosehip jam, how to tell if a Japanese beetle is hiding inside a rose, and how to prevent deer from eating the flowers. During snack breaks, my new friend and I would chat and discuss everything from mountains to middle school, laughing and learning the joys of a friendship across generations.

One day, I opened up to him about my fears for the fall.

"I'm just not ready for school," I said, biting my lip. "What if I have no friends?"

John said nothing, but took me instead to the terrace that overlooked the four-quadrant garden.

"Look, Dana. Do you see these two quadrants?"

I looked at them and nodded.

"Now look at the other two. What's different?"

I squinted my eyes and looked back and forth. Then it clicked. "The two on the left are shorter!" I smiled with triumph.

"Exactly. This garden was styled after Italian Renaissance gardens. The point of the garden is for people who stand there," he pointed to the wrought-iron gate on the left, "to see the garden beds as if they were all the same size.

"It's called perspectivism," he continued, "and I think it's what you need. You can look at your new school as something scary, or you can look at it as an opportunity." He shrugged. "The choice is yours."

I don't think I said much in response. I often didn't. But three months later, after I had started high school, it was time for the Yaddo Gardens volunteer celebration. I saw John — my first friend in upstate New York — and gave him a hug.

"You were right," I said. "I just needed a little perspective."

— Dana Drosdick —

39

A Simple Change

Smile in the mirror. Do that every morning,
and you'll start to see a big difference in your life.
~Yoko Ono

In my early thirties, I decided that my career in teaching was not what I dreamed it would be. I left the job and moved in with my parents for a year while I tested out a new career in the corporate world.

Living with my parents proved to be an even bigger challenge than my new job. Truth be told, it was probably harder for them than it was for me because I was a big jerk. I yelled at my mom for buying junk food and ignored my dad when he offered advice. I complained that my mom never did my laundry the way I wanted and my dad never let me choose what show to watch. Instead of being grateful for their hospitality, I was mean to them and most likely made them regret their offer.

"This is only for a year," I would repeat to myself on a daily basis, sometimes hourly. Instead of living in the present, I would wish for the future and to have it all figured out. My life wasn't what or where I wanted it to be. By this age, I expected to be firmly rooted on a career path with a huge circle of friends who liked to hang out. I did not expect to be living with my parents and starting over.

My attitude grew worse. One day when I was tearfully talking about something that was making my life miserable, my mother interrupted me. She nearly shouted, "Why don't you just try smiling more?" I am pretty sure I laughed at her, but she went on to explain that sometimes things don't work out the way we thought they would. "Don't wait for things to get better," she said. "*Make* them better."

Angrily, I walked away, muttering words under my breath that one should never say to her mother. I cried myself to sleep that night, thinking about how unfair life was and how no one understood me.

In the morning, things felt different. I wasn't suddenly all happy and smiley... I was just different. I decided I was going to show my mother just how wrong she was. I would follow her advice and try smiling more.

Weeks passed, and somewhere along the way, I forgot about *trying* to smile more as it became a habit. I worked on approaching situations with a better perspective and slowly started to feel the weight on my shoulders lighten.

The second half of that year was better than the first. It was still a challenge to be living with my parents at age thirty-three. I was still ashamed and embarrassed that I had fallen so far from the path I had envisioned for myself. But it was definitely better.

At the end of my stay, I bought my own place and realized I had begun to love my job. I had made friends at work, and started to feel like I had purpose and drive. The days raced by, and I learned to love the silence. I started running again, and pushed light and joy into everything I did.

As cheesy as it sounds, I started noticing the birds singing and appreciating nature for what felt like the first time. Smiling had lifted the cloud that had hung over me for years. I even started dating again, although I continued to date the wrong type of guys. But at least I was out there.

Then I met someone. He was the first person I had ever met who made me feel light and happy. For the first few weeks of our relationship, I would tell him one or two great things about each day of the week. And if I forgot, or more likely thought he might be growing tired of all my positivity, he'd ask me, "What's so great about Monday anyway?" And I would share some silly thing I had thought of to get me through a particularly rough Monday.

On one of our dates, I asked him what he first noticed about me. He said that I was always happy and smiling. At that moment, my mother's suggestion rushed back to me: "Why don't you just try smiling more?"

That simple advice, which I initially fought so hard against, had changed me.

— Courtney Wright —

40

The Ice Cream Truck

Winners never quit, and quitters never win.
~Vince Lombardi

"Never give up! Never give up!" chanted my two young children, Max and Charley, as they marched barefoot behind their grandmother Mimi. My mother was clad in her favorite faded-denim, button-down shirt thrown casually over her swimsuit. Wild tufts of her short, auburn hair peeked out from a wide-brimmed, yellow straw hat.

Mimi was leading Max and Charley on yet another adventure, straight off the beach where they had spent the day building sand castles and splashing in the waves. This time, they were seeking the elusive ice-cream truck. As always, shoes were optional.

Over the years, Mimi had become our family's beacon of positivity. It was not a title she earned without concerted effort, however. Having been widowed at only forty years old and left to raise me and my ten-year-old brother alone, she faced heart-wrenching tragedy powerful enough to cloud just about anyone's upbeat outlook. She had been the one who had to make the decision to remove our dad from life support fourteen days after he was in a car accident.

My mom could have lived under a black cloud. Instead, she challenged herself to find joy every day. She was always up for a new challenge, whether that was hiking across the steep, rocky terrain of a mountaintop in Austria to get a better view of the breathtaking landscape while my brother and I looked on terrified, parasailing over the Gulf of Mexico, or signing up for tap-dancing classes at fifty. Leading by example, Mom taught us just how much one could accomplish with a positive attitude.

She has taken the same approach in her relationship with her grandchildren. Prior to starting her adventure with Max and Charley on that hot July afternoon, Mimi heard the familiar clang of the ice-cream man's bell from her beach chair. She turned and saw him briefly, spotting his fluorescent green shirt and catching the gleam of his waving bell before he turned and disappeared over the dunes. Happily, the ice-cream man's visit is a daily occurrence at the beach, although the lag time between the sound of his bell and the departure of his truck is not long. One must be quick to catch him.

Max and Charley were disappointed when they didn't catch him in time that day. That was until Mimi's eyes sparkled and she said, "Never give up!" She explained that the truck might be gone, but they could hustle off to find it at its next stop.

They walked block after block. Not knowing which direction the truck had taken, they had to make their best guess about where to search. My kids' tiny legs were tired, but they forged on, continuing to chant their mantra, "Never give up!"

After about twenty minutes of walking, Max's faith in the mission began to waver. He wondered out loud, "Maybe we should give up. We have been walking pretty far and haven't seen the truck yet." Charley squealed a quick, "No way! Never give up!" and resumed her chant with Mimi. Somewhat skeptically, Max acquiesced.

Just two blocks later, they found it. Mimi threw a triumphant fist in the air, and Max and Charley screamed with excitement, "Never give up!" In that moment, my mom had done for my children what she had done for me countless times. Simple though it was, that phrase has become our battle cry for the challenges we face. Whether studying for a difficult test, pushing through a challenging cross-country practice, or practicing lines to audition for a school play, I know I can always look at Max and Charley and say, "Never give up!" Upon hearing those words, they are instantly transported to a positive state of mind — where the next ice-cream truck is just around the corner.

— Samantha LaBarbera —

41

Why Not?

If you're alive, kick into drive. Chase whimsies.
See if you can turn dreams into a way to make
a living, if not an entire way of life.
~Kevin Smith

My husband had given me an early Christmas present—a comedy show with my favorite screenwriter and director, Kevin Smith. The year had been filled with more lows than any other year in my life, and I was ready for a break.

We waited in the tightly packed bar area until the doors opened and we filed into the theater in line. We started chatting with three other people behind us and admiring the Kevin Smith apparel they had worn to the show.

"Are you five together?" the lady at the door inquired. We looked at each other hesitantly.

"We can be…" I replied cautiously.

"Well, I have a table for five up front. Otherwise, I can seat you separately upstairs in the balcony," she responded.

"We are definitely together," I replied, trying to act nonchalant. Up front? No way! We followed the lady to our seats, and I tried to contain myself as the lights went down and people started clapping and cheering. Music was playing, and the announcer gave a brief introduction before Kevin Smith walked out and appeared on stage. I was in awe; I had never had such amazing seats at a comedy show before.

Halfway through the show, Kevin told us that he was essentially a person with a dream who never gave up on it. Then these life-changing words came out of his mouth: "You've got to get rid of the 'why people' in your life and spend more time with the 'why not people' you meet."

That simple, yet profound, advice completely changed my outlook. I had always been a bit of a risk taker in terms of going skydiving, dirt-bike riding, or backpacking in the mountains, but this made me reflect on how cautious I had been about pursuing my personal goals.

> *"Get rid of the 'why people' in your life and spend more time with the 'why not people.'"*

A couple of weeks after the show, I applied for a new job within my company, and I got it. I was finally working in a much happier environment and I was thriving. Even my husband told me how good it was to see me smile again when I came home from work.

I also started writing again, for the first time in eight years. Writing had always been a passion of mine, but once I graduated college, I would come up with excuses that were essentially reasons "why" I couldn't write.

I had lost both grandparents and our dogs, and writing became a cathartic and therapeutic process for me. My new "why not mentality" helped me through my grief, and I decided to submit my work to publishers, not really believing anything would come of it. But my new attitude brought me the fulfillment of a dream that I had had since childhood; my first written works were published the following year — by Chicken Soup for the Soul! In addition, my husband and I decided to finally search for a rescue dog after losing both of ours. Our new hound nourishes and rebuilds a piece of my soul each day.

These may be small things, but together they create something bigger than I could ever have imagined. I had gone to the comedy show expecting to cut loose and laugh at some raunchy jokes, but what I got out of the experience was life changing. It was the greatest gift I could have received at that time in my life, and I am forever grateful. Two simple words change my life every day: "Why not?"

— Gwen Cooper —

The Words That Changed My Life |

42

Everything We Need

While we try to teach our children all about life,
our children teach us what life is all about.
~Angela Schwindt

I knew I had it easier than most single mothers. We had a roof over our heads, I managed to pay the electric bill each month, and there was always food on the table.

After my divorce, I had returned to graduate school and finished my master's degree. I had a job I loved as a case manager for medically frail and low-income elder adults. My duties involved arranging home services to enable the elderly to stay in their homes as long as possible, a service I believed was vitally important. Yet, as with most social-service jobs, it barely paid a living wage. One day as I was filling out forms for one of my clients to receive food stamps, I realized that if I didn't receive child support, my salary would have qualified us for the same entitlements! I was fortunate I didn't need the supplemental government assistance, but I was aware that many single-parent families relied on the help, and I was grateful it was available for them.

I was fortunate to have the basics covered for my daughters and me, but it was the unexpected costs that kept me up at night. If something broke in our home, it was probably going to stay broken. What if we needed a new roof? What if the air conditioner went out in the 100-degree Oklahoma summer? What if the car needed repairs? My children's father provided health insurance for them, but I couldn't afford insurance for myself. I was very healthy, but I knew one medical catastrophe would financially destroy me.

Then there were all the things I wished I could do for my children. Their friends were usually off on exotic vacations in the summer while I scrambled to make a picnic and trip to the zoo feel like a real vacation. I wished my children could have new furniture and cute clothes and all the latest gadgets.

I thought I was doing a good job keeping my worries from my children, but I wasn't. Children are very sensitive to their parents' moods, and they are often listening when we're not aware. A neighbor had been pressuring me to share the cost of a new fence, and I was talking about it with my sister on the phone, wondering how I would magically make money appear to cover the cost. After I got off the phone, my six-year-old daughter approached me and said, "Mom, please don't worry. We may not have everything we want, but we have everything we need."

> *"We may not have everything we want, but we have everything we need."*

That statement, made by an innocent but very wise child, forever changed my perspective. Whenever I found myself giving into my anxieties concerning finances, I would remember her words. I would focus on being grateful for shelter over our heads and food on our table. I'm so thankful to my little girl who was smart enough to remind me that we often confuse wants with needs. Listen closely to children; it is from their hearts we may learn great wisdom. We had shelter, food, clothing, and love for one another — we did, indeed, have everything we needed!

— Diane Morrow-Kondos —

Serendipity

*Family faces are magic mirrors. Looking at people who
belong to us, we see the past, present, and future.*
~Gail Lumet Buckley

It was New Year's Eve. Eleven adults swapped stories while seven kids, ranging from six to nineteen, laughed in the living room. Right after dinner, I gathered everyone together and proposed a ritual that would connect the old year with the new.

"Think of a valuable lesson you learned in the past year and write it down as a piece of advice for someone else," I said. "Then drop it into this bag for a random drawing."

Everyone dove into the exercise, even my little granddaughter who needed help with writing.

I asked Lulu, "What was the best thing you learned this year?"

She said, "French." (She's in a French immersion program at school.)

"Why?"

"Because it's different."

I asked for clarification. "So would your advice be to learn French because it helps you to think differently?"

"Exactly," said the six-year-old.

Her advice went into the bag with seventeen other slips of paper. We all sat in a circle, excited to see what would happen next.

"Now, it's time to think of a goal for the coming year. Say it out loud, and then pick a slip at random and read the advice aloud," I said, "Let's see if chance advice coincides with your goal."

The room was filled with positive energy as each person stated his or her goal and then chose a random piece of paper. It was eerie how well the advice seemed to fit each person's goal for the coming year.

Teenager Zach wished for his driver's license, and he pulled a slip that read: "Know all the facts. Don't be impulsive. A lack of knowledge can lead to a fatal mistake."

Rich hoped to pass a very tough accreditation. His slip read: "Don't waste time watching so much TV. It's time you never get back." It took a while for the laughter to die down since he's such a movie fanatic.

Sheila, new to college, yearned for a best friend and wondered how to go about it. She pulled the slip I had written: "One size does not fit all. Discover and encourage individuality. Be compassionate with people very different from yourself."

Danielle planned a trip to Europe in the new year, and out came little Lulu's advice, "Learn French. It helps you to think differently."

For me, I wanted to teach a meditation/journaling program for prison inmates. I had volunteered to do it in the past and enjoyed it, but I struggle with too many demands on my schedule. How would it be possible? I pulled a slip that read: "Let God fight your battles." I interpreted this to mean that the path would open when a Higher Power deemed the time to be right. My heart simply had to be in the right place, and meanwhile, I could work toward readiness. In time, I came to realize the prisoner who needed stress relief was me.

Often, we ignore guidance from other people. Yet that night, whether it was serendipity or magic or family bonds, the advice we received seemed so tailor-made for us that we all listened. And we were better off because of it.

— Suzette Martinez Standring —

44

Happy Cells Are Healthy Cells

Very often a change of self is needed more than a change of scene.
~Arthur Christopher Benson

The server, with her forearms covered in bracelets, and I, in my mid-twenties, were close in age. So why did she seem so much older and wiser?

I don't remember how we came to be talking in the hallway outside the pub's restroom. Had we both been using the facilities, and I mentioned something as we washed our hands? Had I been grumbling about having a bad day? Probably. I was always grouchy back then.

It's been more than twenty years since the encounter, and while I may not remember exactly how we ended up in that hallway together, I'll never forget what happened there. She was the first to show me how powerful my thoughts were.

"You must always guard your thoughts," she advised. "They do more than form in your mind. They influence your body."

"What?"

There I was in my business best, meeting up with co-worker friends for happy-hour drinks. She was in her "work clothes," too — a flowing skirt and basic T-shirt, with her hair wild and free to match her spirit. We were the yuppie and the hippie. One was about to teach the other a valuable lesson.

"All that negativity. It doesn't do you any good. In fact, it does exactly the opposite."

I've often wondered what she saw in my eyes in that moment. She could've stopped and gone back to her job. Instead, she took the time to show me what she was talking about.

"Here… stick out your arm." She demonstrated how she wanted me to hold it stretched out perpendicular to my body. "I'm going to press on it while you think about something that makes you happy. What fills your heart with smiles? Think about that."

That was a good question. What filled my heart with smiles? His furry face filled my mind — with a tennis ball in his mouth. Budly, my Cocker Spaniel.

"I'm going to try and push down on your arm," the waitress said. "Don't let me."

I kept my arm stiff, and she wasn't able to press it down. I was able to resist.

"Okay, now think of the exact opposite. Think of something that fills your soul with anger or sadness, maybe even both. Something negative."

That one came easier: my mother. Nothing I did was ever good enough for her. She was always criticizing me about one thing or another.

"Okay, we're going to do the same thing. Try to resist when I press down again."

I couldn't. No matter how hard I tried, thinking of my mom and the way she made me feel literally stole my strength.

The wise waitress told me to think my happy thoughts again. My strength returned. She was pressing equally hard each time, but she was proving my thoughts dictated my strength. I had the power to resist with one, and absolutely no strength with the other.

Fast-forward twelve years. I was battling cancer that I was convinced was brought on by all the stress I'd been under taking care of my mother during her own struggle with cancer. I was diagnosed only five months after her death.

I'd taken on caregiving responsibilities in a last-ditch effort to prove I was worthy of her love. Why I expected her to be different when she was dying, I don't know. But nothing I did was good enough.

Worse, I found out what I'd always suspected: She loved my sister more. I had the last will and testament to prove it. She never said "I love you" to anyone. She wasn't like that. She was very big on material rewards, though. My sister was worth 70 percent of her estate. I was only worth 30 percent.

My sister had known all along how the will had been written, but it had come as a surprise to me. It turned out my mom had expected my sister to care for her. My sister had shrugged off that duty on me, and in my desperation to make one last grand gesture, I'd accepted it willingly — which meant exposing myself to my mom's toxic energy 24/7.

After a chemo treatment that hit me particularly hard, I thought about that waitress from so many years ago. I was on the couch, drifting in and out of consciousness, wondering which would hit first: the next round of nausea or a pain flare.

I tried not to think about my mom or sister, but it didn't work. I was still hurt and angry about how everything had turned out.

But I also knew those feelings were what had gotten me into the mess I was in. If I didn't change my thinking, I was going to die. I was doing what that waitress had shown me all those years ago: letting negative thoughts zap my strength. But these were potent enough to threaten my life. If I wanted not only to heal but to live and thrive, I had to change my thinking. And that's when it hit me: Happy cells are healthy cells. That was a mantra to live by. Sad and mad thoughts made me sick. Happy ones could make me better.

The trouble was, my heart had been shattered. One can't face the level of betrayal I had experienced and expect not to think about it. The more I tried not to, the more I did.

Again, it was the waitress's wise words that helped. I asked myself, *What fills my heart with smiles?* The key was to flood my mind with as many of those thoughts on a daily basis as possible. Make it so there was no room for bad thoughts.

I set about filling my moments with as much "happy" as possible. I made lists not only of what brought me joy in the present, but also things to look forward to once I got better. I listed things I wanted to try, places I wanted to see, and people I wanted to visit. I watched sitcoms and romantic comedies. I cherished

> *Happy cells are healthy cells.*

the time with my husband, friends and pets even more.

And whenever the bad thoughts threatened to take over, I'd gently but firmly remind myself, "Happy cells are healthy cells."

I just passed the "ten years in the clear" remission mark, so when I say this is a mantra I live by, I really mean it.

— C. L. Pryor —

45

Chicken Soup for the Soul

The Can Man

Know that you can, believe that you can, and know
with ALL of your heart that you will. You will succeed
in spite of any obstacles that may try to hinder you!
~Stephanie Lahart

W
hen I was a teenager, my favorite word was "can't." I can't dance. I can't do this homework. I would usually do these things anyway, but only after first saying that I couldn't.

The summer after I turned fourteen, I was in Spokane for my annual three-week visit with my father and he got to hear my constant "can't" mantra firsthand. As he often did on my yearly visit, he took me to sit in on the marketing class he was teaching at the local community college. I was getting ready to tune him out and tune into my book when one of his students said "I can't understand" in reference to something in the curriculum.

My dad stood up at the front of the room and said, "No!" It seemed out of character for a laid-back Southern guy, but there he was going off on the word "can't."

"'Can't' has no business in this classroom," he said. "It's bad enough I get it from her," he pointed at me, "but she's young yet and hasn't figured out that 'can't' is the worst four-letter word in the English language."

His students just stared at him for a minute, and I put down my book. My dad's tangents were the stuff of legend in my life and always funny, but that's why companies paid him to come in and motivate their employees for a couple of hours. He had a great stage presence and a knack for making things understandable. I think his classes were probably pretty interesting for his students.

With everyone's eyes on him, he started pacing the front of the classroom, turning off the projector and changing the day's lesson plan. "Four-letter words are impolite in mixed company — and my daughter is sitting there — but we all know what those words are. A few four-letter words get thrown around like they aren't offensive, and chief among them, is 'can't.' If you're going to stand there and tell me you can't, you've already failed. You've already convinced yourself that you can't, and nothing I say or do is going to convince you otherwise," he explained.

"Your homework — and yours, too, daughter dear — is to go home and find yourself a can. Get one of those big markers and write the words 'Can Can' on it. Every time you say 'can't' this week, I want you to write down what you can't do and put it in the Can Can. At the end of the week, go through them and see how many opportunities you missed because you think you can't. Turn each of those 'can'ts' into a 'can' and see how much you can achieve."

When we got back to his house after class and dinner at my favorite restaurant, he actually made me make my own Can Can. All the things in my Can Can were things I actually could do; I just didn't want to put in the effort.

As a kid, his Can Can made me roll my eyes, but as an adult I think he was pretty on point. Twenty-five years later, going through his things after he passed, I found the printouts he'd made for his class for several years after that first one. Joe's Can Can became a regular lesson in his classes, and the point was that there are enough obstacles in life without becoming one for yourself. Now my children are the petulant teenagers with great affection for the word "can't," and I'm seriously considering having them make their own Can Can.

My dad was the ultimate can man. He never met a "can't" he couldn't turn into a "can."

— Sarah Wagner —

Could I Trouble You?

No life is so hard that you can't make it easier
by the way you take it.
~Ellen Glasgow

I t was about five years after my divorce was finally over. I was broke. I was depressed. There were far too many days when the bottle of sleeping pills on the counter looked less like a coping mechanism and more like a permanent solution. Every day was like running a marathon, except there was no medal and no cheering at the finish line. I was utterly alone, and life felt hopeless.

In one rare moment of lucidity, I signed up for a free weeklong trial membership at a local gym. To my mind, gyms were where already fit people went to admire each other. They weren't where sad, out-of-shape single mothers went in their worn-out sweatpants and T-shirts. And yet, I trudged to the gym for seven mornings in a row. Each morning, I pulled myself onto an elliptical machine and watched the minutes tick by. Each morning, I resolved to come back and do a little better the next day.

This is not a story about how getting physically fit is a path to happiness. This is a story about a book on tape (that's right — a good, old-fashioned cassette) that I listened to at the gym, and the four words I heard that helped me change my life.

Cruising on an elliptical machine is not exactly the height of entertainment. To wile away the time I spent there, I picked up an old pile of cassettes that I inherited somewhere along the way — probably from my mother, an avid reader of self-reflection materials. Since I am a keeper of all things nostalgic, I still had my portable cassette player from high school and an old set of foam-covered headphones. I spent the week listening to Dale Carnegie's *How to Win Friends and Influence People.*

Mr. Carnegie, a brilliant author without question, packed a lot of information into his book. But just four little words have stuck with me for years: When faced with the opportunity to ask for help, preface every question with, "Could I trouble you?"

The idea is simple, really. According to Carnegie, when you use these four words, you tell people that you understand you need something from them. You acknowledge them as people. You understand that you may be asking them to go out of their way for you. You put them before yourself, and you respect them. Simply put, you focus on someone other than you.

I heard the words he spoke, and I admit I had my doubts. After all, wasn't I worthy of pity? Hadn't I earned the right to put myself first for a change? Didn't I deserve more from the world than what I'd gotten? What right did the world have to expect anything else from me? I was the one who had been victimized. I was the one suffering. I wanted the world to ask *me* if I could be troubled to help.

But those words tugged at me somehow. I heard them over and over again in my mind, long after I was off the elliptical. At last, in a moment of true self-reflection, free from the mental agony that made up my life, I decided to try.

At first, it was simple. When a waitress breezed by my table and ignored my empty glass, I didn't bark at her. The next time she stopped, I asked simply, "Could I trouble you for a refill?" She paused and looked at me as though I'd spoken a different language. Eventually, she responded, "Of course, it's no trouble at all!" And she came right back with my drink and delivered outstanding service the rest of my meal.

When I stopped at the bank and they were out of deposit slips, I didn't tell the teller they had a problem. I said to her, "Could I trouble you for a deposit slip?" And she hurried to give me one and replace the stack on the counter as well.

To the grocery clerk, I said: "Could I trouble you to make change for this ten-dollar bill?" I was rewarded with two fives, a thank-you, and a huge smile.

To the customer-service rep, I asked: "Could I trouble you to explain something on my bill?" I was given the credit I asked for and treated like a long-lost friend.

It took practice. First, it was like a game. Could I remember to say the words correctly, and how would the other person respond? Then it became a challenge. Could I make every person I interacted with smile that day? Before long, it was second nature. "Could I trouble you...?" became part of my everyday vocabulary. I often reflected on the title of Carnegie's book, *How to Win Friends and Influence People*. I realized I was, in fact, influencing people. They were doing what I wanted, when I wanted, and they seemed happy to be doing so.

The real kicker was the influence I'd had on myself. I had been so focused on making those words a habit that I had stopped focusing on my misery. I enjoyed making other people smile so much that I began to smile more often myself. I started to see other people as they were. For that brief moment, I felt their pain, sacrifice, gratitude, and happiness. The people I encountered every day mattered. They were individuals and I had a chance to be a positive presence in their days.

It took years before my situation righted itself. It took months of hard work and dedication to make my life better. But it took only moments to make myself happier. Every single interaction with another human being is a chance to make someone feel special. In the moment it takes to ask, "Could I trouble you?" a seed of happiness is planted. Over a lifetime, those seeds grow into a bountiful harvest of joy.

— Karen Haueisen Crissinger —

47

Never Too Old

*It's never too late to start something new, to do all those
things that you've been longing to do.*
~Dallas Clayton

When I was turning thirty, a friend asked me to share my biggest regret in life. It didn't take me long to say I most regretted not finishing college. I explained that I was considered smart in school, made great grades, and had big dreams. By giving up on it all, I felt like I was not only letting myself down, but also everyone who ever believed in me.

My friend said, "Why not now?" But with a son in elementary school, a job, and loads of other responsibilities at church and home, I had a million excuses. The one I thought was the strongest: If I went back, I would be thirty-two when I graduated.

What I heard back was something I will never forget: "You're going to be thirty-two anyway."

> **"You're going to be thirty-two anyway."**

It was the simplest and wisest advice I could have received.

I could turn thirty-two with a college degree or without one, but I was going to be thirty-two anyway.

So I did it.

I earned my journalism degree and could not have felt prouder, thirty-two or not. And I have recycled this advice a dozen times. Aside from becoming Miss Teen USA or high-school valedictorian, there are very few things for which I am too late.

Do I really want to write my first book at forty-two? I'm going to be forty-two anyway.

Do I really want to learn how to dance in my forties? I'm going to go through my forties anyway.

Do I really want to run a half marathon in my fifties? I'm going to be fifty anyway.

Do I really want to be traveling in my sixties? I'm going to be in my sixties anyway.

I hope you never hear me say, "I'm too old for that." Instead, I hope you hear me say, "I'm going to be eighty-five anyway."

—Jen Chapman—

From Lemons to Lemonade

48

Chicken Soup for the Soul

A Positive Message from a Time Traveler

It is often hard to distinguish between the hard knocks in life and those of opportunity.
~Frederick Phillips

Recently, I was cleaning out a closet and came upon several curious letters. They were all written on letterhead from various television stations around the country, all dated in late 1979. It took me a minute to recognize what they were, but as I read through them, I realized they were all rejection letters to me from various television news executives.

I wondered why I kept them. I vaguely remembered applying for the jobs. It was during a time in my television career when I was looking to make that next step toward more responsibility, a bigger city and a bigger salary.

I tried to get inside the brain of that 1979 version of myself to understand what I was feeling at the time. Why did I save these rejection letters? Was I trying to keep myself humble? Was there some hidden streak of masochism causing me to flog myself for my inadequacies?

Finally, I decided that I must have kept the letters specifically for this particular moment forty years later. I concluded that it might very well have been my version of time traveling, a way of sending a message to my "future self." Yet, at the time, I could not have been sure of what that exact message might be.

Strange as it sounded, that rang true. After all, there were many times in my life when I felt that a particular event held some sort of special meaning, but I wasn't sure of the full meaning at the time. The loss of a loved one, a failure in romance, a layoff, a poor investment — they all were life events whose significance only my future self could fully appreciate. My younger self must have sensed significance in those letters, but also suspected that it would require a future self to totally understand what that significance was.

And my present-day self did understand. Each of those letters represented a path not taken — not because I didn't want to take it, or didn't try to take it, but because someone else decided that for me. It was a reminder that my future is not totally in my control; I am not the master of my own fate.

And there was a second part to the message: The fact that I am not in complete control of my life is not necessarily a bad thing. Closed doors guided me as much as open ones had. That's the message the present-day version of me now understands, but the 1979 version of me could only take on faith.

Closed doors guided me as much as open ones had.

That 1979 version of me who was rejected for TV jobs in Green Bay, Wisconsin, Greenville, South Carolina, and Jacksonville, Florida, didn't know that his 1981 version would get a job in a much bigger TV market in the Pacific Northwest. He didn't know that his 1985 version would marry a woman there who was to be his lifelong companion, and that his 1991 version would be given a new opportunity for advancement. That early version of me didn't know that my 1999 self would eventually be laid off from that job and then move his family cross-country to take a job at a national network. But the present-day version of me can look back on all those events and see that, although none of them was completely under my control, each had positive results.

So I'm thankful that my 1979 self sent me that message, even if he didn't fully understand it at the time. I can't travel back in time to thank him, but what I can do is send a message ahead to my 2029 and 2039 selves. That message is this: Life is most productive when you make the most of the path you're on, not when you fret about what the other paths might have held.

So, to my future self: Stop trying to be in control. Don't dwell on what might be on the other side of that closed door. Continue to make the most of every open door. And, one more thing, future self... you're welcome.

—Nick Walker—

49

A Little Exercise Class

*Movement is a medicine for creating change in a
person's physical, emotional, and mental states.*
~Carol Welch

Years ago, I went through an extremely difficult breakup. My ex
was an accommodating, kind gentleman who did everything
for me. When our relationship ended, I realized I had become
completely dependent on him. I felt frightened and helpless,
thinking I was incapable of doing anything for myself.

The first time I went to the grocery store on my own, I felt vulnerable,
lost, and alone. Having lost hope in myself, I turned into a pessimist.

To boost my spirits, a co-worker suggested that we attend an
exercise class at the gym. I doubted an exercise class could make me
happier, but I went along. As I stood inside the exercise room alongside
my co-worker, the instructor turned on some loud music. Soon, the
class kicked into high gear. Awkwardly mimicking the moves of the
instructor, I was doing every cardiovascular move incorrectly. I was
kicking to the left when everyone else was kicking to the right, and
I was doing jumping jacks when everyone else was doing squats. I
looked and felt ridiculous. On top of that, I was exhausted because
the routine was very vigorous.

I desperately wanted to leave, but I stayed until the bitter end.
The next morning, I woke to discover muscles I didn't even know I
had — and those muscles were extremely angry with me. I was so
sore I could barely turn the steering wheel in my car or sit up straight

in my seat.

Later that day, my co-worker asked, "Are you going to class with me tonight?"

For some inexplicable reason, I said, "Yes." My second appearance in class was as humiliating as the first one and I vowed I would never return.

However, several days later, to my great surprise, I asked my co-worker if she was planning on attending the exercise class. She told me she had already moved onto another fitness regimen. I was now left in the uneasy position of going on my own. I thought of how powerless I felt the first time I went to the grocery store by myself. I wanted to overcome that feeling so I decided I would attend the exercise class alone.

For weeks, I flew solo in the class. Although I was uncomfortable, I kept going. Luckily, the moves became more familiar to me. I started to relax. Before long, I began to really enjoy myself. The music was catchy, the students were friendly, and I could feel that I was becoming stronger physically. I was now eager to attend the class.

What I didn't notice until later was that I was also growing stronger emotionally. Outside of the gym, I began to regain my independence and optimism. I did errands on my own, drove myself everywhere, and even dined at restaurants alone. Although these things may not sound like meaningful accomplishments, they were important milestones at that time in my life.

Months passed, and I became a regular in the exercise class. By now, I had mastered most of the moves. My squats were deeper, and my jumps were higher. I was having fun, and I was much happier. And the best part was that I was burning off tons of calories.

My renewed strength and independence led to hope and optimism I had not felt for a while. During class, I admired the students' smiles and enthusiasm. Everyone had so much energy and their vitality was infectious. As I watched the students striving for excellence in their performance, I was inspired to rise to new levels of achievement, thinking of the endless possibilities for me to tackle new, challenging endeavors. After finishing a strenuous class, I felt like I was capable of accomplishing anything I set my mind to. It was a truly amazing feeling.

During the class, I thought occasionally about physically handicapped people who were unable to exercise, which filled me with gratitude because I was reminded of how lucky I was to be healthy. Consequently, I began to see all of the gifts that had been bestowed upon me. Being happy felt effortless when I realized how fortunate I was. I started counting my blessings, which made me feel even more happy and optimistic.

On the days when I felt less than inspired, there was no shortage of enthusiastic students to jumpstart my energy level. If I felt tired, someone would "high-five" me and encourage me to keep going. When I was feeling less than motivated, I would see people wearing T-shirts with logos that exemplified positivity and perseverance. It was easy to maintain my "can-do attitude" because I was literally surrounded by positive, motivated people. Being around them was like taking a vitamin for my body and soul, so I did my best to pay the positivity forward.

If someone around me was feeling down, I tried to infuse optimism into their mood. Whenever I was able to lift someone's spirits, I felt tremendously fulfilled. On one such occasion, a woman asked me why I was "always positive." She probed me for the "secret" to my happiness. I told her my good spirits stemmed from my fitness routine and the motivational people I encountered at every class.

Since the exuberance I experienced was highly contagious, I was inspired to be joyful in my life as well. My positivity attracted good people into my life, and I met my husband Paul. We laugh all the time; we share enough silly stories to start our own comedy club. We truly enjoy our time together, and Paul often reflects that we have a "very good life." Because we do whatever we can to remain positive and grateful, we celebrate the simple pleasures of life, such as delicious food, breathtaking sunsets, witty humor, and our incredible friendship. There are so many joys in life when we stop to notice them.

I have taken the exercise class for twenty years now. Every time I attend, I feel invigorated, positive, and truly happy. I never thought an exercise class could change my life, mind, body, and heart in such wonderful ways.

The other day at work, a co-worker complimented me on my positive, optimistic attitude. After my shift was over, I smiled as I got into my car and drove to class.

—Kristen Mai Pham—

50

Filling a Need

The people who get ahead in this world are the people
who get up and look for the circumstances they want,
and if they can't find them, make them.
~George Bernard Shaw

Two years after he was diagnosed, my husband's battle with ALS came to its tragically inevitable end. I was subsequently left a widow in emotional and financial ruin, with an eleven-year-old daughter who was also overwhelmed by grief. I required major emergency surgery only three weeks after Mike's death. Four months later, my wonderful father died. Without having so much as a glimmer of hope for a once-bright future that had been destroyed, I felt rudderless. Adrift. Alone.

In an attempt to be proactive with my healing, I visited a bereavement support group for the widowed. However, I simply could not fall into step with the conversations that I heard during that one-time visit. Participants were saying things like, "I'm just waiting until it's my time to go," or "I guess I'll be with him soon." No effort was made to steer the discussion in any positive, life-affirming direction. While I had no clue what the future looked like or where my place was in the new world into which I had been catapulted, the one thing that I knew with certainty was that a "hang around until I die" attitude was not what Mike wanted for his wife and daughter. Therefore, it was not an attitude that I would model for my daughter, Kendall, or embrace for myself.

When we hear the word "poverty," we tend to think only in monetary terms. However, I was suffering from a different kind… emotional poverty. I knew no widowed people who were remotely close to my age, and there was no one in my immediate orbit who could truly understand what I was feeling. Worse still, there was no clear direction in which I could turn to seek help, guidance, education or support.

Finally, I decided that I was finished with emotional-poverty thinking and the abject hopelessness that it brings. This particular headspace served only to keep us in a place of sorrow, fear and hopelessness. I had healing to do. I had a new purpose to discover and fulfill. I had a life to live — as did my daughter. It was time to turn the worst of negatives into something positive, promising and life affirming.

I was determined to grow through tragedy, rather than let tragedy define the course of my life, so I set out on a journey to healing. The going was slow, the challenges were many, and a genuine sense of anything resembling happiness hardly seemed within immediate reach. However, as I remained resolute in finding my place in the new life that I had been handed, the hours and days that initially seemed to pass so slowly suddenly became months — and then years. Kendall had happily re-discovered her childhood, something that had been missing for a very long time due to her dad's illness. I was once again healthy after the major surgery. Eventually, I emerged from the pain and grief following the death of my beloved father. I rebuilt my small business to solid success.

Once again, I became active and genuinely engaged in the world around me. Kendall and I both made our way back into life. Like experiencing sunshine on your face after a winter storm, it felt fantastic to have found our places in life once again.

One day, I was thinking about the strides we had made in finding our way, and how I had initially been unable to find the help and support that I needed. I realized that if I'd once had fears, doubts, questions and issues that were going unanswered, there were likely millions of other widowed people who had similar questions and issues. Widowhood does not come with directions, and I thought that perhaps I could help based on my own experiences.

I have long believed, "If you can't find it... create it," so I began writing. I had no idea that what was originally intended to be one book was going to become both the positivity and the purpose for which I'd been searching. Our family's tragedy could actually help others discover their voices, find the "fight" within, and move forward from an emotional-poverty headspace to a place of peace. The one thing that was missing from the widowed community was an actual, cohesive *community* — one that could rise as a singular voice and declare, "We're here, and we matter, too." Happily, I have been able to play a small part in the creation of such a community, with four books, a website providing education, resources and direction, and an online support community.

No matter the circumstances or the seemingly insurmountable obstacles, there is always a way through. If I cannot immediately find that way through, I'll surely do my best to create one. Meanwhile, I can look back, take a deep breath, smile at my daughter and think to myself, *We did it.*

—Carole Brody Fleet—

51

On Hair with 'Tude

Smile from your heart; nothing is more beautiful than
a woman who is happy to be herself.
~Kubbra Sait

I had retired. I no longer needed to impress or please anyone but me. So, I decided to take the plunge. I became a senior blonde! What, you've never seen that color? Even though I was now sporting it, neither had I. Surprisingly, with all the colors my hair had been, I had never been a blonde, senior or otherwise. It was really a combination of platinum and silver, much like an expensive piece of jewelry. I had it cut very short, except for a great swag of bang that swept across my forehead and dipped kind-of-sexily into my right eye. I was mad about the look. So were most others.

Walking into my yoga class after a few weeks' absence, I saw students trying to figure out who I was. As it dawned on them, comments ranged from "It looks great" to "Wow, you look so much younger." By far, the best was, "Now, that's hair with 'tude."

Posting a picture on Facebook brought more comments than I'd ever received before, many from long-lost friends. Best of all, they were 100 percent positive. Among my favorites: "I like! How long did you sleep on it before you did it?" "Very cute!" and "On to Hollywood!"

A few people weren't crazy about it, including my husband. He was stunned — not in a good way. When I came into the house from the beauty shop, he just stared and said nothing. Indeed, he is a smart man who knew that silence was better than an ill-fated comment. Later that day, he happened to be near the beauty shop and stopped in to chat with my hairdresser.

"There is a strange woman in my house, and I think you had something to do with it," he told him. I understand my hairdresser just gave him a menacing grin. It was my hair, so I got to choose what to do with it. I thought I'd be a senior blonde for quite some time.

Then, as it often does, life took a turn. My beautiful senior-blonde tresses starting to fall out in clumps. Not just a strand or two, but in big handfuls. Could it be the chemicals used in the color? My hairdresser changed things up a bit, but to no avail. Even though I was pretty much in denial that anything was happening, the clumps of hair in my hairbrush told me otherwise.

Reality finally sunk in when I looked at photos of a trip I had just taken. I had to face facts: My hair was not just thinning; it was disappearing! I made an appointment with a dermatologist.

Within a short time, I had a diagnosis. I was suffering from something called lichen planus, a chronic, inflammatory autoimmune disease that affected my scalp. Usually, it just runs its course. In my case, it took my hair with it. The dermatologist did say there was medication that could help save my hair, but I would need to see an ophthalmologist before I could use it. On questioning why, I was told a possible side effect was blindness. *My hair or my sight?* Hmmm, I didn't even blink when I said, "No, thanks."

Walking out of the doctor's office and getting into my car, I was upset and angry, and then very sad. My hair was disappearing. What was I going to do?

I wallowed in self-pity. I started a mental list of all the "wouldn'ts." I wouldn't be able to look like myself again. I wouldn't be able to swim because a wig would get wet. I found myself sinking deeper into a dark place.

Looking in the mirror just made me miserable. The little bit of hair I had was fuzzy and growing in funny patches. It was no longer a senior blonde, but a barely there gray. When I could see myself through my tears, I found nothing attractive about how I looked.

Then one day, running my hand over that ugly fuzz, I had a

moment that would turn me around. I would take control. I found a wig shop and bought two very cute wigs. One was short and sassy, great for exercising or walking and informal occasions. The other was a bit more sophisticated with bangs that swooped over my eye. Oh, yes, they were both blondish. Then I went boldly to my hairdresser. After shaving my head, he turned me around so I couldn't see. Then he put one of the wigs on my head and styled it. Finished, he turned me around. As I came into view, I let out a slight gasp.

"Who is that woman in the mirror?" I asked.

"The new you," he replied, with a huge smile.

I smiled back.

It was only hair. I knew it would never grow back, but that wouldn't stop me from doing what I wanted to do in my life. While I wasn't thankful for what had happened to me, I knew that I did have much to be thankful for in my life — family and friends whom I love, experiences that enrich my life, and so much to look forward to. So, while I may not have any hair with 'tude, I am most fortunate to have a life with 'tude, whether I am bald or a senior blonde.

— Ina Massler Levin —

Coffee with Dad

What greater thing is there for human souls than
to feel that they are joined for life — to be with
each other in silent, unspeakable memories.
~George Eliot

I n January, with just six months left (although we didn't know it at the time), my conversations with Mom were about love, fear and the future. Mom wasn't worried about her own eternal fate — that was secured by her faith in Jesus, firmly established over the previous two years. Instead, her heart was heavy with thoughts of how Dad (her true love of fifty-six years) and I (their only child) would manage without her.

Lying in the hospital bed with Mom, I promised her that Dad and I would hold each other up whenever the time came. She was brave, so I tried to be, and I promised her we would continue to be brave as we moved forward.

An idea came to mind, and it took hold. When Mom returned home from the hospital, we would start a new routine where I would come by their house for coffee every day before work. The benefit would be two-fold. First, by laying eyes on her before going to work each day, I could be more "present" when I got to the office, knowing exactly how she was doing that morning. The second benefit was establishing a routine that included my dad as much as my mom. I had always been Daddy's "princess," but the relationship between Mom and me was so tightly wound that others could really only watch from the outside.

That had to change. It was time for Dad and me to really get to know each other on our own, without Mom as the intermediary. We had to start laying the foundation for a new future together.

Nearly every day for the next four months, I stopped by for coffee and a short visit with my folks. Often, Mom wasn't up to much talking, but she loved the ritual and welcomed her "care bear" enthusiastically. And something really special happened during those visits. A stronger connection grew between Dad and me right before Mom's eyes. We didn't talk about it, but I like to think that the greatest gift we gave Mom at the end was proving to her, and to ourselves, that we were taking care of each other and would continue to do so as things progressed.

Now, from the crack in my broken heart, something new and beautiful is sprouting: a rich and fulfilling relationship between father and daughter. I see this man in a whole new light. As I have told Mom several times in my mind, "I get it… I see why you loved him so much for so long."

During our morning visits, Dad and I talk about current events, history, politics, his grandsons, my job, and the number of steps our Fitbits registered the previous day. I have learned what classes he enjoyed in high school (history and auto shop) and other things he loved in high school, too (pitching pennies and sneaking a smoke).

We talk about our pain, too, although not a lot — that's hard. But we share the pain, and that's enough. We shared a great love for a great woman, and now, more than ever, we share a very special friendship that is all our own.

— Cheryl M. Scott —

Even a Cold Fish Needs Love

*Never forget the three powerful resources you always
have available to you: love, prayer, and forgiveness.*
~H. Jackson Brown, Jr.

Have you ever felt as if someone hated you before you were
even introduced? That's how I felt about a co-worker named
Carolyn who I met when I was promoted to a new position in
a new department.

On my first morning, every person was welcoming except Carolyn.
Her cubicle was next to mine, and she was the last one I met.

I extended a hand and smiled. "It's nice to meet you, Carolyn."

She didn't smile. She unenthusiastically shook my hand and then
squirted sanitizer into her palm. "Hi," she said.

The next day, my supervisor, Ben, told me that one of my first
assignments was to write a brochure about a project that would help
salmon. A culvert under a road was blocked, so when salmon tried
to swim back to the stream where they were born to lay eggs, they
hit a barrier.

I was excited to work on the salmon project until Ben said, "Carolyn
has the folder with all the background information. You'll need to get
it from her."

All afternoon, I stalled. Finally, I asked her for the folder.

"I handle anything to do with salmon," she said. "If you need a
brochure, I can write one."

"Actually, the brochure is my first assignment from Ben."

She didn't look up.

I waited for her to say something. I noticed a sign on her wall that said: "Even cold fish need love."

"I like your sign," I said.

She glanced at it and then kept working, as if I weren't there.

I walked back to my cubicle. *Cold fish Carolyn,* I thought. *How appropriate. Well, she's not going to get any love from me!*

The next day, as much as I hated taking this matter to Ben, I didn't know what else to do. He shook his head and walked into Carolyn's cubicle. "Can I see you in my office?" She followed him, and he shut the door. I heard him talking to her in a raised voice. When she came out, she got the folder and plopped it onto my desk.

"Thanks," I said.

She glared at me.

For the next few weeks, the tension between us grew. For the most part, we avoided each other. If we did pass in the hallway, we huffed or sneered.

Initially, I felt I had won a small victory by securing the folder, but as time passed, I dreaded coming to work. I had always gotten along with people, and this situation gave me a nervous stomach each morning.

When I finished the brochure, I gave it to Ben.

"Good job," he said later that day. "Why don't you run it by Carolyn to see if she has any comments?"

Run it by Carolyn? No way. She'll rip it apart. I went home without giving it to her.

Unable to eat dinner, I took out a book I often consulted: *There's a Spiritual Solution to Every Problem,* by Wayne Dyer.

I found one section where he talked about how holding onto pain and seeking revenge against someone would keep one stuck in pain. "Practice letting go of injured feelings with love and pardon… Let go, and let God."

I knew that as hard as it was going to be, I needed to make peace with Carolyn if I wanted peace at work. I started by treating her in a friendly way the next morning.

"I know you've been working on these types of projects for a long time," I said, handing her the brochure. "Could you take a look at this and let me know what you think?"

She looked surprised.

Let go and let God, I thought.

She took the brochure from me. "Okay," she said.

The next day when I came in, the brochure was on my desk. She had made some suggested changes in red, but not as many as I had expected. I actually agreed with some of them.

I poked my head around her cubicle. "Thanks, Carolyn," I said.

No response.

I continued saying "Good morning" when I came in, and I smiled when I ran into her during the day. It was hard, because she continued to ignore me. I felt like a salmon trying to swim upstream. But each time, I would say to myself, "Let go, and let God."

Carolyn's birthday was coming up. I found a nice card with a fish on the cover and put it on her desk. Around noon, she stuck her head around the corner and said, "Thanks for the card."

As time went on, we began getting to know each other and talking. I learned that she had been at this job for a long time and no longer felt appreciated. She had been trying to find another job closer to where her family lived and wasn't having any luck.

After the new culvert was installed, we went to the stream together to see if we could spot any salmon. The sun was out, and it was hard at first to see through the stream's current.

"There's one!" she said, pointing.

"There's another over there!" I shouted.

The new culvert was working — and so was our friendship.

— Wendy J. Hairfield —

54

Halloween Heroes

*A kind gesture can reach a wound that only
compassion can heal.*
~*Steve Maraboli*, Life, the Truth, and Being Free

A week before Halloween, my young children were parading around our home in their Halloween costumes. Then the babysitter called and canceled. I knew that emergencies do occur, and I told her that I completely understood. But what was actually going through my mind were feelings of frustration and self-pity. Now I would have to pile the kids in the car, drive to my appointment, and get the kids out of the car and into the elevator, all while making certain they behaved.

On the drive, I thought about how life should be going. I was thirty years old, a mother of three daughters — twin five-year-olds and a one-year-old. I should be playing in the park with them or visiting the library. But there I was, once again, going to see the oncologist.

It had been a year since I had been diagnosed with ovarian cancer. I knew that I was one of the lucky ones. I was grateful that surgery and chemotherapy were over, and this was just a routine blood test. As always, there was the lingering fear that they would find the cancer had returned. But today, it was more than that. I felt alone, tired, and sad. My family and friends had been great during the past year, but they were also busy with their lives, and I did not want to burden them with my feelings of unhappiness. I just wanted to see the positive things in life and be truly grateful — without reservations.

When we finally arrived, we sat in a crowded waiting room. It was pretty uneventful until my youngest daughter, dressed up like an angel, walked up to a complete stranger and said, "Tweet." This was how she said, "Trick or Treat," having been coached previously by her twin sisters. The woman, who was in a wheelchair and accompanied by her caregiver, knew exactly what my daughter meant. She ordered her helper to take her over to the vending machine. She put in enough money to give each of my girls a treat. This caring act started a run on the vending machine. Soon, everyone had a candy bar or bag of chips ready for impromptu trick-or-treating. The nurses managed to find three plastic bags, and the angel, dog and cat collected their treasures.

Everyone was smiling and laughing, and my daughters were overjoyed at their good fortune. The happiness in that room touched me to my very core. Here were these people, facing who-knows-what health difficulties, and they only thought of giving three little girls some Halloween fun. It was a lesson for me about how good, kind and generous people are. The gratitude I felt was overwhelming, and the thankfulness didn't fade away.

I have shared my story about the best Halloween ever with my children and grandchildren. Even this many years later, I still feel extremely beholden and grateful to those waiting room Halloween heroes.

— Diane St. Laurent —

55

Angelica

It is literally true that you can succeed best and
quickest by helping others to succeed.
~Napoleon Hill

They were a group of at-risk, inner city teen girls; we were a group of childless career women, at risk of living only for ourselves. A professional women's organization was matchmaking us to help these kids focus on their studies and get them into colleges, and to help us workaholics find meaning in mentoring them.

Our first meet-up took place at a bowling alley. The girls were instructed to recite their first names and follow up with a few words to describe themselves. One by one, they stepped forward. Some got stumped on the brief description of themselves. Girl by girl, the names came with giggles as punctuation: Mary, Leticia, Cindy, Toni, Lourdes, Maria Elena. Silly, good at science, kind to animals, loud, love my sisters. One girl was too shy to make an audible sound, so great was her shame. We were all teary-eyed.

The final, poised young person rose and said, "My name is Angelica, and I am intelligent." *Oh, yes, she is!* I thought to myself. *Both angelic and very intelligent.* She was slender with long, straight, thick hair and a big smile made shinier by silver braces. When the bowling began, she and I drifted into one another's lanes. I would certainly not be guiding anyone out of any gutters in the bowling department, but our chortles about it created a natural bond. When we were later asked to tell the organization our choices, Angelica and I had chosen each other.

It was a relief to feel mutual enthusiasm. I was in a very dark period of my life. Two years before, I'd learned that the man I loved was neither father nor marriage material. I was left with a waning career in an ageist business and no life to enjoy at the end of hard days. As an actor making a living with my imagination, this mentoring would be my first real-life responsible role, not ending at the curtain or the word "cut." This was not pretend, and I wanted very much to be a reliable point person to someone beyond myself.

I met Angelica next at the women's tennis finals. We'd come with homemade lunches, and she helped herself to chicken from my bag, offering me some spicy rice from hers. Serena Williams' war screams of victory provided a powerful background as we shared confidences over the roar of the crowd.

I came from an English-speaking Jewish family of four living in five rooms on the East Coast. Hers was a Spanish-speaking family of five from Oaxaca, living in two rooms. Sharing family-style came naturally to her, as she had shared one bed with her two sisters for years. To me, that sounded crowded but cozy. Angelica's parents both worked as cooks, and she was their translator, accountant and attorney. Her own goals and dreams were hard for her to figure out with so much responsibility and so little opportunity.

When I was invited to her home for Christmas, her mother made me her version of matzohs, and her father prepared a delicious brisket, both with a Mexican spin. I was touched beyond the burn on my tongue by their warmth, and tickled by their laughter over my attempts at Spanish. I was much funnier in Spanish than English, apparently.

As Angelica went on to amaze me, acing her sophomore finals and earning an award at our organization's spring dinner, I felt a pride I'd never known. When she thanked me from the stage and called me her "angel," I was shocked and humbled to tears. From my perspective, I was just relishing her company, encouraging her and, in the guise of "benefactor," benefiting one hundredfold from what I was receiving in return.

In the next few years, I drove her to her first horseback ride, and her first experience with snow and sledding. I shared in her yelps of delight as she slid down snowy hills on a trash-can cover. That was the most fun I'd ever had anywhere with anyone. I could feel tight things inside me letting go around this freedom-loving female.

Things that were easy for me to provide were monumental for her. I gave Angelica an old bicycle, and she taught herself and her sisters how to ride it. When I gave her an old computer, she mastered it. Fast learner, generous soul, grateful, proud person — Angelica came in with all that. I wept at her quinceañera and screamed "Bravo!" when she graduated high school with honors. I cheered her decision to get her B.A. and become a social worker. She hugged me tight and tenderly, and said, "I love you!"

Then, out of the blue, I had to have emergency foot surgery. Unable to drive, I needed someone to get me to the hospital, fetch me in a post-op drug haze, and stay in my home to get me through the first druggy night and day. With no local family and all my career girlfriends too busy to help, I was humiliated by how helpless I was. Taking control, Angelica took a sick day from school, and her uncle brought her in his gardening truck to drive me to the surgery at 6:00 a.m., wait for me, and drive me home.

That night, her sisters came by bus and took care of me. They iced my foot, helped me to the bathroom, cooked for me, and undressed and dressed me. The three slept in two of my spare-room double beds, which they declared, "*Muy grande!*"

As I stumbled my way online through date after date looking for love, Angelica's hugs and kisses eased many disappointments. Her screams of joy on my wedding day, and her screeches when she and her older sister fought for the bouquet, made me laugh and cry. They didn't catch it, but they caught the infectious fever of getting married, and both wed soon after.

Now, Angelica is a grown-up, married woman, with a B.A. in social work, so she can help other people as she did me. She's now living a life in which I'm no longer much needed. But I will think of her forever as my precious angel — despite the fact that she always calls me hers.

— Melanie Chartoff —

56

Snapshots

Life is all about perception. Positive versus negative.
Whichever you choose will affect and more than
likely reflect your outcomes.
~Sonya Teclai

It's funny how we live so much of our lives based on snapshots. Still photos of an instant in time, a specific location, looking in one direction with our attention focused on just a tiny corner of the viewfinder... and that snapshot becomes our reality.

This morning, I'm sitting in a restaurant eating breakfast. At the table in front of mine sits a woman and her young daughter, who is wearing a pink hat. I only notice the hat because it is exactly the sort of thing my own daughter would wear.

Across the aisle from my table sits an old man staring out the window, a cup of coffee held, as though forgotten, in his gnarled hands. His face is creased with years, and his mouth droops slightly at the corners. A bushy, white mustache and matching stubble give the distinct impression of a moody walrus.

He looks tired. Worn.

As he sits, slump-shouldered and lost in his own thoughts, the little girl whispers something to her mother that I cannot hear.

Her mother responds in a hushed voice, "I don't know. Maybe he doesn't have any family or friends to have breakfast with."

I hear another undecipherable whisper.

"Yes, I think it's sad, too. But sometimes that's what happens when we get older."

Then their breakfast arrives, and they move on to another subject. The moment passes.

That is their snapshot.

What the mother (my assumption) and the girl in the pink hat don't have, can't have, is the picture from *my* perspective.

My view from just a few minutes earlier, a few feet away, at a slightly different angle, is an entirely different reality.

When I arrived at the restaurant roughly a half-hour earlier, a dozen old men had been sitting at three adjoined tables.

They were loud and joyful. The room rang with their gravelly, unrestrained laughter, sometimes-bawdy jokes, and much back patting and leg-pulling.

I overheard (yes, I'm a shameless restaurant eavesdropper) plans to meet up for a round of golf later that afternoon, an invitation for dinner with the wives, and even talk of a deep-sea fishing trip this summer.

One man had shared about a recent business trip to Florida. Another (our old man) spoke about a trip to Greece with his granddaughters.

One by one, his friends had finished their breakfasts of eggs, thick bacon, and coffee with heavy cream, and then dropped bills from nearly identical creased and weathered leather wallets onto the tables. Then they excused themselves (after several handshakes and a couple of hugs), and most of them flirted with the young waitress, who appeared to know all of them by name.

Finally, only the old man remained. The tables were cleared and separated. As his cup was refilled, he turned toward the window to watch the geese waddling around the rain-speckled parking lot.

Just then, the bell above the door jingled, and a woman walked in with her daughter, who wore a pink hat.

They saw an old man, seemingly lonely, perhaps embittered, obviously reflective and cognizant that his better days were behind him.

A sad, old man, all alone.

My snapshot, however, showed me a man full of joy, a life rich with friends old and dear, a loving family, a man of appetite who laughed freely and embraced life.

What a strange thing perspective is… and what a powerful force on how we perceive this thing we call reality.

Each of us fashions our world from our own small collection of snapshots.

I hope I remember this… Life is not always what it seems in my viewfinder. Some things may be gold even if they don't glitter.

The grayest, bare walls may shelter the most beautiful gardens… ones that are just around the corner from my view.

— Perry P. Perkins —

Step Outside Your Comfort Zone

57

How Losing My Home Improved My Life

*Coming out of your comfort zone is tough in the
beginning, chaotic in the middle, and awesome
in the end... because in the end,
it shows you a whole new world.*
~Manoj Arora

"I'm sorry, Lisa, but Debbie and I are going to move back into the house. You're going to have to find another place to live."

I couldn't quite believe what Neil, my landlord, was telling me on that warm April night. *I'm going to have to move? But I want to stay right here where I am. This is my home!*

I had tears in my eyes, and so did he. I had lived on the first floor of his Staten Island two-family house for more than twelve years — longer than I had lived in any place since my childhood home. Ever since I moved back to the New York City area in 2000, Neil, a butcher in his fifties, had been like family to me.

Originally, Neil lived on the second floor of the house. But a few years ago, he had moved a few miles away into his girlfriend Debbie's house. He renovated his old apartment and the attic, and rented out that space to some young members of the Coast Guard. But after a torn rotator cuff had ended his grocery career, he and Debbie had decided to sell her house and move back here.

Neil had never raised my rent, which was $750 a month, dirt-cheap for New York City. This was a big comfort when I was laid off from my newspaper job during the height of the recession and couldn't find more than piecemeal work for two years. He promised me that I would always have a home, even if I had a hard time making the rent. However, I always made sure that I paid the rent before any other bill.

Now, I was still recovering from the recession, and I was going to have to find a new apartment and pay more. *A lot more,* I thought.

That was part of the problem. Neil was making a lot more money from the new tenants upstairs, so it made sense for him to keep those tenants and move into my apartment. He was very nice about it, and gave me six months to find a new place. Nevertheless, I was devastated and worried. I was so upset that I got into bed, pulled the covers over my head and cried. It was only 8:30 p.m., but I just wanted to go to sleep and forget this was happening.

Around 12:30 a.m., my upstairs neighbors had a few friends over, and they were making some noise. I stormed out of bed, opened my front door, and yelled up toward their apartment: "Can you keep it down already? I have to get up in five hours to go to work!"

I was so wound up afterward that I couldn't sleep. So I called Jon, my best friend, to bemoan my bad fate. But Jon surprised — and annoyed — me.

"Look on the bright side," he said. "Maybe you will find a place you like better. Let's face it. Your apartment isn't exactly the Taj Mahal. And you complain all the time about that crowded bus to and from the ferry. Why don't you find a place where you don't have to take that bus?"

"How can you say that?" I snapped at him. "This is way out of my comfort zone!"

"C'mon, Lisa. Did it ever occur to you that change could be good?"

"No!" I screamed, and hung up on him.

I fumed for the next few days about our argument. But what if Jon was right? Why was I so afraid of change? Why did I assume that every change would be bad? Why was I so negative all the time? Yes, I had a bad break losing my job, but why couldn't change be good sometimes? Maybe my life needed to be shaken up. Maybe I was in a rut.

The fact was I had let myself go in too many areas. When was the last time I had tried to do something with my writing skills? Or with my weight, which had gotten out of control in recent years? When was the last time I did anything outside of my routine? When was the last time I felt positive and hopeful about anything?

That summer, as I started looking at apartments, I began to think about new possibilities. Maybe I could get better furniture, be a better housekeeper, and have an apartment I could be proud of again.

It was a good thing Neil had given me six months to find a new place because I needed most of that time to save money and find an apartment, which was frustrating. I loved the view from the first place I looked at, but the landlord had already promised the place to someone else. Other apartments had parking issues, or were too small or expensive. And some of them had landlords who seemed just plain weird, like the woman who asked me four times whether I was planning on having a baby even though I was in my late forties.

But as the leaves started falling that year, I wondered if I was being a little too picky and was in denial about having to move. I prayed that I would find a place that was right for me. When was it going to happen? Time was running out.

Finally, that October, I spotted the apartment of my dreams in a new home in a nice neighborhood. The place had a stainless-steel refrigerator, stove, and microwave oven. Great overhead lighting. A built-in washer and dryer. Central air conditioning and heat. No more having to rely on crummy AC window units. The floor was beautifully tiled, unlike my old apartment's worn-out wood floors. This apartment also had a luxurious bathroom that looked like a spa. My old bathroom looked like a crime scene.

The new place was also close to the train and the express bus. While it was farther from Manhattan than my old place, the public transportation was better and more convenient. Plus, the neighborhood had a pharmacy and grocery store less than two blocks away. I could get along well without a car, something that wasn't the case at my old place.

But the apartment was $200 a month more than my current apartment, and it was more than I wanted to spend. It took me two weeks of agonizing, but I finally decided that it was the place for me. I signed a lease and agreed to move in right after Halloween. Moving was very stressful, but I got through it.

Once I had a new place, I was motivated to have new — and better — furniture. I was able to get a fancy new bed at a great discount thanks to one of our clients at work. I also saved a few pennies and bought some good, gently used furniture. My brother bought me a dresser. And Jon put together a bookcase, TV stand, and coffee table for me.

It took a few weeks to get the place fully in order, but I remember how proud I was to show my new digs to my friends, Jon and Ann, one Saturday night when they came over for dinner.

As time went on, I found myself doing more things out of my comfort zone and feeling more positive about life. I started to address being overweight. I began a regular exercise plan and started making meals in my new kitchen, instead of wolfing down junk food. I became more conscious and mindful, and ran regularly — another thing way out of my comfort zone — which helped me lose eighty pounds. I became so dedicated to running that I completed over 250 road races, including eight marathons.

I also started to get out of my comfort zone professionally. I took a risk and pitched *The Washington Post* website about an article idea. To my surprise, they said "yes." Not only did they run "The Redemption of A-Rod" on the website, but they also ran it in the Outlook section of the Sunday edition, which I consider the most prestigious section of the paper!

As change upon change built up in my life, I felt like I was a different person. My life had improved in so many ways, and it all started when I shed the cocoon of my old apartment, took a risk and found a new place to spread my wings. There's a reason they say that the end of your comfort zone is where the magic happens.

— Lisa Swan —

58

The View from the Back Seat

If you surrender completely to the moments as they
pass, you live more richly those moments.
~Anne Morrow Lindbergh

T he back seat is not a place I ever sought out — literally or figuratively. I loved being behind the wheel, enjoying the adrenaline rush while navigating unpredictable traffic. I was a control junkie in all the other areas of my life, too — the take-charge person who could sort out a situation and make things happen.

But that all changed abruptly when the career I loved ended with no notice. My world turned upside down. No longer did I oversee any people or projects. I was shattered.

When two part-time jobs came my way some months later, I was ready to take them on. One required some travel, including two road trips with co-workers. Each time we spent as much time in the car as we did at the events. While preparing for the trips, we talked about who would drive. It turns out that all three of us preferred to drive. Being the newest to the team, I felt it was expected of me to step back.

> *Not driving*
> *reinforced the*
> *fact that I was*
> *not in control.*

This was a new experience for me. Sounding more confident than I felt, I said I would leave the driving to them and sit in the back seat. Surprisingly, I found contentment there, as well as a new direction.

Not driving reinforced the fact that I was not in control. I did not have to focus on directions, road conditions, traffic, or timing. I set up the entire back seat as my little kingdom (perhaps using that word "kingdom" means I still needed a bit of control). I had my thermal bag with my drinks, a book, my phone and charger, a blanket, sweater and assorted sundries.

Now I found myself in the position of a learner. I listened to the conversation in the front seat and picked up subtleties I might have missed if I had been driving. I wasn't idle in the back seat. Instead, I was asking questions, seeking clarification, and learning to use new tools and get to know my traveling companions. By the time of the second trip, I was looking forward to riding in the back.

As I journeyed, I found that these trips gave me a framework for the next phase of my life. Most of my years of work had focused on creating, developing and leading various aspects of ministry and teams. I enjoyed that and found it was a good fit for my gifts, passions, and that stage of life.

My other part-time job did not require travel, but it placed me in a subordinate role to my co-workers. All but one were significantly younger than me. Many were on track for future promotions and career growth. Not me. My responsibility was to copy, scan, index, confirm appointments, make transactions, and assemble mailings. But it was good. I learned I no longer wanted or needed to prove myself. I was content to do what I could to help my colleagues shine.

And changes were taking place in other areas besides in my employment. My marriage improved when I let go of the need to control or always be in charge. A weight came off my shoulders. I'm not saying I never try to step into the position of leader; long ingrained habits change slowly, but I'm working on them.

I learned that the view from the back seat is beautiful. I am more aware of others and situations around me. I am not anxious to change that any time soon. If someone had told me years ago that I would find joy and fulfillment by stepping back I would have scoffed. Now, after a few years as a supporting player, I find it refreshing.

—Joan M. Borton—

59

The Review Is In

*You must be the person you have never had the
courage to be. Gradually, you will discover that you
are that person, but until you can see this clearly,
you must pretend and invent.*
~Paulo Coelho

I t was a beautiful summer day in 2000. I had just returned to my desk from my lunch-hour walk along Mirror Lake in the small city of Camrose, Alberta. The scenic walk was just what I needed after being cooped up inside the children's library all morning. I loved my job, but the sun glinting off the water and wind murmuring through the poplars always left me feeling refreshed and ready for the rest of the day's challenges.

Back at my desk, I found a message saying that the editor of a prominent regional magazine had called while I was out. In addition to my job in the children's department at the library, I was a part-time writer. Very part-time. I was so part-time that, back then, I would never have called myself a writer, even though many of my poems had been published in literary magazines and anthologies across Canada and the United States. I had noticed several months earlier that this magazine published poetry now and then, so I sent their editor a few of my best poems for consideration.

Immediately, I returned the editor's call.

"Hello, Carol! I received your letter and submission, and I wonder if you might be interested in reviewing for us. You'll have a month to turn in your review. And we pay."

Reviewing?

It's amazing how quickly your brain sorts and weighs through options, scenarios, and possibilities in the few seconds between pauses in a conversation. I had never written a review before — at least, not of the sort that would appear in a glossy magazine with a substantial readership. I had written short, enthusiastic book synopses for our library newsletter, created to entice our library patrons to read new acquisitions. Any assessments were always positive because I only discussed books I liked. This would be something quite different.

Could I do it? I questioned if I had the skills, but more to the point, I questioned whether I had the right to critique the work of others. After all, who was I? I was an occasional poet and library assistant in charge of the children's library. My heart fell. They didn't even mention my poetry. They wanted me to review other people's writing.

"I have a novel here. It's by a fairly well known author. Would you like me to send it to you?"

For a split second, my internal critic quieted and I heard another internal voice speak to me even louder: *You can do it. It's a writing gig. Go for it! Worry about the details later and say "yes" now!*

"Certainly," I said, trying to sound confident. "Send me the novel."

The book arrived the next day. Holding the review copy in my hand, I felt like quite the imposter. Whatever gave me the idea I could do this?

Again, that little voice spoke up. *Take it one step at a time. First, read the book.*

So, I did. Initially, I read it through as I would any book for pleasure. Then I re-read it carefully, taking notes. I was relieved to discover I enjoyed the story.

Now what? I sat at my computer, fingers poised, frozen. *Think! Think! Think! What are you going to say?* I remained still for several minutes.

"This is ridiculous," I muttered to myself. "Just start typing. Anything. Just start typing."

My fingers dutifully responded by typing a sentence, then two. Before long, I had a paragraph. Then two. After that, I was immersed in the task, oblivious to everything around me. Many hours later, I reached the end of the review and let out a huge sigh. First draft completed.

I had been writing long enough to know that you need to let a piece sit for a while, and then edit it with fresh eyes. Since I had a deadline, I couldn't let the review languish too long, so I began my edits two days later. Then, I put it aside again. In the meantime, I read through the novel once more. I revised the review again. And again.

When it came time to e-mail the finished piece to the editor, I sat motionless at the computer, hand on mouse, cursor poised over the Send button. I knew once I hit the Send button, it would be out of my hands. I pulled my hand off the mouse. I re-read my review and accompanying e-mail one last time to make sure it was clear of typos and obvious grammatical errors. I took a deep breath and hit Send.

I was certain I would receive a reply from the editor immediately, one that called me out as the imposter I was. "You're not a reviewer! You can't even write properly! Who do you think you are?"

I was right on one point. I received a reply from my editor a short fifteen minutes later.

"Hi, Carol. Thanks for sending in the review. I did a quick read-through, and it looks great! I'll send you updates on any edits I make. Cheers."

A month and a half later, I held the glossy magazine with my review in my hands. Shortly after that, I received another call from the editor. She had two books that she wanted me to review for upcoming issues. I accepted both assignments.

I enjoyed the work so much that, on one particularly optimistic day, I decided to approach two of the largest reviewing magazines in Canada and the U.S. to see if they would take me on as a reviewer. I sent them copies of my published reviews as examples. I cannot say that my imposter complex had disappeared by this time. It had not, but that little voice that kept telling me that I could do these things only had to win out long enough for me to hit the Send button. Both magazines said "yes," and I went on to write hundreds of reviews for their publications as well as for other magazines.

Reading and reviewing so many books over a relatively short

period of time increased my knowledge of contemporary literature tremendously. It also inspired me to do more of my own writing. In 2002, I sold a story to a prominent children's magazine, the first of many magazine and anthology pieces I've had published. In 2017, my first picture book for children, *Lily in the Loft*, was published. Today, I no longer write reviews. The quiet but persuasive voice that I listened to all those years ago when I said "yes" to the book-review assignment suggested that I should focus on my own writing for a while. I'm so grateful I found the confidence to listen.

—Carol L. MacKay—

When the Blind
Taught Me to See

*It's a funny thing about life, once you begin to take
note of the things you are grateful for, you begin
to lose sight of the things that you lack.*
~Germany Kent

A number of years ago, I experienced a lot of frustration and sadness related to a number of things that were happening in my life. It was a daily struggle to simply think about something positive, let alone take action to change my circumstances.

One of my challenges was having recently moved to Chicago from a small Canadian city. I was trying to get used to living in such a large, bustling city.

One day, I saw an ad asking for volunteers to help at a resource center for the blind and low-vision community. I hadn't thought about this kind of volunteering opportunity before and I was a little afraid of it. Nonetheless, I signed up to attend a volunteer orientation session. I was hoping I'd feel better by doing something good for the community.

At the orientation, I sat around a large table with about ten other prospective volunteers. As the orientation facilitator asked each of us why we wanted to volunteer to assist blind and low-vision folks, I began to feel uncomfortable. Every person who answered mentioned they wanted to volunteer because they had either a family member or a friend who was blind or had low vision. I didn't have either. When it was my turn, all I could think to say was that I loved helping people. I was pleasantly surprised when the facilitator commented that helpers were just the kind of volunteers they were looking for. Suddenly, my nervousness began to melt away.

I started volunteering within the week. One of my first assignments was to accompany a blind woman for a walk to a downtown department store. Since I was fairly new to the city, I wasn't completely familiar with the area. Trying to figure out how to get to a certain store proved a bit daunting. As we approached one street corner, I suggested to my companion that we "go to the right." "No, we actually want to turn left," she replied.

I wasn't prepared for her to answer this way, so I asked, "What makes you say that?"

She smiled and said, "Because I can smell coffee coming from the left. The store I want to go to is just past the coffee shop."

As I continued to volunteer at the center, I learned a lot. I discovered that we all strive to do things in life to make us happy. However, we just do them in different ways. One day, I heard a group of folks talking about attending a local theater production. I was trying to figure out how it could be enjoyable for them since they couldn't actually "see" the performance. Slightly hesitating, I asked, "Can you tell me about your experiences at the theater?"

A gentleman replied, "The theater we go to is great! We get to attend a 'touch tour' before the performance. We walk onto the set and are shown where things are placed by touching them. When the play begins, we know what the actors are referring to, such as where the couch is located. Getting to touch all of the props on the stage helps us enjoy the play a lot."

"Don't forget about the headphones," another person said.

"Yes, we get to wear headphones. An assistant lets us know whenever there is movement by an actor, or if there is a particular facial expression," commented the gentleman.

Yet another person said, "We always get the best seats in the house!"

Over time, I started a reading group focused on inspirational and uplifting books and anything with a slice of humor. I'd read the book to everyone, and we'd discuss it. The meetings always morphed into incredible talks. I remember reading a passage in a book that mentioned a character's hair color. A member of our group asked, "Cher, what color is your hair?"

"I have blond hair," I replied.

"What color is my hair?" the same book-group member asked.

"Your hair is a beautiful, shimmering gray that catches the sunlight coming from the window," I answered.

"Oh, it sounds nice," she said.

"Yes, it certainly is," I replied.

Once, I was rushing past someone in the center's main hallway because I was late for an appointment. All at once, I heard, "Hi, Cher!"

I stopped and asked, "How did you know it was me?"

"Everyone has a distinctive walk," the woman replied. "I heard yours, so I knew it was you."

My time volunteering at the center was truly life changing. Describing the visual world to these dear souls gave me a monumental appreciation for every single thing I could see. Hearing the joy in their voices over the ability to "watch" a play or to recognize someone by their footsteps was humbling. Describing someone's hair to them while knowing they'd never seen it was overwhelming, to say the least.

During the time I volunteered at the center, I became a U.S. citizen. Little did I know that my book group had organized a party for me. Walking into the meeting room, I was greeted by clapping and, "Yay, Cher!"

A cake, coffee, and an envelope with my name on it were placed in front of me. As I slowly opened the envelope, I could feel a lump in my throat. Inside, I found a beautiful card and a note written by a volunteer on behalf of the group.

The note congratulated me for becoming a U.S. citizen. There was also an additional note referring to a gift that was given to me. The group had donated their own money to a reforestation project and purchased a tree to be planted in my honor.

I tried to hold back the tears, but everyone could hear my shaky voice. Without thinking, I said, "I'm crying with happiness," to which several members replied, "We know."

Never again will I take my many blessings for granted. I hadn't realized how many I had until meeting the wonderful people at the blind and low-vision center.

They significantly impacted my life for the better. Now I embrace the positive and look at things in my life from a brand-new perspective.

"Seeing" the world from a different perspective changed me. It has made me incredibly grateful and happy for the little things in life — the smell of fresh pastries coming from a bakery, the sound of children playing, tasting new foods, puppies wagging their fuzzy tails, and smiling babies.

I could never give to them what they have given to me. I will never forget how they changed my life for the better.

—Cher P. Garman—

More Important than Fear

*When we share our stories, what it does is, it opens up
our hearts for other people to share their stories. And it
gives us the sense that we are not alone on this journey.*
~Janine Shepherd

"**Y**our body listens to everything you say, so be careful what
you tell it!" my oncologist, Dr. Gordon, warned during
my last visit to his office. "Life's a celebration, so start
living it," he added with a sparkle in his eyes.

It was the end of my breast cancer treatment. I should have been
jubilant, but Dr. Gordon's words struck me as a "warning" to change
my way of thinking. I took him at his word and made a conscious effort
to live and think positively from that day forward — just in case my
body was listening. I posted his words on the bathroom mirror so I'd
see them when I got ready for work. I pasted them on my computer
screen at the office and over the kitchen sink where I'd see them while
doing dishes. It became my mantra: "Life's a celebration!" And behind
that exclamation mark were the sobering words: "Your body listens
to everything you say."

Before breast cancer at age forty, I was more of a glass-half-empty
type. But after the completion of treatment, I became a glass-half-full
woman. It was the fall of 1996, and I loved my job in health information
management. But I knew if life was going to be a true celebration, I
needed to change career paths. More than anything, I wanted to make

a difference — not just go through the motions of bringing home a paycheck.

As I researched the possibilities, I decided that I wanted to share with others how to overcome the challenges brought about by cancer. I contacted my public library, and they agreed to allow me to present on the topic: "What to Say and How to Help When Someone Has Cancer." The only thing I forgot was that I had a paralyzing fear of public speaking — so much so that I gave up graduating from college because I never took Speech 101.

I had one month before the evening's presentation at the Milanof-Schock Library in Mount Joy, Pennsylvania. Every time I passed the library on the way home from work, I felt more fear creep in. How was I going to present a two-hour seminar without my voice quivering, my hands shaking, and my palms sweating? Maybe they could dim the lights through the entire presentation, and no one would have to see me. Or maybe, like in *The Wizard of Oz*, I could hide behind the screen as I narrated the PowerPoint.

> *"It's not about you; it's about the people you're trying to help!"*

I knew from past research that public speaking was the number-one fear of most people. In fact, it was greater than the fear of death. I took some comfort in that, but I was still afraid. Every time I thought about standing in front of a crowd, my palms started to sweat, and my throat became dry.

Two weeks before the seminar, I called my best friend, Kim, who planned to be in attendance that evening. As a high-school Spanish teacher, she was accustomed to getting up in front of students and teachers.

I blurted out, "I don't think I can do the seminar!"

"What are you talking about?" Kim questioned. "You'll do fine. Your passion will override every fear. Remember, it's not about you; it's about the people you're trying to help!"

That's all I needed to hear. How selfish of me to be concentrating on myself when the message was to help others.

"Thanks, Kim. I'll see you in a couple of weeks."

The evening of the seminar, as people poured in and filled the room, more chairs had to be brought in to accommodate the crowd. One of the first to arrive was the head of the medical practice where I worked, followed by my friend Kim. More friends and guests came to offer support.

After the introductions were made, I walked numbly toward the podium with my syllabus and PowerPoint, ready to share my heartfelt message. As I began telling my story, I saw people in the audience dabbing at tears. Others nodded in affirmation, and Kim smiled warmly. I realized that the shaky voice was absent, and my hands weren't sweating. My focus was on the crowd — not me!

As I delivered my last PowerPoint slide with the words "Life's a Celebration," there was silence followed by a standing ovation. I was both relieved and excited that I had not only overcome cancer, but also my lifelong fear of public speaking!

It's been fifteen years since I gave my first speech, but it wasn't my last. Since that time, I've been traveling across the country giving my hallmark speech, "Living the Passionate Life." On November 2, 2007, I was scheduled to deliver a keynote at the Fox Chase Cancer Center in Philadelphia, Pennsylvania, for The Eileen Stein Jacoby Fund for breast-cancer research. As I stepped up to the podium, an entourage followed me with a beautifully framed plaque in hand, a corsage of pink and white roses, and wearing smiles of appreciation.

As it turned out, I wasn't going to be giving a speech at all, but receiving the "Celebration of Life Award" from the Fox Chase Cancer Center. Tears sprang to my eyes as I accepted the award on behalf of all breast-cancer survivors who have discovered that life is worth celebrating — even on the darkest days.

Through my tragedy, pain and loss, I discovered my passion for public speaking and celebrating life — one precious day at a time!

— Connie K. Pombo —

Oh, I've Always Wanted to Do That

Life is short, and it is up to you to make it sweet.
~Sarah Louise Delany

When I was a junior in high school, my girlfriends and I bemoaned the fact that we were bored and there was nothing to do. I decided that my senior year was going to be the best ever, and I began looking for clubs to join. I had always wanted to be a cheerleader, so I tried out for and was elected to the position of school mascot. I applied for and received the position of editor-in-chief of the school yearbook. I auditioned for and made the school dance team. I was even voted Class Most Spirited. My senior year was the best ever!

Attending university became a different matter. I only had time for school and work. Then I got married and had a baby right away. For eighteen years, I stayed home and raised my sons. I volunteered at my church, but that was the only outside commitment that my then-husband felt I had time for.

I had always wanted to join other organizations like Meals on Wheels or to sign up for dance classes. I pored over the community catalog that offered crafting and cooking classes, daylong excursions to museums, and lessons in tennis and golf. There were so many things that I had always wanted to do, but my husband wouldn't allow me to do them. It was only every once in a great while, after much cajoling, that my husband would give me the okay to sign up for a class.

At year seventeen, my marriage began to crumble. Divorce was imminent. As my life fell apart, I cried, ranted, and complained to anyone and everyone. But soon I got tired of hearing myself whine. I knew I needed to get outside myself and focus on something bigger. What could that "something" be? I had always wanted to be a mentor within the Big Brothers Big Sisters organization, so I gave them a call. Turns out they didn't need sisters; they only needed brothers! What else to do? Well, I knew a physical outlet to relieve the tension from my failing household would be good, so I signed up with the Leukemia & Lymphoma Society. They provided marathon training in exchange for raising funds to support their organization. I had always wanted to participate in a marathon. By the day of the Rock 'n' Roll Marathon, I had accomplished several things that I had always wanted to do — purchase a home by myself, get a tattoo, and sign up for a 26.2-mile marathon.

At the start of the marathon, I began with my team that I had trained with for months. At some point along the course, I was separated from them. I ended up crossing the finish line by myself. Deliberately, I focused on watching my feet cross the finish line, to be in the moment and feel that sense of accomplishment. I had accomplished something that I had always wanted to do!

A few weeks later, the professional photographer for the race sent me a photo of me smiling at the camera. I looked so proud and happy in that photograph. As I studied that photo, I realized that the words, "Oh, I've always wanted to do that," had become my mantra and guiding life philosophy. I was back to living my true, authentic life. If the words, "Oh, I've always wanted to do that," come out of my mouth, then I have to do it!

I keep that framed photograph on my bathroom vanity so I see it every day. It's a visual reminder that I can do whatever I put my mind to.

Since then, other accomplishments that I've achieved because of my new life philosophy include: Walking the Great Wall of China, becoming scuba-certified, skydiving twice, managing a funk band, becoming a published writer and paid speaker, taking my mom to

Step Outside Your Comfort Zone |

Paris, swimming with dolphins, and going snowmobiling.

What's next? Recently, I received an e-mail from an associate who is a racecar driver. He invited me to ride along with him as he drives his Porsche 911 GT3 at the Auto Club Speedway. I didn't realize that was something I'd always wanted to do, but I accepted the invitation! Some people may call it a "Bucket List." For me, it's not a list — it's a lifestyle. With a life philosophy of jumping out of my comfort zone and into whatever "I've always wanted to do," the possibilities are endless!

— "Sunny" Esther Valenzuela —

63

Mommy, Molly and Magic

I am not the same, having seen the moon shine
on the other side of the world.
~Mary Anne Radmacher

It's 1984, and several mommy friends and family members have told me that I'm crazy. I'm audacious and foolhardy for taking off alone with my toddler daughter to explore the South Pacific islands of Fiji, New Caledonia and Vanuatu. They said I was reckless and irresponsible.

"Traveling with a toddler is so hard and dangerous, especially because you're alone."

"She's in the terrible twos. Are you sure you can handle this by yourself?"

As we stand in the crowded, chaotic International Terminal at LAX, waiting to board our thirteen-hour flight to Fiji, I have to admit they might have a point.

But I have a point to make, too. I want to share my own confident, free spirit and the words that I live by: "Be a leader, not a follower. Be daring and bold." This blond, curly-haired little person, this trusting, radiant being, looks to me wide-eyed for guidance and reassurance. I do my best to provide that. Our bond is unmatched and joyful. We're an inseparable duo, just Molly and me.

Besides, we're protected by magic. She's wearing her brand-new OshKosh B'gosh pink-striped overalls and Rainbow Brite T-shirt. She clutches her favorite doll, a baby girl, who she has named Edward. Her other tiny hand holds mine firmly. The oversized Strawberry Shortcake backpack she proudly wears dwarfs her two-and-a-half-year-old frame. It's filled with Cheez-Its, Cheerios and apple slices, a Care Bear puzzle, Elmo coloring book and a small stable of My Little Ponies.

Magical!

Finally on board and settling into our seats, she jabbers excitedly. "Mommy, when are we going to be there? How fast does the airplane go? Do they have cookies?"

An hour into the flight, she yawns and asks, "Mommy, are we there yet?"

Not yet, baby girl, but soon.

We stop over in Honolulu and visit the gift shop. My intrepid traveler, on her first airplane flight and clearly feeling the spirit of Aloha, suggests that Edward needs a hula skirt and lei. Of course, she does!

Back onboard for the longest leg of our Qantas flight, Rick Warneke, our handsome, friendly flight-service director, leans into me. With his endearing Australian accent, he whispers in my ear, "I'll bet you and your little girl would be more comfortable in first class. Come with me." Obediently, and not needing any arm-twisting, we follow.

Now well fed, cozy and warm, snuggled in our thick, first-class blankets, we stretch out in our cushy seats and drift off to sleep. A bit later, I jolt awake, and Molly is nowhere to be seen. I know she hasn't gone far, but I am still panicked. I bound out of my seat and run down the aisle looking for her.

She's in the back of the plane playing with the flight attendants and several passengers. Happy as a lark, she's laughing, chatting, and eating a cookie. Clearly, she's not missing me or worried in the slightest.

That's my fearless, adventurous girl… born to travel. Wanderlust is imprinted in her DNA.

Crossing time zones and losing an entire day, we land bleary-eyed in Fiji. Looking up at me with her big, blue eyes, Molly asks again, "Mommy, are we there yet?"

Almost.

I've reserved a cabin at Castaway Island resort. It's only accessible by boat or seaplane, so we hop onto a little ferry for the ninety-minute ride to our first tropical paradise.

The staff meets us at the water's edge and forms a ragtag band in the sand. Music fills the air, and Molly's giddy as she's hoisted off the boat onto a crewmember's broad shoulders. Our *bure*, Fijian for a wood-and-thatch hut, awaits. The scent of frangipani, jasmine and gardenia fills the air. Ripples of warm, aquamarine waves gently kiss the shore. Trade winds blow tranquilly as we settle in and unpack.

But we're not alone. Little green geckos are everywhere. Initially alarming, they're actually pretty adorable. We learn that geckos do all sorts of noble and noteworthy things, such as eating bad bugs. Watching them scurry about endlessly makes Molly squeal with delight.

We see fishermen catching our dinner at dusk right outside our door. I use a scarf to make a tiny sarong for baby doll Edward, and then the three of us, dressed in almost matching sarongs, stroll barefoot through the sand to dinner. We dine by candlelight under balmy, starry skies while a funky little band serenades the guests. The island kids join in to sing, dance and pound on drums. I delight in watching my little girl joyously jump around on the makeshift stage with the other kids while we parents enjoy a delicious dinner of freshly caught fish, taro and tropical fruits.

One thing becomes clear almost instantly: Fiji is one of the happiest countries in the world. It's no wonder since they are a tight-knit, village-based society where kids are cared for by everyone and are free to roam around and play. Elders are revered, and children are supported by aunties, uncles and cousins. They have a nearly perfect climate year-round. The national drink is kava (known to be mildly hallucinogenic). Music, fresh food and blazing colors are everywhere. The laidback culture is steeped in ceremony and tradition.

They have a rich, storytelling folklore filled with mythological gods. One myth describes how the islands are protected by Dakuwaqa, the shape-shifting shark-god. The islanders live in harmony with, and have great respect for, the many sharks in their waters.

I find myself identifying with this mighty ocean guardian and hope that he or she doesn't mind me borrowing a bit of fearlessness. But then I realize that I've come here for a reason that I didn't quite

Step Outside Your Comfort Zone | 203

understand before — to find my own strength and power. And the Fijians are sharing and showing me how I can seek my own shark-god.

And here's the point I'm trying to make: Had I listened to the fear-inducing, unsolicited advice that others gave me, we might never have had this magical experience.

I know there are plenty of things in life to be fearful of. Some are reasonable: Don't hitchhike alone at night when the Zodiac Killer is on the loose. Never walk between a mother moose and her calves on a lonely mountain road in Montana. (Hmmm, did I do that?) Other fears are unreasonable and designed to do nothing more than make me fret and worry. Like raising a child — especially on my own.

Other moms told me that if I made it over the hurdle of morning sickness and the agonizing pain of childbirth, I could look forward to postpartum depression, aching breasts, sleep deprivation, and loss of any type of self-care. Life would be an endless loop of dirty diapers, snotty noses, throw-up, and laundry — and that is if I had a "good" baby. If my baby were colicky or fussy, I was warned, my life would be a veritable nightmare.

Nope, not me. That would not be my story. I have never been afraid of much, except those scary moms. I ignored them all. Then and now.

By traveling abroad together, we were growing from life's magically unpredictable, teachable moments. No building blocks and circle time for my toddler. This big world is a living, breathing experiential classroom, where life's richest education happens. Together, we learned that we can live bold lives without fear.

Today, Molly has three rambunctious, adventuresome kids of her own, and they've traveled the world, too. Happily, gloriously exuberant, and fearless.

One day, I hope to take them all to Fiji and introduce them to the legend of Dakuwaqa. I'll tell them how the mystical shark god protected their mother and me, and gave us strength and courage.

And that magic happens.

— Stephanie Blank —

64

Aftermath

One of the greatest discoveries a man makes,
one of his great surprises, is to find he can do
what he was afraid he couldn't do.
~Henry Ford

The numbers seemed to melt together. I felt the tears coming, again. It was lunch period, but here I was, standing at the blackboard trying to solve a multiplication problem. Mrs. Harris had said, "You are going to finish that problem if it takes all lunch period." And then I thought I heard her mumble, "You are just dumb."

That was third grade and the beginning of my dislike of math. I did everything possible to avoid it. Even when I worked as a bank teller after graduating from junior college, the computer did the work for me.

But then, I had a chance to get a four-year degree. There was only one problem. I had to take a math class in order to get in.

When I read the course description, I saw that the class involved many mathematical procedures such as percentages, powers and permutations. I shuddered. If I wanted a chance at this dream, I had to face up to my fear, or I could work behind the teller desk forever.

The ultimate question was: How badly did I want to go to the university? Was it enough to face not just multiplication, but powers and permutations and all the other concepts I had no experience with?

When I decided to brave the class, I learned that it was already full. And it was the only class that would fulfill the math requirement.

I would need to talk to the instructor, Mr. Thorpe. I called his office after rehearsing what I would say.

Holding the receiver to my ear with a trembling hand, and ignoring the stares of customers at the teller windows, I said, "Mr. Thorpe, if you could see me, you would know how much I want to be in your class. I am on my knees."

He agreed to make an exception. My supervisor gave me one morning off a week to attend the class.

I got an F on the first test. The second was a D-. After a week, I decided perhaps it wasn't meant to be. The ultimate humiliation would be to finish the course but fail the "test" I had set for myself. I couldn't endure it. I would be confirming what my third-grade teacher had mumbled about me — I was dumb.

I called Mr. Thorpe the next morning, thanking him for giving me the chance to succeed, but admitting that I just had to face it. Math would never be my strength, and it would not be the way into the university. I would find some other way another time.

There was silence on the other end of the phone. Then I heard him take a slow, even breath and say, "Leah, I don't know if you have noticed, but the class is smaller. There were 257 students enrolled in this course, and now there are sixty-four. You can't quit now... You are a survivor."

He waited for my response, and I tried to sound unemotional and detached as I said, "I've decided I cannot continue... especially after seeing my grades. I want to thank you for admitting me."

There was another long silence. I waited for him to accept my decision and end the conversation. Instead, he continued. "I wasn't going to tell you this, but there is a woman from the university who calls me weekly. She says, 'I have the admittance papers here ready for Leah. How is she doing? Do you think I'll be needing these?'"

I closed my eyes. I really didn't want to hear this.

He continued, "And I tell her, there is not a doubt in my mind. She has hung on. She is a survivor."

The tears flowed down my face.

"I wish you hadn't told me that," I managed to say.

"Do you still want to leave the class?" he responded, ignoring my last remark.

I was quiet, sniffling, feeling backed into a corner.

"No," I said softly.

"Fine. I'll see you in class on Tuesday."

I was stunned. Didn't I just call to drop out of class?

After that, I never thought about those test grades again. I studied every weekend with a friend over coffee and doughnuts.

When it was time to see our grades, I said a prayer before I looked. C+. I had passed.

Months later, I found myself walking up the steps to start at the university They seemed to be welcoming me... leading me to the beginning of a new life. An overpowering sense of gratitude brought me to my knees again, and I found myself leaning down to kiss the steps. I didn't even feel my knees on the cement.

All around me, I felt eyes on me. I didn't care. I had grabbed my second chance by the tail.

Then, I got up and rushed off so I wouldn't be late for my first class.

Take *that*, Mrs. Harris!

—Leah Cano—

65

The Lake Weekend

Don't be afraid to expand yourself, to step out
of your comfort zone. That's where the joy
and the adventure lie.
~Herbie Hancock

I t was a beautiful morning, quiet with the fog still suspended over the lake. Every now and again, we'd hear the slap of a fish jumping out of the water. This was probably the tenth year our two families had come to the lake for Labor Day. It was everyone's favorite weekend.

Kristen and I were the early risers. We loved waking before anyone else. Now we sat on the deck with steaming mugs of coffee. Best friends since college, we cherished this uninterrupted time to catch up and talk.

Kristen was telling me the details of her latest competition. She was deep into working out and fitness, and it showed. She looked fabulous and had competed in fitness competitions — the kind with the tiny, glittering swimsuits and muscle-enhancing poses.

"I don't talk about them a lot. People think it's weird. But here's the thing," she said. "I do it for me. Not for anyone else. And what else in my life is all about me? It challenges me and takes me out of my comfort zone."

All of a sudden, after all the months and years of competitions, I understood.

"The other thing," she continued, "is that it gives me a new confidence, especially at work with all the men." Kristen is a lawyer and works in a male-dominated office. She's brilliant and insightful, but often has to work extra hard to prove herself. "I don't mean confidence in a great body; I mean confidence on the inside. It's like an internal, personal strength has grown from this. I can do this thing I never thought I could. That's what it's about. Sure, the buff arms are a perk, but the confidence is more of what it's about."

"It's like my writing," I said. "I never thought about it, but they're essentially the same thing. I mean, we're both baring ourselves, letting ourselves be vulnerable and be judged." Now I understood her figure competitions. I told her about a novel I'd begun writing and a story I had submitted for publication.

Like Kristen and her fitness, I didn't talk much about my writing. It's my thing, the challenge I have taken on for me and me alone. It doesn't bring in much money, I'm not on any bestseller list, and it doesn't provide for my family. And yet, it does have an effect on them, because taking on this personal challenge has made me a better, stronger person. And that makes me a better wife, mom, friend. I've increased my confidence, something I was always lacking. Yes, I have goals and dreams of where I'd like to see it go, just like Kristen does with her fitness. But we are both okay for now if things just stay the same, as long as we keep pushing ourselves and doing these things that are just for us.

Growing up, I didn't really push myself. I did okay at things, but I didn't try new things, put myself out there, or push my limits. As an adult, I have grown into a stronger, tougher, more confident woman, and I think it's because I've undertaken this challenge of writing fiction. Now, I encourage my kids to try new things, go out for leadership positions, and speak up for themselves. The younger me wouldn't have been a good role model, but the new me, who has put herself out there, is a good example.

Throughout the weekend, our families laughed until we cried, ate until we were stuffed, played until we were worn out and sun-kissed, and let the lake soak into our souls. We knew Monday would come quickly, and we'd have to pack up and go home. Kristen would be back in her office in her high heels, with make-up and a fabulous outfit replacing sunscreen and a bathing suit. I'd be back in front of my computer, writing the unglamorous stuff that brings in enough money to enjoy lake weekends.

On Sunday night, as we cleared the last of our dinner and listened to the kids laughing as they roasted marshmallows, Kristen asked her husband, "Did you know Claire wrote a short story, and she's working on a novel?"

"What? How would I know that?" he said.

"Her story's incredible. Y'all should read it. I'm sure it will get published. Claire's a great writer," my husband, Alex, said casually. But when I looked over at him, his face shone with pride. *That pride is for me,* I thought. I had challenged myself and found something beautiful and shiny.

I remembered the first time we had come to this lake ten years earlier. We were all much younger. The kids were underfoot, and we drank much more wine. But this trip was better. I could tell Kristen felt the same, too. Sure, we tried to leave our stress and baggage at home, but that wasn't always easy. Sometimes, it came with us, especially the social baggage that often follows women around. This time, we were more relaxed and carefree... more confident.

Did the writing do this to me? Did the fact that I had the nerve to send in a story make me a different person? I think by challenging myself to step outside my comfort zone, it helped me become this stronger person who might have been inside all along. Who would have thought I'd like the middle-aged me more than the younger me?

The weekend drew to a close. We dried our towels, packed our bags, and headed home. The air had a taste of fall in it; it was time to re-enter reality. Good news arrived that week, though — my story was accepted. It was just an online magazine, but still, my story was accepted! I called Kristen to tell her, and the buzz of excitement and pride in her voice was almost tangible through the phone. Even better, I felt it inside me, too.

By the way, this wasn't my first submission — I'd had a few rejections along the way, too. But those didn't hurt as much as I'd thought they would because I was growing with each one, getting stronger and owning myself. The positive growth from stepping outside my comfort zone was worth every bit of anxiety, and I've noticed there's much less of that anyway. Now it's my turn to go support Kristen in her next competition. We've got this!

— Claire Chargo —

Chapter
8

Find Your Inner Strength

66

The Miracle of the Potatoes

I have sometimes been wildly, despairingly,
acutely miserable, but through it all I still know
quite certainly that just to be alive is a grand thing.
~Agatha Christie

World War II was raging throughout Europe and was getting more intense in our area of France, which bordered Germany's Western Front. Those of us who lived in outlying areas were being rousted from our homes and loaded onto trucks to be transplanted to abandoned houses elsewhere in France. It was a harrowing time for all, as fighting raged around us, and we feared for our lives.

We were living a frugal farm life, but our home was comfortable, and we always had enough to eat. We worked long, hard hours on the farm, but our tight-knit family managed to get by reasonably well. We considered ourselves lucky and were quite content despite the circumstances.

Then a series of disasters struck. My grandparents both passed away in quick succession, while my father got called up for the draft into the French Army. Meanwhile, my mother began feeling poorly and was soon diagnosed with terminal cancer. Then the soldiers appeared at our door, evacuating the town. Being uprooted from our home just added to the chaos and suffering. We weren't allowed to take anything with us, so we grabbed what cash and trinkets we could lay our hands on and hurriedly got into the transport trucks.

After what seemed like a lifetime, we were deposited in front of a tumbledown shack where we were told to take up lodging. It was an old, abandoned house that we would have to stay in for the rest of the war.

We began gathering sticks to build a fire in the hearth. The only food we had was the dry rations left for us by the transport soldiers. All the wonderful provisions that we'd stockpiled at the farm had been left behind.

My sickly mother gave me some meager funds and asked me to canvass the neighborhood to see if anyone would sell us some eggs, butter, or anything else to eat. I trudged from dawn until dusk, only to come back discouraged and empty-handed. Everyone realized that the situation was dire, and no amount of pleading or crying could convince them otherwise. "You can't eat money," they said, as one after another refused to sell me even one solitary egg, often slamming their doors in my face.

I was being forced to grow up fast, and I didn't like it very much. Looking at the innocent faces of my four younger siblings, I knew I had to do something. But what? As I contemplated my next move, I began exploring the surrounding property and the outbuildings. I was hoping to find anything of value.

Soon, I had scoured everything but found nothing of interest. Except for some junk, the place had been totally cleared out. The final area to check was the creepy dugout basement, which I purposely left for last. With a fretful sigh, I screwed up my courage and went down there.

It was musty and dark in the basement, but I moved around quickly and hoped I wouldn't be there long. If the grounds were stripped of goods and nothing of value was in the house, what could possibly be down there? No sooner had that thought crossed my mind than I saw a huge, shadowy object in the corner. It seemed to be a tarp covering something very big. It was an ominous thing to discover while exploring the dim basement by myself, but my desperation gave me the nerve to proceed. As I moved closer, I saw that a thin ray of sunshine had passed through the dirty basement window and was illuminating the area.

Gathering my last shred of courage, I edged toward the large, dark object. Holding my breath, I lifted the corner of the tarp. I couldn't believe what I was seeing. It was a massive stash of potatoes, enough to last us for quite a long time. Better still, on closer inspection, they all seemed to be in perfect condition.

The next day found me in the streets again, bartering potatoes for all kinds of other foodstuffs. Soon, I became a young businesswoman by day as I learned to trade fairly and expertly. The rest of the time, I was a homemaker, nurturing my siblings and my ailing mother.

My mother didn't survive the war, but thankfully my father did, as well as my siblings. We returned home to rebuild our lives and the house that had been razed to the ground.

In the midst of both personal and worldwide devastation, I learned to be a strong and capable young woman. The experience set the tone for the rest of my life, empowering me to push aside fear and take on whatever the world would bring.

I've never forgotten how, in our most desperate moment, we were saved by the Miracle of the Potatoes.

— Denise Del Bianco —

67

Walking Back to Me

Walking is man's best medicine.
~Hippocrates

I pulled my chemo-battered, exhausted body off the couch and headed out the door. *Put one foot in front of the other. That is all you have to do,* I told myself. I had determined that if I made myself walk every hour for five minutes, regardless of how terrible I felt, it would help me feel better. It would at least make me feel that I had some control over my life again.

My husband and I had been told by my therapist, Tiffany, that my coping strategies needed to change to effectively manage my fatigue. Walking was a key part of my hoped-for transformation. Cancer had taken so much from me, and it was time to start working my way back. With that goal in mind, I set out into my yard and began walking around the property. Each step defeated me. Chemotherapy-induced aching bones made every step painful. That first five-minute walk felt like a daylong forced march. When I was done, I limped back in and crumpled exhaustedly on the couch. My husband just flashed a "way to go" smile in my direction. I slept for the next hour until it was time to do it again. It was a very long first day.

Limiting myself to the yard was protective. If the walk became too much, I could always stop and go inside. Some days, during those five minutes every hour, I plodded along in tears, forcing myself to put one foot in front of the other. But I had to do this for myself and my family. That first week was exhausting. My body fought against the change and ached more than before. I also slept more between walking sessions. Little by little, though, I began to feel stronger.

At our second meeting, Tiffany helped us set long-term goals. One of my goals was a day at a theme park, walking instead of using a wheelchair. After our session, I carried on with her assigned tasks and my self-imposed step challenge. I determined to add two extra minutes to my hourly walks every week. As time went by, these became easier. Some days, the bone pain still overtook me, and I'd cry through the effort, but I could feel that I was not as tired as my body traveled the track etched in my yard. The grass wore away, and the ground smoothed under my steady footfalls. With each week, my walks grew lengthier, but I always trod the same path.

As the weeks progressed, I began meeting other program goals, but I still had the theme park to conquer. It frightened me to risk a whole day on my feet. It wasn't just me that I would disappoint; my family also wanted this so desperately for me.

The day finally came, and we ventured off to SeaWorld. As we walked into the park, the sun was shining and there was a cool breeze. Over the speakers, Rachel Platten's "Fight Song" played. "This is my fight song, take back my life song…" she sang. Tears glistened on my cheeks, and my husband looked at me with concern. Our teenage daughter saw the worry in his eyes and glanced at me. When we shared a knowing smile, my daughter reached for my hand and said, "Don't worry, Dad. That's Mom's song."

In the early days of this leukemia journey, she had forgotten something at home after leaving for school and had found me balled up in bed, crying from the pain, with "Fight Song" on repeat. I told her it was my anthem and reassured her that I would be fine eventually. She gave me a hug before returning to her father's waiting truck. Apparently, she hadn't told him about that.

I walked from show to show that day. I climbed stadium stairs with purpose. I offered to get the food while my family saved us a table. I walked around the park practically overflowing with accomplishment. I was so proud that you would have thought I had run a marathon. In a way, I had. Walking my way back to a life not controlled by fatigue was an exercise in perseverance. Every day, I tried to go a little farther than I had the day before.

My body cooperated on some days and let me down on others, but I kept going. Through my walks, I began to see myself as an unstoppable force. Yes, cancer was and is a part of my life, but I will not let it be the prime descriptor of who I am. Walking gave me my life back and changed the way I saw myself. Even now, when I have a difficult task ahead of me, I remind myself to just put one foot in front of the other.

—Amy Michels Cantley—

68

Creating a New Story

That last page turned is a perfect excuse
to write a whole new book.
~Toni Sorenson

W hen the Woolsey Fire first began in Southern California in November 2018, I didn't think I had much to worry about. After all, it was a good twenty to thirty miles away. It would have to jump a freeway and spread through miles of canyons to get anywhere close to my Malibu home.

With that in mind, I happily went off to a dance class thinking all was safe. By the time class was over, I had received three recorded mandatory evacuation alerts on my cell phone. I barely had time to race back home and grab my dogs, laptop and my mother's jewelry before driving away. I lived with friends and in hotel rooms for days, glued to the TV, desperate for any news about my little piece of paradise by the sea. Finally, I got word that my home had burnt to the ground.

After the mandatory evacuation orders were lifted, I grabbed a friend (for moral support) and drove through the blackened canyons and up a twisty road to where my home once stood. It was a modest house, built in 1980, but it had a glorious, peaceful view of the Pacific Ocean. Seeing the charred ruins of what had been my sanctuary for eighteen years broke my heart.

Now what? I was grateful that my dogs and I had survived, but now I had literally nothing but the clothes on my back.

Well-meaning friends and strangers tried to comfort me by saying that what I lost was just stuff. I had to bite my tongue, for I knew, deep inside, that wasn't so. Finally, when a friend said those words yet again, I couldn't hold it in any longer. I burst out, "It's not just stuff! It's my mother's portrait. It's the American flag given to honor my father, a World War II vet, at his funeral. It's the first picture of my sister as a baby." My friend stared at me for a long moment, and then said, "Oh, you lost your story." He was right. He totally got it.

And almost immediately, I had a knee-jerk reaction: *It's time for a new story.*

With that realization, everything changed. Oh sure, I cried. I still cry. I had nightmares, and there were days when I would have loved nothing more than to hide under the covers and stay in bed. But when I started to see how wonderful people were, dear friends as well as perfect strangers (which has forever changed my definition of "perfect stranger"), I realized that I may have nothing in terms of "things," but in truth I have everything.

With so many people displaced by the fire, finding a place to stay for months (or possibly even years) was a huge challenge. A week after the fire, I went to my usual ballroom lesson. I was in the parking lot when a woman in my class who had heard about my loss approached me. She said that she owned a rental property, and the tenant had just left that morning. Did I want it? My jaw dropped. After recovering, I asked, "How much?" She quoted a price that I couldn't afford, but then she decided to drop it substantially. I moved in the next week.

The fire happened in November, and Christmas was right around the corner. While at a Sunday service, a fellow parishioner, whom I had never really met, came up to me with a huge box of holiday ornaments and lights. She said, "I'm pretty sure you don't have any of these. I want you to have a happy Christmas." I cried tears of joy.

Other people helped me write a new story. My ballet teacher made sure I had slippers until I could get my own. A woman at the local CVS who overheard me struggling to get a prescription refilled for a medication that had been lost in the fire offered to buy me anything in the store. Her kindness was sincere and will forever touch my heart. I experienced countless examples of these acts of compassion in the months following the fire.

Creating a new story isn't easy. It's tempting to dwell in the land of "Why me?" That's a sure path to depression and misery. I loved my home of eighteen years and all the memorabilia of my entire life that it contained. They will always be in my heart. I know, however, that if I'm going to live the rest of my life to the fullest, I have to look forward. By appreciating what I have today and surrounding myself with people who care, I am creating a new story, even in the most difficult of circumstances.

—Dr. Noelle C. Nelson—

What's Next?

Once in a while, it really hits people that they
don't have to experience the world in the
way they have been told.
~Alan Keightley

I had recently become single again and the world was my oyster! Monday through Friday, I was the director of a fledgling nonprofit working for social justice in the local community. On Sundays, I was organist and choirmaster at a small Episcopal church. Other than that, my life was mine to change as I wished.

I had left my former life with little more than an armful of clothes and my blow dryer, so I was truly starting with a clean slate. I loved my new apartment, which looked down on a duck pond. I decorated the window with lace curtains and filled the balcony with plants. At the age of fifty-one, I was as giddy as a young woman furnishing her first apartment. I dreamt of the possibilities my new life would hold. This was my time!

A mere six months into my new life, Christmas arrived, bringing with it my annual cold. When I still had my cold two months later, the doctors couldn't figure out why. They chalked it up to stress.

By February, all I could manage was work and basic self-care. I was falling asleep at my desk and at stoplights! My cute new apartment was a mess. Then one morning, after taking a shower I was too weak to dress myself. I called a friend, who took one look at me and called 911. Fourteen days later, I emerged from the hospital with a diagnosis of systemic lupus, kidney disease, and autoimmune hemolytic anemia.

As sick as I was, I was determined to return to work. I refused to give up on my dreams and surrender my independence. Soon, I had no choice. By May, the rector of the church announced that I was being let go as the organist and choirmaster. He wished me well and encouraged me to concentrate on my higher-paying job. By September, the pastor at the church that hosted the nonprofit informed me that there was no money to fund my position.

Now I was sick, jobless and alone. A month later, a kidney biopsy confirmed class V, membranous lupus nephritis. The treatment? Chemotherapy. I wept.

As I went through treatment, I spent my days and nights in excruciating pain and profound exhaustion. Every night, I put my head on the pillow, praying that I wouldn't wake up. I couldn't work. My identity was gone. I was eating through my meager retirement savings just to keep a roof over my head. Why go on?

I still had enough presence of mind to realize that I needed professional help. An appointment with a psychiatrist was anything but helpful. He just didn't get it! I was so angry with him that I was propelled into action! *I'm going through this,* I thought, *and other people have gone through it, too. Some of them made it to the other side. Some of those people wrote books. I will find the books.* I went directly to the library. I learned about lupus. I learned about chronic illness. I learned about grieving for lost identity, hopes, and dreams.

> *I learned that what I think causes what I feel.*

As my wounded spirit healed, my health improved. And then a low-stress church job opened up, and I jumped at the chance. I had been volunteering for a lupus organization and I was offered the position of part-time program director, so I took that, too. I became a master trainer for Stanford University's Chronic Disease Self-Management Program. I added another part-time position as pastoral musician in a school. Now I was very busy. I had purpose and my life had meaning. I also had some money!

But lupus never goes away. Thirteen years after my initial diagnosis came a crash far worse than the first. Profoundly anemic, I needed four blood transfusions. This time, I got a blood clot. As I lay in intensive care, I periodically roused myself, waved a finger in the air and said, "This is not my first rodeo. I got better before. I will get better again. If you are going to treat me, you must believe this, too." On the seventh day, I was discharged. I spent the next two days training community leaders in chronic disease self-management.

Periodically, lupus makes dramatic intrusions into my life. Each time, I bounce back faster. I work half time at a school and freelance as a musician on weekends. I blog and create online courses, and I am launching a podcast and YouTube channel. My third book is nearly complete. In that book, I offer daily reflections for living well with chronic illness based on more than fifteen years of personal experience. I found purpose when I decided to "make my mess, my message" and hold the light for others on this journey.

What did those books teach that enabled me to reclaim my life? I learned that what I think causes what I feel, and that those feelings impact my physical health. I can observe my thoughts and choose thoughts that better serve me.

Early in my lupus journey, I embraced a negative explanatory style. Lupus was pervasive, personal and permanent. I was hopeless and helpless. That one encounter with the psychiatrist flipped the switch, leading me to embrace a positive, explanatory style. I embraced the challenge, made a personal commitment to live well with lupus, and took back control of my life.

Once again, the world is my oyster, full of new adventures, challenges and possibilities.

The question isn't "Why did this happen to me?" It's "What's next?"

— Linda Ruescher —

70

Good Morning, Five Toes

You teach people how to treat you by what you allow,
what you stop, and what you reinforce.
~Tony Gaskins

I looked down at the hospital bed where my leg used to be and resisted the urge to hold my breath and ball my hands into fists. Instead, I let the pain wash through me as I focused on my husband's hand resting where my leg should have been. Whatever they had given me for pain wasn't working. How could something that wasn't there be so excruciatingly painful?

"Please, just massage it for me," I begged. "It hurts so much!"

He ran his hand up and down the bed where my leg should have been in an attempt to ease my phantom pain. Oddly enough, just watching his hand slide along the crisp sheets as he rubbed my missing limb made me feel better. I was thirty-two and had just lost my entire right leg, hip and pelvis to bone cancer.

Now what would I do?

The two-legged me was a hairdresser, reflexologist, mother, wife, sister, daughter, and friend, and I couldn't help feeling that my life as I knew it was over. I had to redefine myself as a one-legged lady and find something that gave me purpose. If I was going to survive cancer, I promised myself that I would never waste a minute of precious time ever again.

Two weeks after my surgery, I was recuperating at my parents' home. My husband couldn't afford to miss more work, and I needed help just to get in and out of bed let alone look after our energetic three-year-old. The phone rang. My long-time friend had been admitted to the hospital for a ruptured appendix and had developed peritonitis. They didn't know if she would survive. I knew I had to go see her... and possibly say goodbye.

I thought it was fitting that my first trip out of the house as an amputee would be to see a sick friend in the hospital. If I fell, I'd be in good hands there. My mom drove me to the hospital and came inside with me to lend a hand and carry my full-length winter coat. It was too hot to wear it in the hospital, so Mom draped it over her arm, which also made it easier for me to walk using my crutches. The visit went well, and my friend eventually recovered, but I was proud of myself for making the effort to go see her.

As I made my way through the hospital, I was prepared for looks of curiosity, empathy, sympathy, and even shock. But the one thing I had not prepared myself for shook me to a depth I had never experienced before. Two young children, about six or seven years old, were playing with toys in the hospital lobby. As I passed by on my crutches, they looked up at me, and I flashed them a smile. They didn't return my smile. Instead, the little boy pointed his chubby, little finger at me and started to laugh. "Look, everyone! Look at that lady!" It seemed to me he was shouting loud enough for the entire hospital to hear. "She only has one leg! Doesn't that look funny?"

Both of the kids howled with laughter. Heads turned, and I felt the blood rush to my face. I couldn't speak. I put my head down and rushed out the door as fast as I dared on my crutches, not even stopping to put my coat back on. I felt the tears coming, and I held them back until the car door closed. I slumped into the passenger seat as Mom slid into the driver's seat. I started to sob. "How could they think this is funny?"

Mom tried her best to comfort me. "Honey, please don't cry," she said softly, looking almost as upset as I felt. "They are just kids. They don't know any better." Her words struck a chord in me, and my tears stopped as I felt the steel return to my backbone.

They were just kids, but that did not excuse their rude behaviour. I lifted my head to meet my mom's eyes, and I felt a wave of conviction flood through me. I knew what I had to do, what my purpose would be. "Well, someone has to teach them!" I said. And I knew that someone would be me.

As my strength returned, my conviction never wavered. I decided that when I was well enough, I would visit elementary schools and talk to children about being different. It is okay to ask someone why they look the way they do, but it is *never* okay to laugh at them because they are different. Thirty years ago, there were no anti-bullying programs and not really even a name for what I was doing. I was teaching children to be respectful of people who are different and teaching them that everyone is different in their own way. People come in all shapes, colors and sizes. We are each special and unique. How dull and boring it would be if we all looked and sounded the same.

Kids are like little sponges. They absorb new thoughts and ideas easily. It was an honor to touch their little lives with a big truth — a truth big enough to carry into adulthood. The strangest thing is, in the thirty-plus years since I became an amputee, I have never had another child laugh at me like that. I truly believe that those children were there for a reason. They were sent to push me in the right direction in order to find my purpose. Sometimes, our true purpose in life is found through the hardest lessons.

Speaking to children was just the beginning for me. I volunteered for the Canadian Cancer Society, The Terry Fox Foundation, Optimist International, the YMCA and even the March of Dimes. The word "no" was not in my vocabulary back then, and whenever someone asked for my help, I gave it gladly. My husband would laugh because he said it was hard for people to say no when a one-legged lady walked up to their door on crutches collecting for the less fortunate!

I became an inspirational speaker and author. I learned that being grateful for all the parts of me that were still intact was the only way to start and end each day. Teaching that attitude of gratitude to people of all ages and sharing my story in a book I wrote called *I Am Choosing to Smile* has given my life a purpose I never dreamed of when I had two legs. I do, indeed, choose to smile every day. Waking up in the morning, I look down at my one foot that is remaining and say with all sincerity, "Good morning, five toes. I'm very glad to see you!"

—Glenda Standeven—

71

That Smile

It's your reaction to adversity, not adversity itself,
that determines how your life's story will develop.
~Dieter F. Uchtdorf

It began with a phone call that no parent wants to receive. "Your son is in the hospital with a broken back." Jay was not a child. He was almost fifty and a professional trumpet player for the Army's 3rd Regiment Old Guard Fife and Drum Corps.

Jay was hurt in a freak BMX bicycle accident on an indoor track in Pittsburgh, Pennsylvania. To make matters worse, my wife Margaret and I lived 2,500 miles away in California.

Margaret booked a flight so we could be by Jay's side. We arrived after his emergency surgery at a Level I trauma center to learn that he had suffered a concussion, broken collarbone, broken ribs, and a crushed cervical spine with paralysis from his upper chest down.

We felt helpless as we looked at our son strapped into that specialized hospital bed. Jay's wife Angela stood next to us, doing her best to keep her emotional pain in check. When Jay saw us, he looked up and smiled. I wondered how he could do that after the pain of such a life-changing event, but I had seen that smile before.

Jay wore that same smile when he started playing the trumpet in elementary school. His horn became the center of his world, the fulcrum that got him through high school, college, and graduate school. It helped him ride out the ups and downs of life from adolescence to adulthood.

Jay's horn ultimately brought him to the Old Guard Fife and Drum Corps with support and encouragement from Angela and his daughter, Madelynne, born after he entered military service. Jay also practiced yoga and added BMX bicycle racing to his list of activities, for the adventure and camaraderie.

After we returned to California, we learned the full extent of our son's injuries. On the positive side, his spinal cord was damaged but not severed. That gave us hope, even though some doctors believed he would never walk again. The paralysis had also affected his core strength, which trumpet players need to perform.

Had he lost too much of himself to live a full life? He could no longer stand, walk, or perform his job as a trumpet player. His mother and I felt hope slipping away, but then we thought about that smile.

While we waited on the West Coast, the Army was busy helping Jay rehabilitate his body and his spirit. They moved him to the Walter Reed National Military Medical Center in Maryland, and from there to the Hunter Holmes McGuire VA Medical Center in Richmond, Virginia. Their caring specialists taught him how to get dressed, drive a car and live independently.

The Army continued to help Jay normalize his life. They supplied funding to modify his home, making it wheelchair-accessible for his return. Then they partnered with a nonprofit organization, Help Our Military Heroes, to provide him with a new wheelchair-accessible van.

We were encouraged by Jay's progress, but like many parents, we prayed for a miracle, some magic or medical breakthrough that would restore his old life. We visualized him walking and playing his horn, even knowing that the prospect of a full recovery was slim.

When we talked with Jay on the phone, nothing had changed, yet he sounded surprisingly upbeat. Our son had a lot more going for him than we had first understood. We saw a different kind of miracle in the making. Rather than dwelling on the past, Jay focused on what he had right in front of him.

Jay had his family — a caring wife and a talented teenage daughter — who remained at his side and worked with him to redefine their relationships after that life-altering event. Injuries like Jay's traumatize all family members, but Angela and Madelynne gave our son the support he needed to begin rebuilding his life.

Jay also had friends. Margaret and I were amazed at the number of caring souls who visited and wrote to him through this troubled time. Friends from the Army, high school, college, graduate school, the Old Guard, and the BMX community were all there for him. A young cyclist, who Jay had coached, visited him in the hospital and gave Jay the first trophy he won. He wanted to honor his mentor.

His cycling friends drove him to the local track where he coached other riders, young and old. The local track even sponsored a "Jay Day" that raised $10,000 to help their friend. A later "Jay Day" funded the construction of a new BMX track for the friends who supported him.

Jay also had adventure. The Army selected him to participate in the 2019 Department of Defense Warrior Games as one of forty injured soldiers to compete for Team Army. This competition includes injured servicemen from other branches of the military, along with participants from Britain, Denmark, Norway, Canada, and Australia. Jay competed in air rifle, wheelchair races, hand cycling, shot put, and discus. We received a picture of him sitting on a specially designed platform after a shot put tryout, and there was that smile, broader than Margaret and I had ever seen it. Jay went on to win two bronze medals at the games.

We once believed that Jay's family, his horn, and his bicycle were the things that held his life together, but we were wrong. He had resilience. Like the Serenity Prayer, Jay accepted the things he could not change and focused instead on the things that he could do here and now.

Margaret and I have not given up on the dream of seeing Jay marching and playing his trumpet, but we are proud to see that he has found fulfillment right where he is. Perhaps Jay's zeal to embrace his current life will move other miracles into the realm of possibility.

We have enjoyed watching Jay grow from childhood into a remarkable and gifted man. I learned from Jay that our value depends less on the challenges we face than on the way those challenges are handled.

I sincerely hope that Jay has benefited from my role as a parent, but someday I want to grow up to be just like him.

—Jim Grayson—

72

Four Little Words

Never bend your head. Always hold it high.
Look the world straight in the eye.
~Helen Keller

With my arms trembling and sweat dripping from my face onto the mat, all I could think about was how I wanted to give up. Even on my knees I could barely complete a push-up.

Just then, the coach came by and said, "Keep your head up!"

While she was referring to my form, she had no idea that those four simple words meant so much more.

At that moment, everything hit me at once, causing tears to mix with the sweat pouring off me. I could taste the salt running into my mouth, a taste I had become accustomed to over the past year.

The prior twelve months had devastated me emotionally, mentally and physically, leaving me a shell of the person I was.

In October 2016, my husband and I found out we were expecting our first child. Our joy was short-lived. The following month, we knew something was wrong with the pregnancy. After multiple doctors' appointments, tests and misdiagnoses, we were told that the pregnancy was ectopic, meaning that the baby was growing outside of my uterus. In my case, it was in my right fallopian tube.

We were informed that there was no way the baby would survive, and I was in physical danger the longer the pregnancy continued. The best option was a methotrexate shot, which works in 90 percent of cases. A week after the shot, I found out I was part of the 10 percent in which it does not work. My husband and I were asked to come into the doctor's office on a Friday afternoon.

It was the first and last time that we witnessed our baby's heartbeat.

The doctor stated we needed to head immediately to the emergency room to remove my fallopian tube along with our baby. I asked if I could have the weekend to process this information. She said, "No, there is a strong possibility you could die if you wait."

In that moment, I had the out-of-body experience one reads about in books or sees in movies. I was present in the room, but not truly there. I could hear words, but not process them. I was aware of what was happening, but not understanding that I was at the epicenter of the situation.

After the surgery, I was a zombie just going through the motions of my life. Go to work. Come home. Eat. Sleep. Repeat.

I ate to soothe myself, spent the majority of my free time sitting on the couch, and cried more tears than I thought possible.

During this time, we met with a fertility specialist and started intrauterine insemination (IUI) treatments. After a failed first attempt, we received a positive result with the second. It ended in an early miscarriage.

I felt like a failure. I felt like I was failing my husband. And I felt as though my body was failing me.

We made the decision to take a break from treatments.

One day shortly after I stopped the constant doctor appointments, daily pills and endless shots, I truly looked at myself in the mirror. I didn't recognize the person staring back. I had gained more than twenty-five pounds, the spark had been extinguished from my eyes, and the person staring back looked defeated.

Something needed to change.

I had always enjoyed working out, but after the surgery and fertility treatments, I had cut back my daily gym sessions to walks around our neighborhood. Having stopped treatments, I decided to ramp up my workouts again.

I kept hearing about a group fitness class near me and decided to sign up for an introductory class. Walking in, I was intimidated immediately. Everyone was in such great shape. At the conclusion of class, I could barely walk.

I signed up anyway.

A week later, my muscles were telling me to quit. It would be so easy to give up.

During the second week, my coach uttered those four little words: "Keep your head up."

Something clicked.

With wobbly arms and my vision blurred with sweat and tears, I picked up my head and finished that push-up.

From that day forward, I made a conscious effort to keep my head up, both literally and figuratively.

I never realized how often I looked down while going through my day.

During my walks, I would shuffle along, looking at the gray concrete. I told myself to look up. In front of me was life — trees ablaze with the dazzling colors of fall, a clear blue sky with the sun offering warmth to my upturned face, and neighbors waving and offering friendly greetings.

During dinner, I would stare down at my food as I quickly ate my meal. I told myself to look up. There was my husband sitting across from me — this man who had been by my side throughout the entire ordeal, who held me in his arms as I sobbed, who told me he loved me even when I didn't love myself.

During workouts I would stare at the floor or at my feet as I jogged. I told myself to look up and I saw myself in the mirror, someone who was not giving up and who was gaining strength.

On the surface, it was evident that I was becoming stronger physically, but there was also a transformation on a deeper level.

My view on the hand that life had dealt me was shifting. I had a choice to keep pursuing fertility treatments or to change course. While my husband and I had previously discussed adoption, it had been put on the back burner.

Over the next few months, we explored adoption more seriously.

We attended workshops, met with adoption agencies, and spoke with others who had gone through the process.

Ultimately, adoption was the route we chose. Exactly one year from our first baby's due date, our beautiful son was born.

During this time, I have regained parts of me I thought were buried, found new strength I didn't know I possessed, and found my fitness family.

When we brought home our little boy, we received a thoughtful gift bag of baby gear from the same coach who had such an impact on my life. I realized I had never told her how her words were a turning point for me.

In my thank-you note to her, I thanked her not only for the gift bag, but also for how those four little words had impacted my life.

Even now, over a year later, she sometimes says, "Way to keep your head up," and I smile.

I don't know what the future holds, but more likely than not, there will be curveballs thrown my way. As long as I keep my head up, I know I can handle them.

—Laura Niebauer Palmer—

73

Can't Take My Smile

Mothers and daughters together are a powerful force
to be reckoned with.
~Melia Keeton-Digby

Mom said the unforgettable words, "I have cancer," and clasped me in a tight hug. I could feel her chest shaking as she tried not to cry but failed.

If adulthood is bestowed in a moment, that was it. For all of my twenty-four years, my mom had been sturdy, supportive, and an unchanging presence. For a moment, I was the adult, and she the child. Strength and compassion had always flowed from her to me. Now I knew it would have to flow the other way. I felt a wave of protectiveness I had never felt before, and I promised her with a smile I would help her through anything.

But Mom didn't stay down for long. After the initial shock of the breast-cancer diagnosis, she armed herself with a purple spiral notebook and pen and a thousand questions for the doctors. She took notes on white blood cell counts and medications with eight-syllable names as though she were studying for entrance exams into medical school. "The not-knowing is the worst," she said.

Almost before we could blink, she was waking up from surgery that claimed her lymph nodes and dictated she would need both chemo and radiation. She couldn't use a towel on her tender, bruised chest, so she took to air-drying the area with a blow dryer on the cool setting. Dad offered to get the job done more efficiently with the leaf blower. Mom laughed until it hurt.

We knew chemo would take her hair, so before it fell out, Mom and I went wig shopping together at a tiny salon that catered to cancer patients. You would have thought we were picking out outfits for a costume party. We tried on everything from Betty Boop-style brunette bobs to electric-pink, rock-star locks like a pair of middle-school girls squealing at a makeover. Other customers stared. Was it sacrilegious to belly laugh at a cancer shop?

Trying on new hairdos in the mirror was a chance to reinvent ourselves. As a new adult, I was in the habit of reinventing myself anyway: new clothes, new diets, new jobs. But Mom had been loyal to the same short perm for over two decades. I had never seen her with any other hairstyle. When she put on a shoulder-length wig, straight and banged, I paused the festivities and stared. Honestly, I had to double-check to be sure it was her before I spoke. I didn't recognize my own mother. But then she grinned, and I saw the same sweet smile as in black-and-white pictures I had seen of her as a twelve-year-old with the same hairstyle.

Mom was one of my closest friends, but I realized there were still parts of her I didn't fully know. She held stories inside she hadn't told me. Neither of us knew the end of her cancer story that day in the wig shop. It might turn out to be an inspirational story, or a tragedy, or even both. It was still being written. I had never considered that mothers, too, are still growing into their most adult selves.

I went with Mom to every chemo treatment and watched as soft-shoed nurses hung bags of her chemo cocktail over her head. "Cocktail? Sounds like a party!" I said. So we called her bi-weekly treatments "chemo parties" and made an event out of them. During the two-hour IV drips, she joked about life, medical issues and even the pain. We celebrated with hot grinder sandwiches afterward. Mom hasn't been able to stomach one since, but back then they tasted like a victory meal after a sports championship. We spoke on the phone almost daily. She rarely complained, though I heard far more about my mother's toenails and fingernails than I ever wanted to as they fell out one by one. We joked that she could save money on nail polish and put it toward the doctor bills, even though she never wore nail polish. Fear became a guest at our party. It was the guest no one wanted to come, but we invited it in on our own terms.

"Cancer can take my hair, my nails, my health, my very life. But it can't take my smile," Mom said.

Mom learned to share her fears with me, and it formed an even deeper bond between us. Yet I am certain there were fears she didn't share because she was still protecting me — worries she only shared with Dad, or maybe even refused to give voice to. My mom, who never played sports and demurred when she won a hand of rummy, was a warrior determined to defeat breast cancer. Defeat it, and even joke about it. When you look your greatest fear in the eye and laugh at it, you take away some of its power.

I made Mom a survivor's box from a purple and pink shoebox. Every time I visited, I left behind a small gift, like some kind of cancer tooth fairy. Lotion for skin chapped by treatment. (It was called Udder Butter, which we found hilarious for a breast-cancer patient.) A mirror labeled "The Most Courageous Woman in the World." A lock of my hair left over from the eleven inches I had donated to a wig-making organization. A huge hat I had crocheted — somehow I had made a nine-sided octagon even though I had read the pattern. And a whole bunch of silly quotes and puns.

Mom was the most sociable patient the cancer center ever had. She made homemade noodles for the medical staff. She chose to be grateful to the hands that tried to heal her, instead of resentful when fatigue kept her from the job and social life she loved. Each morning, she chose to thank God for the day He gave her, instead of being angry that He allowed her to have cancer.

One day when I went to visit I found Mom sitting at the table doing her crossword puzzle without her wig. The morning light shone on her vulnerable, bald scalp. Her fingertips, raw and nail-less, grasped a pencil over the newspaper. She looked up and smiled, not self-conscious at all. I had never seen a stronger or more beautiful woman.

Months later, after the final radiation treatment, we held a graduation ceremony for Mom. I made a mortarboard out of pink foam sheets and a curtain tassel. She placed it on her hairless head like a crown and paraded around the dining room as Dad played "Pomp and Circumstance" on his baritone horn. We presented her with a teacup to remind her that the finest porcelain only grows strong after it goes through the fire.

Mom was one of the lucky ones. She did beat her cancer, though not without scars. To this day, she wears a compression sleeve to control the swelling from lymphedema, a result of the removal of her lymph nodes. But she lived, and whenever she can, she encourages others in those first scary weeks of diagnosis.

Most of all, I saw a change in Mom. Nothing afterward seemed to worry her quite as much. She was more patient and resilient. Cancer was her fire, and it refined her. From her, I learned I may not get to choose what I face, but I do get to choose how I face it.

—Sarah E. Morin—

Make Every Day Count

74

Choosing Joy

Once you replace negative thoughts with positive ones,
you'll start having positive results.
~Willie Nelson

"**Y**ou're not there for me," I shouted. "I need you more than ever, and you keep pulling away. It's like you've disappeared."

"Lori, are you kidding me?" my husband yelled back. "YOU disappeared! You've been down and out for over a year and a half! I've been pulling more than my weight trying to keep our marriage and our life on track. I didn't go anywhere. You did!"

They say the truth hurts, and after that exchange, we were both hurting. It had been months since a routine surgery to remove an ovary and its cyst had resulted in the loss of all my reproductive organs. Uterus, cervix, ovaries, fallopian tubes — everything had been removed due to the severity of endometriosis that had been found.

Prior to that, I was in the best shape of my life. I was strong and lean with six-pack abs. I had been a runner, bodybuilder, and cyclist. I was strong, joyful, and confident. As healthy as I felt, I had a few minor health challenges, namely a uterine fibroid and an ovarian cyst. I had opted to have both removed, hoping to alleviate the physical pain I had been experiencing for years. I went into surgery expecting routine results and a quick recovery. I woke to the unimaginable: a full hysterectomy as well as a double oophorectomy. Recovery would take a bit longer.

I struggled both physically and emotionally as the removal of my ovaries sent me into sudden, surgical menopause. I didn't know how to help myself as my symptoms included hot flashes, night sweats, fatigue, insomnia, loss of libido, weight gain, lack of focus, a zombie-like state, depression, anger, and an overall lack of passion and energy for anything in life.

I had been an outgoing, vibrant woman filled with joy, and now I was a listless crybaby. I'd lost my curiosity, zest for life, and drive. Everything, from getting up in the morning to getting myself through my workday and finding the energy to socialize and maintain relationships, became laborious. Externally, I was functioning, but many times it felt like I was just going through the motions. Internally, I felt out of balance and weak.

The words spoken the day of that argument were difficult to hear, but they served a purpose as they scared me into action. My husband helped me realize how much I had withdrawn from him and from my life. I began to see that, as a result of my surgery, I had been feeling a huge sense of loss, which required time for mourning. It also required a time to heal and, ultimately, to rise.

I could no longer sit on the sidelines and wait for my symptoms to resolve. If I wanted to live happily, I had to choose joy over my circumstances. I had to turn my setback into a comeback.

I combined everything I knew from traditional and nontraditional healing practices, and I explored new paths and lifestyle changes to reduce stress and improve my life's balance and overall wellness. I worked to bring more peace and calmness to my life through meditation. I spent more time focusing on the positive.

Any area of negativity or toxicity got purged.

I went to work on my mindset and habits. I became more conscious of my thoughts, words, and feelings. Instead of leaning into my sorrow, I needed to move, dance, smile, laugh, be grateful, and think positively. I had to guard what came into my life and my mind regarding television, books, the news, social media, and relationships. Any area of negativity or toxicity got purged. As I focused on the positive, I felt my mood lighten and lift.

I created better habits. I made sure I got a good night's sleep and then began my day with quiet meditation. I followed that with music and dance. I moved my body. Every day, I wrote down three new things in my journal that I was grateful for. Throughout my day, I would watch short video snippets from funny TV shows. When my husband asked me to go to the movies, I always picked a comedy.

Consciously and consistently, I chose to be happy and grateful. Some days, this came with a decision to be happy before I truly felt it.

I learned that feelings are contagious. One day, I noticed that every person I encountered smiled at me like I was their best friend and said "hello." I thought, *Wow! Everyone is so friendly today. It's like everyone's in a good mood.* Then I realized I was the one who was in a good mood. I was smiling. I was calm, relaxed, and walking with confidence. I was greeting everyone like they were my best friends. My smile was contagious, as were my positive feelings.

The twenty months after my surgery were the darkest period of my life. Surgical menopause rattled my cage and threatened to rob me of my confidence, sexuality, and motivation. However, in the journey through the darkness, I was forced to examine my mind and my thoughts so I could reclaim and maintain my balance. It was where I learned to change my perspective, focus on the positive, and find ways to laugh and be grateful, each and every day.

And every day that I choose joy, happiness follows.

—Lori Ann King—

75

A Simple Life Lesson

We tend to become like those we admire.
~Thomas Monson

It didn't take long after meeting my neighbor Josie to realize she ran circles around women twenty years her junior. She was a gourmet cook, adjunct college professor, and all-around know-it-all.

For some reason, she took a liking to me and chose to fit me into her days on a regular basis. She would call me over throughout the week to taste-test recipes, which was a pleasure since my cooking consisted primarily of grilled cheese and tuna melts.

Early each morning, Josie forced me to join her on her "daily constitutional," as she liked to call it. I believe we were supposed to be walking, but it felt more like mini-sprints. I had my rules. If I couldn't talk or breathe, I would stop.

I stopped every day at the end of our block. Josie would return bright-eyed and cheery a half-hour later and make me breakfast as a reward for making the attempt!

Our communal garden was a testament to Josie's green thumb. Every conceivable flower and vegetable made its debut once a year. In some instances, I could not even identify what was growing, but we had the freshest salads in the neighborhood all summer long!

Last month, Josie decided to take up art. She enrolled us in a painting class. Her masterpiece is prominently displayed on her living room wall. The teacher said I could re-enroll next semester without charge in order to finish mine.

Each night around sunset, Josie and I would touch base on our porches before retiring for the evening. We would chat back and forth, exchanging worldviews as easily as off-color jokes.

One evening, Josie was a "no-show." I started over to her door when I heard the ambulance and saw her husband and children running outside.

Josie had suffered a stroke.

When I next set eyes on her, she was leaning in a wheelchair, covered in a thick shawl. She looked smaller and older than I remembered, but her smile, though crooked, was still dazzling, and her eyes still sparkled. Her speech was slower, but her voice still had the lilt I loved.

Josie's world had shrunk overnight from exotic travel destinations to the few rooms in her condo. But it's what she does with her surroundings that gives me pause and perspective.

When Josie feels well enough to eat, her husband brings her breakfast in bed. She calls it "dining out." They listen to soft music in the background and light candles as though they were sharing a table together along a Parisian boulevard.

On days when Josie has some strength, her husband wheels her into the living room, and they watch old movies together huddled under the blanket. She calls it "date night."

And on the most special of days when Josie is doing really well, her husband takes her for a walk outside in her wheelchair. She calls it "going on vacation."

Despite the fact that Josie is not expected to make a full recovery, she continues to dine al fresco, go to the movies and take lots of mini-vacations.

She is grateful to listen to her grandchildren giggle, to smell a summer barbecue, to share a laugh with her favorite neighbor, and to be here for another day.

I am thankful for her simple life lesson: Find the positive, and you've found your reason to live.

— Lisa Leshaw —

76

The Mickey Mouse Watch

I only hope that we never lose sight of one thing—
that it was all started by a mouse.
~Walt Disney

In the spring of 1968, I was nineteen years old and living the life. I had a good job, a new car, and a steady girlfriend. However, that was all put on hold when I received my draft notice ordering me to report for induction into the U.S. Army.

Upon completion of infantry training, I was sent to Vietnam for one year where I served as a combat squad leader. Life in the steamy jungle was miserable. In addition to being far from home, soldiers also contended with the enemy, snakes, voracious insects, and oppressive weather conditions.

The one thing that kept soldiers going was support from home, primarily in the form of mail. During the first half of my tour, I received letters from my girlfriend nearly every day. Her devotion sustained me and kept me focused. As a result, hardly a moment went by when I did not dream of the day I would return home so we could get married.

As I entered the second half of my tour, her letter writing dwindled to the point where several weeks would pass without a word. When an occasional letter did arrive, it read like a high school homework assignment. The passion was gone, and she often wrote about places and events that I had never heard of. It was obvious that my girlfriend had found someone else.

I was devastated at the realization that I no longer had someone waiting for me. My morale fell to an all-time low. I had trouble concentrating and often took unnecessary risks because I no longer cared if I survived the war.

Then one night, a fellow soldier handed me his luminous Mickey Mouse pocket watch so I could keep track of my guard shift in the dark. I stared intently at the timepiece as Mickey smiled back at me. I began to think about when I was a kid and how much I loved sitting in front of the television after school to be entertained by *The Mickey Mouse Club*. I thought about sitting in my parents' home where I was warm, safe, well fed and carefree. I thought about the neighborhood kids and all the fun we had playing baseball, ice-skating and camping in each other's back yards. I even missed my father yelling at me.

Suddenly, something magical happened: All my anxieties vanished! I looked again at Mickey's silly grin. It seemed to tell me not to worry because everything was going to be okay. I smiled back with a nod, as if I were actually communicating with Mickey. I still had to complete a danger-filled tour, but that watch made me care again and gave me the confidence to survive the war unharmed.

Shortly after returning home from Vietnam, I purchased a Mickey Mouse wristwatch, and I have worn one ever since. I wanted to have a constant reminder that no matter how many obstacles life sends my way, no matter how bleak the situation, things could be worse, so I am thankful to be alive. A luminous Mickey Mouse pocket watch on a dark, lonely night did that for me.

—Arthur Wiknik, Jr.—

77

Hymns of Praise

The sun is a daily reminder that we too can rise again
from the darkness, that we too can shine our own light.
~S. Ajna

"What do you mean I have cancer? There's no cancer in my family! That's impossible."

But it was possible. I stared helplessly at the doctor who had performed the colonoscopy. He patted my hand and told me not to worry. My niece and my husband sat with their mouths slightly open, as stunned as I was.

This couldn't be happening! I couldn't take it in. My best friend had just passed away a month before after fighting her cancer for four years. I had been with her at her appointments and chemotherapy treatments. I had watched her fight fearlessly. Her faith grew stronger as her body grew weaker. How I wished Joanie were with me now. But, in a way, she was.

As I navigated countless tests and scans, her face was before me. I tried to emulate her courage as I canceled our twenty-fifth anniversary trip; my surgery would be right on our anniversary. My daughter flew out from Minnesota to be with us during this time and take care of my disabled husband while I was in the hospital.

I had a lot of people praying for me, but I was still in pain when I woke up in the hospital. I asked the nurses to keep the shades shut and the door closed. Every bit of light or noise seemed to intensify the pain.

One morning after being medicated, I had settled down to try to nap in the darkened room. Just as I was feeling drowsy, the door opened a crack, and a man peeked in. "Is it okay if I come in and clean your room?" he asked. He had a big smile on his face, so I refrained from throwing my pillow at him.

"Sure, come on in," I answered without any enthusiasm.

"Can I turn on the lights so I can see to clean?"

Oh, great, lights, too, I thought to myself. But I just said, "Sure."

I closed my eyes against the light and hoped he would finish and go away. Surely with my eyes closed, he would see that I didn't want to "chat."

"You should open these shades and let the sunshine into your life," the man said as he pulled them open. "It's a beautiful day out there!"

I didn't answer or open my eyes. He returned to cleaning the bathroom while humming a hymn! What was wrong with him? Couldn't he read my signals?

"Do you like hymns?" he asked.

"Yes, I usually do, but I'm not feeling very well today."

"Oh, I will cheer you up. I love hymns, too." Now he added words and sang his way around my room.

Lord, I thought, *why did you send this guy to me?* I kept my eyes closed.

"Do you go to church?" he asked.

"Yes, I do," I told him. "Eastside Christian church."

"You do? That's where I go, too. They play praise songs there, which is great, but I love the old hymns, too."

I opened my eyes wide now, and we began to talk to each other.

God, you must have sent this guy to sing to me and break through my fog of pain. Thank you, Lord.

As my new friend finished up the room, he shared with me that he had been an executive with a company that designed high-end wine cellars. He had traveled all over the country installing them in the homes of celebrities and other wealthy people.

"A few months ago, I was laid off," he told me, "and I didn't know what I was going to do to take care of my family. My wife went back to work, but I couldn't find anything. Then a couple of days ago, this job just dropped in my lap. I can tell you, I was glad to get it. It doesn't pay much, but I love cheering up the patients."

"You certainly did that for me," I told him. "I'm glad you came into my room and my life at this moment."

Before he left, he asked if he could pray for me, and it was a lovely prayer of hope and encouragement. He came every day that I was there and filled my room and my heart with joy as he sang his hymns and left me with a prayer.

My attitude really changed after that. I was alive. They had discovered the cancer early, at stage 2, and I didn't even need chemotherapy. I was so grateful.

I haven't had any recurrence of the cancer since the operation, and I am thankful every single day. I look for all the good and happy things around me. My husband and I are starting to travel. Sometimes, we eat dessert first. I donated our old towels to an animal shelter, and we use the good ones every day. We volunteer and open our home and hearts to family and friends. We never end the day without counting our many blessings.

Every day, I "open the shades and let the sunshine into my life." That was the best advice I'd ever heard, received just when I wanted to give up. My heart is filled with joy, and I want to spread that to others like the man who cleaned up my hospital room — and my attitude.

— Judee Stapp —

78

The Bucket List

What you get by achieving your goals
is not as important as what you become
by achieving your goals.
~Zig Ziglar

About ten years ago, a casual conversation with a stranger changed my life. We were taking a one-day course together, and during the lunch break, five of us started talking about things that help us get organized. That's when a young woman told us about something she and her friends do every year. They get together and pick 100 things they want to accomplish in the next year.

That number sounded daunting to the rest of us. We all looked a little skeptical, so she explained that the "goals" could be something as simple as eating a jawbreaker. She told us how they all remembered liking that hard candy when they were kids, so they decided to try it again. Her review: "They weren't as good as we remembered, so no one actually finished theirs. But they're well named because they really *do* hurt your jaw!"

So, while I've never had a desire to eat a jawbreaker, her idea resonated with me, and I decided to give the list a try. It took me a few days, but I came up with twenty-five things I wanted to accomplish. Here's a sample from the original list:

- Cook a dish I've never made before. (That's how I learned how to make a perfect omelet.)

- Try a food I've never eaten before. (I finally tasted poutine — truthfully, I'm still not sure what all the hype is about.)
- Go somewhere I've never been (Rome, Italy).
- Dance.
- Go to a play or concert.
- Visit a museum or art gallery.
- Take a class. (I took Intro to Social Media.)
- Do something good for someone else.
- Volunteer for something you believe in.

Over the years, my annual list has expanded to include 100 things, and the best ones are repeated every year. I go over the list every few weeks and check off the things I've accomplished. Those updates also help me to focus on the next challenge I'm going to tackle.

I can say honestly that because of a chance conversation with a total stranger, I've now been to Europe (I talked about it for years, but never actually went until I added it to my list); learned to kayak; and rode Zero Gravity with my six-year-old grandson. (This is an amusement-park ride that goes really fast while spinning you upside down as well as backwards and forwards — and, yes, it qualifies as doing something that scares me!)

Other things I've checked off my list include spending a day at the Prado Museum in Madrid, joining friends to cook at Ronald McDonald House for their Meals That Mend program, and planning a multi-generation family vacation.

And, in case that sounds overwhelming, I purposely pick a few simple things such as reading a classic novel — I reread *To Kill a Mockingbird* — and watching a classic movie, *The Wizard of Oz*.

I've shared this idea with others who are now creating their own annual bucket lists. It's surprising what you can accomplish if you set your mind to it — and actually write it down. Oh, and developing my list is always the first item I check off — because it feels good to start the year with a "win."

— Lori Kempf Bosko —

79

Think Like a Dog

*Those who find beauty in all of nature will find
themselves at one with the secrets of life itself.*
~L. Wolfe Gilbert

I was excited to take my rescue Beagle to the river the other day, as it's within walking distance of our new home. Having spent her first six years in a cage, Georgie had never seen a body of water, and I wanted to get there before sunset to watch her experience it.

I was growing increasingly impatient about all the stops her little Beagle nose required. She inspected the grass, dirt, and trees, and licked whatever was stuck to the road. These were all new discoveries for her, and she took her time studying them.

When I accepted that it was fruitless to hurry her along, I whipped out my cell phone and began texting. I thought that I needed something to do while Georgie was slowing us down.

Then, for some reason, I heard the cicadas, and I remembered that the sound of cicadas is my favorite sound in the world. That awakened something buried within me that yearned for the simple pleasures that had been replaced by technology.

I made a conscious decision to be present, and to enjoy the journey *to* the river, just like Georgie. The journey was just as wonderful as the final destination would be, and it took that little Beagle to remind me.

Now, I admired the intricacy of the flowers and the wonder of the winding ivy on our path. I felt the occasional warm raindrop on my skin from a gray sky threatening to burst at any moment. I smelled the asphalt, the grass and the flowers, and the dirt and the air. I treasured each one equally, as if discovering them for the first time. I took note of the colors everywhere that people would claim I exaggerated if I were to paint them on canvas.

I tripped over my feet and stumbled in some holes, and I was damp with sweat and rain. A few mosquitoes circled my head and landed on my sticky arms. As we neared our

> *Why must there always be a destination?*

destination, I realized something even more important: It didn't matter if we even reached the river. Why must there always be a destination?

Georgie had no idea that we had a destination. She was present for the journey, and she savored every bit of that sweet experience. There was no race and no finish line.

Now I'm not sure who rescued whom.

—Lauren Mosher—

What My Children Have Taught Me

Children make you want to start life over.
~Muhammad Ali

I began my foray into motherhood with an ambitious list of things I hoped to teach my kids through my words and actions. I wanted to teach them to live in the present, consider others' feelings, see humor in life, never say "I can't," and always make their best effort.

I also had another list of things I hoped they *wouldn't* pick up from me. I didn't want to teach them to procrastinate, criticize their bodies, underestimate their own abilities, lie to get telemarketers off the phone, run red lights, or lose their temper at inanimate objects. The jury is still out on how well I've succeeded at any of the above.

But this morning, watching my seven-year-old daughter Haley strap on Rollerblades for the first time, I was reminded of how much my children have to teach their father and me.

As I watched her progress from inching along with spaghetti legs beside my parked car, to venturing out on her own and falling again and again with complete confidence, I learned more than I'll ever need to know about determination and tenacity. Here are just a few of the things my children have taught me. Many are lessons I learned as a child but had allowed myself to forget.

- If you don't know something, ask.
- Believe in the unbelievable.
- Play in the rain and squish your toes in the mud.
- If you like somebody, tell them.
- Dip graham crackers in milk.
- Handmade gifts are the best kind.
- Save your money for something you really want, and when you have enough, get it!
- Sing, dance and laugh a little every day.
- Share your ice cream with the dog.
- Have dreams.
- Have heroes.
- Sign your letters with Xs and Os.
- Mean it.
- Apologize when you're wrong.
- Smile at lonely people.
- Make wishes.
- Make new friends.
- Make clover chains.
- Circle special occasions on your calendar, and then count down the days.
- Give gladly to those less fortunate.
- Laugh when you're happy.
- Cry when you're sad.
- Stop and study the ants.
- Get dressed up on your birthday.
- Never see weeds. See wildflowers.
- Deep in your heart, believe that people are basically the same.

The list continues to grow daily. How much better this world would be if we adults never forgot these important lessons. But somewhere in the process of growing up—in learning to evaluate, intimidate, and impress—we do forget. I, for one, am glad to be sharing my days with little people who remind me continually of the things that really matter in life.

—Mimi Greenwood Knight—

You Are More Than You Know

I don't want to come all this way, to do this life,
and then decide it's too hard and not show up for it.
~Elizabeth Gilbert

Toward the end of yoga class, the instructor asks, "Is anyone afraid to get into an inverted position?" I scan the rainbow of mats lined up like crayons, expecting to see colorful reactions. Nothing.

Silence.

Complete Zen.

Seriously? Am I the only one who just recently figured out how to touch my toes? Uh... hellooooo! This yoga stuff is interesting, I'll give you that, but a headstand? Is that even possible?

I think about grabbing my mat and making a run for the door.

"Big breath in," the instructor calls out. "Now release slowly... 5... 4... 3... 2... 1." And with each number, my fear dissipates.

I inch my mat closer to the wall, as instructed.

"You won't be able to see the wall, but I want you to feel its energy, its presence," she explains. "We're not going to use it. Just knowing it's there is enough."

Maylo, the instructor, wants me to believe in something I can't see, and find comfort in knowing it's there if I should need it. She's asking me to have a little faith, both in the wall and in myself.

With baby steps, we inch toward a headstand. Each small move seems reasonable, so I follow along. Before I know it, I have one foot off the ground, and the other foot just kind of tags along as if it doesn't have a choice, like some sort of anti-gravity.

> *Each small move seems reasonable, so I follow along.*

I can feel a powerful inner strength kick in and take hold. I can sense that my core, like the world, isn't flat. And it isn't just about abs, muffin-topped or otherwise. To keep me from caving into my neck and creating too much pressure on my head, it requires a whole inner barrel of muscle work. For the first time, I can actually feel the muscles engage around the entire hub of my body, working together like a well-rehearsed orchestra. I'm surprised at my own strength and stability.

"I did it! I'm doing it!" I blurt out loud.

"You can do more than you know," Maylo smiles. "You are more than you know."

Slowly, I breathe in her words.

Lately, I've been asking the Universe to help define me — to disclose my worth, my innate value. This request isn't coming from an enlightened Dalai Lama place. It's more of a, "Please, help me. I'm pretty sure I'm doing it wrong," sort of thing.

Finding my value through a man's eyes for most of my life turned out to be a bad move. It nearly took me down. Now I'm looking for something more reliable.

And there it is: "I am more than I know."

That's not exactly a high-end price tag hanging from my elbow, but it clearly shuts down the idea of giving myself away. And I like how it leaves a little room for interpretation. It's almost like an invitation to get better acquainted with myself, so I can discover my true value piece by piece, like a scavenger hunt.

It isn't that I think I'm a bad person. Not at all. I'm kind-hearted. I'll bring you soup when you're sick and celebrate your birthday in style. But the truth is… I spent the better part of my forties trying to please my partner without even noticing that I was edgy, drained and sad most days. I was walking through my life on a tightrope. To keep the peace, I gave up pieces of myself. I'm no therapist, but I would guess that someone truly in touch with her own worth would have walked away after a few weeks, maybe a few months. She certainly would not have limped away eight years later.

So I graciously accept the gift my yoga practice has given me this evening. I can still feel the powerful force deep inside that's strong enough to support me in whatever position I find myself. I'm starting to see that I don't need to look outside myself for that. And that makes me feel powerful and steadfast, qualities I probably wouldn't have used to describe myself before tonight.

Perhaps that's why I make time for yoga even on my busiest days. Sure, I like seeing my body become more flexible, but the gains are so much bigger than that. It's as if the most valuable parts of me are right there inside my yoga practice, just waiting for me to reclaim them. All I have to do is unroll my mat. Again and again.

— Mindi Ellis —

82

What I Wouldn't Give...

Give every day the chance to become
the most beautiful day of your life.
~Mark Twain

I get up between 4:30 and 4:45 every morning throughout the workweek—sometimes a few minutes earlier. As one might imagine, that hour feels more like the middle of the night than it does the early morning. It is still dark out. My husband is still breathing heavily and deeply, comfortably tucked under the covers, where he will stay, sound asleep, for another two and a half hours. The only sounds are the quiet hiss of air through the floor vents, and the whistle and rumble of a distant train beyond the woods. And as my consciousness awakes reluctantly to the fact that I must pry myself out of my soft cocoon of a bed, where the warm body of my snuggling dog is wedged tightly against my stomach, I think, *What I wouldn't give to stay here for even one more hour....*

On a recent morning, though, it occurred to me to actually think this through. After all, if I just got up and prepared for work, I could sleep till 6:15, leave my house at 6:45 and still get to work on time.

But here's what I'd be giving up: I wouldn't get to read the Bible lesson over breakfast, with my dogs sitting patiently beside me. That would leave me hungry for food *and* for inspiration. I wouldn't get to take my morning walk with my two dogs, the fresh air sweet and invigorating, and the sound of the dogs' tags ringing clear in the pre-dawn quiet. Missing our walk would mean foregoing precious bonding time with them, sacrificing time to mentally prepare myself for the day, and giving up a chance to appreciate the beauty of the outdoors before my daytime obligations become paramount in my consciousness.

Sometimes I wish I could accomplish all these things without having to get up by 4:45, but then I would miss out on some of the other things I love about early morning, too: the intimacy of the early morning hours, the privacy of the darkness, the moonlight, the sunrise, the stars, the kindred spirits I sometimes encounter — neighbors up and out as early as I am. I would miss the chirping of the crickets, and I would miss watching the world wake up. All of these things are as indispensable to my morning routine as is brushing my teeth.

So tomorrow, when I reluctantly throw back the covers and think, *What I wouldn't give to stay in bed another hour,* I will try to remember the answer: nothing. The moonlight spilling onto black asphalt through pine needles; the pale blush of pink or peach or gold dusting the bottom of gray clouds; the sound of my dogs' paws trotting along the sidewalk beside me; the hoot of an owl hidden in the dark of the woods; warm lights blinking on in the upstairs windows of houses lining the street; the occasional shooting star blazing across the purple-black sky; the earliest birdsong of the day — I would give up none of these. Not even for another ninety minutes of sleep.

— Amanda Sue Creasey —

Chapter
10

Reboot Your Life

83

From the Depths to the Heights

When we are no longer able to change a situation,
we are challenged to change ourselves.
~Viktor Frankl

I was lying in bed in the dark ready for sleep when my fiancée announced that her engagement ring was now in my sock drawer because she "didn't want it anymore." It felt like a baseball bat to the stomach and one of the worst nights of my life. It would be months before our actual separation, during which time we saw a counselor—to no avail.

On the day she was to move out, she returned to our apartment in San Francisco to collect the last of her belongings. As if my world wasn't shaken enough, that was the moment the powerful Loma Prieta earthquake struck. I was amazed our building did not collapse.

In the weeks that followed, paralyzed with depression and grief, I decided to continue seeing the counselor on my own. One day, he gave me a homework assignment: I was to write down a list of one hundred life goals.

It took me two weeks to complete the task. When I finally handed over the list, I expected him to read it, maybe even give me a gold star. He did neither. He didn't even look at it. He merely instructed me to pick one goal and take two small steps toward it before the following week.

Looking over my list of one hundred goals, I chose, "Fly an airplane." I bought a flying magazine. That was one step. Then I went to a local airport and arranged with a flight instructor to take a low-cost "Discovery Flight."

During that first flight, as I took the controls at 3,000 feet, I let out a shriek of excitement. The flight instructor grimaced in pain. I assured him I would never do that again.

And so began my journey to become a pilot, starting from scratch. No knowledge. No experience. When I bought $300 worth of textbooks, I began to question what I'd gotten myself into. Then came the fear that accompanies every new challenge thrown at one while flying.

That's when I realized I needed to adjust my mental attitude. Somewhere along the way, I had read that people should tell themselves they were the best at whatever they were attempting to do — but keep it to themselves. I took this to heart. Thus, I decided privately that I was a Top Gun pilot suffering from some sort of amnesia. With that well-hidden core of confidence, I was going to seek the help of flight instructors and ground instructors to chip away at the forgetfulness that had apparently overtaken me.

> *I was now excited to recover all this "lost" knowledge.*

Newfound enthusiasm came along with this new attitude. Unlike the school days of my youth, which I privately viewed as a benign prison system, I was now excited to recover all this "lost" knowledge. No way would I ever miss a ground-school class.

Eventually, the time came for my first flight check with the chief instructor, an airline pilot with 11,000 hours. As if I wasn't nervous enough already, one of my classmates privately confessed to me that he'd recently been through the same routine. Not only did he fail but he actually cried.

Without my internal Top Gun attitude, I probably would have succumbed to the urge to run away and never go back to the airport. Top Gun pilots, however, don't run.

On the day of my first in-flight testing, Paul, my regular flight instructor, approached the chief and me as we prepared to get airborne.

Pointing to the chief and myself, I asked Paul who he thought was more nervous. "I am," Paul replied. I was startled by his reaction until I realized that he, too, was going to be evaluated based on my performance that day.

Climbing into the cockpit of a Piper Cherokee Warrior, the chief informed me that he would be giving orders but not answering questions. I'd never flown with him before, but I was beginning to get a sense of why my classmate broke down. This guy was a tough cookie.

Shortly after our wheels left the ground, I rested my right hand on my knee. This led to a facefull of drill sergeant as the chief yelled at me to put my hand on the throttle. The tone had definitely been set. Would my Top Gun mindset hold up under the pressure?

The flight lasted 1.7 hours. It consisted of everything that could go wrong going wrong, on purpose. Toward the end, the chief told me to take him home. We were out over the San Francisco Bay in the late afternoon. Prior to this, I had always flown in the late morning to take advantage of the light winds. Turning west toward the airport meant heading straight into the late-afternoon sun. The Plexiglas windshield, full of minute scratches, refracted the light in such a way as to be nearly blinding.

Somehow or other, I managed to find the airport and put us safely on the ground. Without a word, the chief climbed out of the plane and walked to the office, leaving me alone for the first time to physically push the plane back into its parking spot.

When I arrived in his office, I was eager to hear what he had to say. He started asking me questions about my performance. He queried me about each landing, forcing me to judge each one and explain what I'd done wrong. I thought I was done sweating bullets back in the airplane, but I was wrong.

When he'd wrung me out like a sponge, he finally offered his opinion, evaluating my performance as "superb." I nearly fainted.

There would be many more hoops to jump through before an FAA examiner would sign me off as a pilot. When that day finally came, and I wound up flying home in a star-filled sky, I marveled at the depths of my despair years earlier when I was told to write a list of goals.

I wasn't done, though. Once I'd racked up enough hours, I applied to become an Angel Flight pilot. That entailed more testing, which, as a Top Gun pilot, I also passed. The missions I would subsequently fly dealt with transporting a variety of deaf children to and from special camps in the mountains.

Were it not for the despair and pain that drove me back into the office of that counselor, I am sure I never would have sat down and made a list of one hundred life goals. My depression would have kept me from taking the simplest of steps in any direction. However, from the deepest emotional hole I had ever found myself in, I have soared to 17,000 feet in a glider, turned corkscrews through the air in a home-built RV-4 at 200 knots, and helped deaf kids have the time of their lives.

— Brian Narelle —

The Dancing Rabbi

Joy does not simply happen to us. We have to choose
joy and keep choosing it every day.
~Henri Nouwen

I was curious when my employer smiled after I mentioned we were attending Beit Tikva's Friday evening service. "The one with Leonard Helman, The Dancing Rabbi?" she asked. Perplexed, I asked what she meant.

"You'll find out," she chuckled.

We were new to Santa Fe and looking for a synagogue to join, so off we went. After the service, we chatted with a lovely couple named Jerry and Alison. Jerry mentioned that he had just joined the choir.

"A choir? How lovely. I sing as well," I replied.

As soon as the words were out of my mouth, Jerry brought me over to meet the cantor.

"Cantor... she sings!" he announced.

"Really?" the cantor said. Leading me across the room, he introduced me to the rabbi.

"Rabbi... she sings!"

With twinkling eyes, the rabbi looked me over and said, "So? What do you sing?"

"Lots of things," I countered, smiling. "What do you dance?"

Breaking into a broad grin, the rabbi shouted, "Vanessie's!" And before we knew what was happening, Charles and I felt hands beneath our elbows as a small group gathered around us and swept us into the parking lot with instructions to "Follow us!" Trailing our newfound friends, we joined a small caravan of the initiated and drove off to Vanessie's, the world-famous piano bar we had read about in several tour guides of "Santa Fe, The City Different."

We were soon made welcome at "the rabbi's table" close to the piano, but were completely unprepared for what was to happen next. The rabbi took his seat and pulled out a gym bag. In a flash, he switched into tap shoes, a clip-on bowtie and a straw bowler.

"Ready, Rabbi?" Vanessie's talented piano man inquired as he played a spirited medley of show tunes.

With a nod, Santa Fe's own Dancing Rabbi rose to his feet and haltingly began shuffling toward the center of the room. It was only then that I noticed the cane hooked around his arm.

"It takes him a little bit to get his motor revved up," Jerry whispered in my ear. "He has advanced Parkinson's, you know."

I hadn't known and was transfixed as the familiar dance tunes propelled the stilted figure forward. Soon, he was tap dancing his way from table to table, joyously swinging his cane and tipping his bowler to the ladies. Then, pulling one laughing woman after another to her feet, he flitted across the room, changing partners constantly. After a few seconds, he'd pull each woman's companion to his feet and hand his partner over to take it from there as he moved on.

In short order, everyone was on their feet, just in time for the grand finale as the rabbi distributed small American flags, and the piano man launched into spirited renditions of "Take Me Out to the Ball Game" and "The Star-Spangled Banner." The rabbi gleefully led the sing-along, as the crowd around him joined in with gusto, waving their flags in time to the music.

It was only later that I learned how this once brilliant lawyer and world-renowned Gold Life Master bridge player had switched careers to serve both God and his community. When stricken with Parkinson's, he simply took it in stride, waking at the crack of dawn to work with his physical therapists at the hospital, confer with his doctors, and then "do rounds" of his own in the wards. Everyone who needed a shoulder to cry on, a hug, or a good laugh received a visit before he'd leave for his office to attend to his rabbinical duties. Yet, the best was always reserved for Friday nights, when he'd deliver the Sabbath sermon and then head off to lead the songfest at Vanessie's. His spirit was both indomitable and infectious. There was no feeling down in Leonard Helman's presence.

Nowhere else, before or since, did we ever welcome the Sabbath with such unabashed joy. That first Friday evening with our beloved Dancing Rabbi was a once-in-a-lifetime experience. We joined the synagogue, and I joined the choir and the board. The Beit Tikva congregation became our family, and Leonard — our wise uncle. It was unquestionably a synagogue reflecting its rabbi's singular standing as "the rabbi different" in "the city different."

As a choir member, I was seated behind him on the bema during the Jewish High Holy Days while he read at breakneck speed from the Torah. I was thrilled as he rattled off the names of the Patriarchs — Moses's sister Miriam included. Later, I told him how thrilling it had been to hear him call out her name.

"Rabbi, you read so quickly, without notes. How extraordinary to learn that Miriam — a woman — is actually recognized as a Patriarch in the Torah! I had never heard that before."

With the same twinkle in his eyes as the evening we met, he confessed, "Well, I sometimes improvise. Just because the scribes forgot to mention Miriam doesn't mean that I have to!"

So, Leonard bent the rules a little. Nobody seemed to mind, and his universal view of worship was recognized by everyone who encountered him, earning him the distinction of becoming New Mexico's honorary legislative chaplain.

It was always an honor to be in his company. One such occasion was when he invited us to join him for Christmas Eve Mass at Santa Fe's towering Cathedral Basilica of Saint Francis of Assisi downtown. Upon seeing the rabbi enter the magnificent sanctuary, Santa Fe's bishop rushed to shake his hand and usher him and his entire entourage to front-row seats. I should have been surprised, but I wasn't. I was in the company of a singular human being... a man admired by all.

We left Santa Fe after only eighteen months due to business

obligations. Between tears, I told Leonard that he would forever be my rabbi, as nobody else could ever fill his shoes — stretched wide by compassion, humor, courage, spirit and... tapping!

—Sue Ross—

Big Red Divorce Boots

Give a girl the right shoes,
and she can conquer the world.
~Marilyn Monroe

My divorce day had finally arrived. After a painful two-year separation that included several reconciliation attempts, our divorce was a reality.

I thought my ex-husband and I had done everything the "right way." We met when we were in high school, but didn't date until he was a third-year medical student. We waited to get married until he was well established in his residency and had our first child only after he was in a successful practice and we were financially stable. I loved my husband, our children, and our life.

In my mind, we had the perfect life, and nothing would ever change our storybook existence. I was insufferably self-righteous, smugly believing my place in Utopia was secured because of my own decisions and actions.

Pride goeth before a fall, and the plummet from my self-created pedestal was far and hard. My husband's unexpected request for a divorce left me shaken to the core. An unwanted and painful epiphany emerged through the darkness—life wasn't as simple as I thought. The good guy doesn't always win, and sometimes the "happily ever after" we assume is our rightful destiny takes a very unexpected turn. People are fallible, and even when we think we've done everything according to the book, things may go terribly awry.

Shame and embarrassment at being the first amongst my friends to get a divorce led me to create a wall of silence and loneliness. I shared my situation with very few people. Even when I did, I presented a façade, a lie that said I was handling things well. My inability to admit weakness and what I perceived as failure left me alone on my divorce day. If this had been the movies, I would have had a posse of friends cheering me up at a margarita-laden lunch. But since this wasn't *Sex and the City*, I headed to the mall alone.

I wasn't normally a shopper, but the need to be among people who didn't know me and wouldn't ask questions drew me to the windowless, impersonal structure. I wandered around the mall obsessing about marriage regrets and consumed with worry about the future. The stores and the people I passed were merely a backdrop for my personal movie of sadness. I was heartbroken and couldn't imagine how I was going to pick up the pieces of my shattered life. But, for the sake of my young daughters, I knew I had to find a way out of the dark.

Through my self-pity, a vision of bright red and black cowboy boots appeared. As if they were on a pedestal, surrounded by an unearthly glow, the boots beckoned me. Never in my life had I even thought about wearing cowboy boots, yet I heard a voice seeming to come from my mouth directing the salesclerk: "Size ten, please." As I coaxed my long, city-girl feet into the unfamiliar feel of the boots, I sensed the possibility of novel adventures. These buttery soft, brightly-colored leather boots were the symbol of a new beginning, a different life. I walked around the shoe-store floor envisioning a future that included swing dancing in the arms of a tall, dark cowboy, dressing in clothes that didn't involve elastic waists, and experiencing the world in a way I'd been shielded from in my previously insulated life.

> *These buttery soft, brightly-colored leather boots were the symbol of a new beginning.*

Absurd as it sounds, those boots were the catalyst for a transition from the life of a suburban, married mother of two to a single mother ready to take on whatever challenges were surely awaiting. I felt empowered. My mopey shuffling turned to confident strutting in those big, red boots. My 5'10" height became elevated to an Amazonian, six-foot level of strength. Floating out of the store with a big box of boots in my arms, I was poorer financially, but rich with feelings of renewal and possibility.

I wore the red cowboy boots almost constantly for the next year, designing outfits around them and even dancing the Country Two Step with a tall, dark cowboy. Fondly referring to it as my "Western Mommy" stage, my daughters remember hearing me walk down the hall of their preschool, knowing it was their mommy approaching by the "stomping" noise of the boots.

I like to think that my little girls felt safer when they heard my sure-footed, cowboy-boot stride. Their emotional security was dependent on me, and they needed to know their mom was strong enough to take care of them. We were still a family, and despite the changes, I was determined we wouldn't be broken.

Before long, I was able to put my magical boots farther back in the closet. Soon, I stopped wearing them all together. I was healing, as if the big, red cowboy boots' power had created courage in me, and I was moving forward bravely.

Over twenty years and many closet purges later, the magical boots still reside in my closet. They represent strength and independence, and the decision not to be a victim of sadness and bitterness but to take charge and move forward. The red boots were my touchstone, my talisman, as I became stronger than I imagined possible. Like Dorothy in *The Wizard of Oz*, I had the power all along; I just needed my own version of her shiny red shoes to discover it.

— Diane Morrow-Kondos —

86

Never Give Up on Your Dreams

Let me tell you the secret that has led to my goal.
My strength lies solely on my tenacity.
~Louis Pasteur

My dream in high school was to live in a big city and be an international marketing executive. After that, I would settle down with a wonderful husband and raise a family. I was a high achiever in high school and was well liked. The world was my oyster. Why couldn't I have it all? If I worked hard and stayed focused, it should work. Unfortunately, this dream was demolished in April of my senior year in high school.

April 16, 1978 was the first day I can remember after emerging from my fourteen-day coma. I had been hit by a car speeding at fifty miles per hour while I was crossing the street. I had two shattered legs, a broken pelvis and fractured skull. My eyes were skewed to the right — an indication of bleeding within the brain cavity and a severe coma.

My parents were worried that I might be paralyzed and spend the rest of my life in a wheelchair. But the reality of the situation was far worse. My rating on the coma scale was a 4 on a 3–15 scale, with 3 being the worst. This meant that even if I survived, I could have permanent brain damage.

After being released from intensive care, I was moved to a regular hospital room. Even though I was now awake, my neurosurgeon did not give my parents much hope that I'd be able to do much more than take care of myself. Plus, I would probably have a permanent limp. But at least I was awake, which meant it was a good day.

I stayed in the hospital for two months with my left leg in traction. Once my left femur had a long rod in it to hold it together, I only had breaks below my knee, so they let me out of the hospital with crutches. Whereas I hadn't felt any pain when I was in traction due to the aftereffects of my coma, the real pain started when I tried to walk again.

Soon after I got out of the hospital in June, I was valedictorian at my high-school graduation. I hobbled onto the stage with my crutches and note cards and started my speech. "Always remember the simple things in life. Enjoy life," I told the audience. "Everyone here is alive. Always remember how good life is." I received a standing ovation after my speech, and it was the start of my long journey back.

I was scheduled to start at State University of New York in September of that year. When my tutor had come to the hospital so I could finish my English class and graduate from high school, she rated my overall cognition at the level of a twelve-year-old. I looked normal, but my mind was in turmoil. There had been no therapy for my injured brain. I could pick up a book and verbalize the words, but I didn't understand what they meant unless I was reading a book for an elementary-school student.

The old Carol (pre-coma) was kind, had a 3.97 GPA in high school, was never stressed, had a lot of friends, and was very focused. The new Carol (post-coma) was still nice, but was always stressed, got headaches, slept a lot, fought off depression, and found it hard to remain focused. My personality was different than it had been. Life had been turned upside down, and my old dreams were a thing of the past.

College was enormously difficult. I fought short-term memory deficits and cognitive issues all the way, but I eventually taught myself how to learn again. Graduate school was even harder, but I made it through with a lot of effort. Although my neurosurgeon had told my parents that I probably wouldn't be able to go to college, I earned one bachelor's degree and two master's degrees. I beat the odds.

When I started working in San Francisco, I had earned my degrees, but I fell a bit short in knowing how to put it all together and work in a business where one had to respond rapidly. Everything wasn't as organized as it had been in college, and this was the real world — a world in which I needed to figure out how to excel.

Although my previously shattered legs left me with arthritis in my knees, I did not have a permanent limp. The greatest trouble, however, was with my memory. I was forgetting about many of the tasks I had been asked to complete. And even when I did remember to get some information from a given source, I'd forget what I had just learned ten minutes after I retrieved it. I felt the same as I had during my first year in college because I couldn't seem to remember a thing.

Depression came back with the memory failure, but this time it was different. I was more in control now; I knew where I had to go and was closer to getting there, but I just didn't know the route.

Over time, I came up with an effective method to recall and retain new information. At work, I carried a pen and pad with me whenever I went to speak with anyone on a business issue. If I wrote things down, I could remember what was discussed. I still do that today, and it works.

I have found that what I have been through sets me apart from others. I've experienced an awakening by way of a deep sleep. I don't take things for granted, and I have learned that I can do just about anything I choose to do. My goals are realistic, yet high enough to motivate me to reach them. They are truly an essential part of me, of my life, for they are the means to furthering myself, to growing and learning and strengthening myself.

I've been successful in my career as a senior financial analyst, operations manager, and finance manager. After I met my husband, I no longer wanted to travel the world as an international marketing executive. But I didn't give up on my dreams; I just altered them a little. Today, I work at a university and live in the East Bay area of San Francisco with my husband and three teenage daughters.

I would be a different person today if my accident had never happened, and I'm thankful for what I have accomplished and who I am. I have a wonderful family and a professional life I'm proud of. I discovered that even if your initial dreams are disrupted by something unexpected, success is still possible. Never give up on your dreams.

— Carol C. Lake —

87

I Don't Have Arthritis

When you treat a disease, first treat the mind.
~Chen Jen

For the third time in two months, I sat on my orthopedist's examining table explaining once again how debilitating the arthritis in my knees had become. Together, we'd tried everything — medication, injections, physical therapy, ice packs, hot compresses and, most recently, arthroscopic surgery. The procedure only left my knees more swollen and sore. As I implored him, my doctor just shook his head. Though I would eventually be a candidate for knee-joint replacement, he said, he hesitated to do the surgery at this point since he felt I was still too young at age fifty-six.

First diagnosed with osteoarthritis in my thirties, I accepted it as my destiny. My grandmother had terrible arthritis at a young age. My mother spent her last two years in a wheelchair. A favorite aunt required a hip replacement. Of course, I had arthritis; it ran in the family.

Regardless, I did everything I thought I could to remain limber. I avoided eating inflammatory foods, walked two miles daily and practiced yoga. Yet, I'd come to accept certain limitations the condition had placed on my life. When I was unable to open a jar, I'd blame it on my arthritis. When I found it difficult to walk stairs, I'd blame it on my arthritis. Climbing a ladder to trim a tree branch or climbing on a step stool to reach the top shelf had become out of the question. So, it came to be that whenever I was unable to keep up physically with some task, I'd say, simply, "Well, I can't… I have arthritis."

Yet, at some point, even daily activities became agonizing. One evening, after having dinner out with my husband and his sister, I was unable to walk across the restaurant parking lot to the car, even with the help of my cane. The pain was excruciating. Dressing was difficult. Getting up from the sofa was tough, too, and I'd find myself having to push my hands against its frame in order to stand. And that yoga class I loved? I had to quit. But the final blow came when I was out shopping at the mall one day.

On what was one of my better days, I was able to spend part of one afternoon strolling the mall. Before leaving for the drive home, I decided it would be a good idea to visit the ladies' room. And here's where it gets a bit embarrassing. I was unable to get up from the commode. The fixture was apparently lower than mine at home, and my knees were not strong enough to help project me upward. Eventually, I was able to pull myself up somehow, with tears streaming down my face.

"Is this what's become of me?" I asked myself. "If this is my predicament now, where will I be in ten years? In twenty years? Will I be wheelchair-bound like my mother, only at a much younger age?"

That was my turning point. I was fed up with arthritis. I decided to give arthritis back to wherever it came from in the first place. I didn't want it anymore. So, I started walking daily again. First, I could only go one or two painful blocks at a time, gritting my teeth, and repeating over and over, "I don't have arthritis." I resumed a yoga practice at home, initially

I screamed louder: "I don't have arthritis!"

doing seated poses that didn't strain my knees. Soon, I worked up to some easy standing postures, reminding myself with each movement, "I don't have arthritis." Each time I had to raise myself from a seat, with my knees screaming at me, I screamed louder: "I don't have arthritis!"

At first, I noticed subtle improvement. Even the smallest victory was encouraging, so I continued affirming to myself that I did not have arthritis anymore. Last week, I walked to my library, a four-mile roundtrip, pain-free. I can get up off the sofa — and other places! — with no problem. Six months ago, I returned to my yoga class. Joint pain and limitations are no longer a part of my life. Just ask me the reason, and I'll give you my answer: I don't have arthritis.

—Monica A. Andermann—

88

Dragonflies

To forgive is to set a prisoner free and discover
that the prisoner was you.
~Louis B. Smedes

I t was two hours past the time that I was supposed to be moved
to jail from the city cells. I was sick of Hungry-Man dinners and
toast, and tired of sleeping with one itchy blanket in a cold, dark
cell. I made all the calls I could, asking friends and family for bail
money. No one accepted. They all had their reasons.

After three days inside, I was truly scared. When the guard came
and unlocked my cell, I thought it was time for the move, so I steeled
myself for whatever was going to happen next. In silence, he led me
upstairs. Not knowing what to expect, I trudged along behind him,
anxiety coursing through my veins. When I finally looked up, there
stood my mother, the last person I expected to see.

My parents split up when I was very young, and though children
of divorce are often raised by a single mom, my dad raised my brother
and me. I don't think I ever forgave my mother for leaving. Because of
that, among other reasons, we never saw eye-to-eye, never got along,
and never enjoyed a good mother/daughter relationship. So, seeing
her there left me stunned, especially since she was one of the many
who had declined to bail me out.

But now she had bailed me out, and we quietly drove to my dad's
in her car. I had no clue what awaited me, but as soon as I opened the
door to the house, I had a pretty good idea.

And so it began — an intervention just like the ones on TV. All the people who loved me most were gathered there, but they were dead serious. They told me that I needed to change and clean up my act. They loved me, but they were not willing to stand by and watch me destroy myself. It had already been agreed before I got there that I was to move to my mother and stepdad's farm. If I refused, they would "disown" me. My dad and my brother meant everything to me, and I couldn't imagine my life without them, so there was no decision to be made. Of course, I agreed.

> They were not willing to stand by and watch me destroy myself.

Mom lived just outside a tiny town of about 800 people, forty kilometers away. I started out there going through withdrawal. I slept for most of the first two weeks. I was so sick that I wanted to die. I didn't think I could get by without the drugs, the partying, and the friends, let alone live in the sticks with the woman whom I felt had once abandoned me. Everything about the situation seemed impossible.

Then came the day I still recall clearly. Mom came into my room and told me I had to get up. I had to get some fresh air. I just wanted her to go away and leave me alone, but she persisted. Muttering under my breath, I got up and went outside with her.

The sun was blindingly bright, and the breeze smelled like pasture. Believe me, that is not as pleasant as it sounds. We talked, enjoyed her flowers and admired the gathering of dragonflies. It was an especially hot summer, and they were plentiful that year. I have never seen that many since. She raised her pointer finger in the air and told me to do the same. I rolled my eyes, but complied begrudgingly. Then I watched, mesmerized, as the dragonflies landed on our fingers.

At that precise moment, I realized that I was missing the small things in life. I had a sudden awareness that there was so much to appreciate and so many experiences that I had yet to live. I had my whole life ahead of me, a life more valuable than I had ever thought possible. I realized then that the parties, drugs, and fake friends weren't really living at all. They were just a way to pass the time, a way to bury my anger, hurt and feelings of abandonment that I refused to let go. More importantly, I realized that I did have a mother. She didn't abandon me, and she was here now when I needed her most. I was still her daughter, and she hadn't given up. On that day out on the prairie, in the afternoon sunshine, she became not only my mother but my friend.

That was more than twelve years ago. Since then, my mother and I have formed a relationship I had never dreamed possible. She has become a big part of my life and that of my two wonderful children. They think the world of their granny. She has held me when I've cried, consoled me when I was in pain, celebrated my successes, and carried me through my failures.

Most of all, I admire how she held my hand through recovery, teaching by example the true meaning of life and love. It took me far too long to forgive her for not being there when I was young. And as much as I regret that, I understand. Because of her, I was able to get clean and begin a relationship with her that would be unbreakable. My children are also blessed with her unconditional love. Because she taught me how to forgive, they enjoy an amazing granny who shares with them the simple things in life, like catching dragonflies. I am forever grateful that she saved me and has shown me the depth of a true mother's love.

— Celeste Bergeron Ewan —

89

Chicken Soup
for the Soul

Born at Age Fifty-Five

Some day you will be old enough
to start reading fairy tales again.
~C.S. Lewis

My uncle Art is 102 and 1/2 years old. When you get that old, you get to count your age in half years again. He is still a broad-shouldered man, about 5'10", with a shock of white hair and a handsome face, sporting high cheekbones and a straight, classic nose.

Alas, he is now blind after botched eye surgery when he was eighty-five. But he has a better memory than people half his age. And every morning, while he's riding his stationary bicycle, he uses his good memory to recite to himself some of the poems he memorized in earlier years. He knows short poems — Shakespeare's sonnets — and long, narrative poems, such as "The Cremation of Sam McGee" by Canadian poet Robert W. Service.

Art has a twinkling sense of humor. When he could still see shapes, he walked with the aid of two white walking sticks.

My son said to him, "Hey, Uncle Art, those remind me of ski poles."

Instantly, Art shot back: "Well, I am on the downward slope, y'know."

But here is what is most remarkable about my uncle. He says he started his life at age fifty-five.

In his teen years, Art was "a runt that nobody noticed." His older brother (my dad) was part of the popular crowd in high school, but

Art was so shy and insecure that, even now, he remembers, "It was worse than not being liked. I felt like nobody even saw me."

He grew nine inches the year after he graduated, but his insecurity stayed with him during his Army service in World War II. Though he won a Bronze Star for his actions in the Battle of the Bulge, he never told anyone about it. Still insecure after the war, he became a U.S. mail carrier in his hometown, so he wouldn't need to work around people.

What did make Art feel more comfortable during his twenties was alcohol. There were plenty of bars lining Durango's Main Street at the time, and a few shots of bourbon helped Art forget his self-doubts. Unfortunately, he said, "I was a mean drunk. Had a chip on my shoulder and got in some real barroom brawls."

One morning, he woke up in an alley, smelling of booze and vomit. Unable to remember the last twenty-four hours, he realized, "I've gotta stop this."

So no more bars. Just like that, Art stopped drinking.

He moved in with his widowed mom and began what I call his "cloistered years." Both my mom and dad were born in Durango, so we went for a visit every summer. Art was just the quiet guy who sat in a corner and never said much. I did notice that he seemed to read a lot — especially books of poetry — and apparently he liked classical music. Mostly, he was invisible to me. I didn't pay him much attention.

Then came the morning of Art's fifty-fifth birthday. "Why did that birthday seem so different?" I asked him many years later. He shook his head and shrugged. "Can't really say what it was. I just looked into the mirror that morning and realized that life was passing me by. And it was up to me to start doing something about it."

In Durango, the VFW sponsored weekly dances for people over forty, sometimes with live music. On Sunday afternoons, people could go early and take lessons. Pretty soon, Art was learning the foxtrot, waltz and jitterbug. He even learned to tango.

So this shy, reclusive man started dancing. And since one needs a partner, Art summoned up the courage to ask a woman to dance. One evening, he spied a pretty widow who, he learned, was five years younger. Lucille was outgoing and spunky with eyes that sparkled, and she seemed to like this tall, somewhat gawky man. When he asked her to dance, she accepted. Pretty soon, they began attending dances together.

At the age of sixty-two, Art summoned up the courage to propose. At that moment, his life changed. He retired from the postal service, and he and Lucille bought a trailer in Yuma, Arizona, where they began to spend their winters. "Regular snowbirds we were," Art said. "And in Yuma, we went dancing five nights a week." He began to quote poetry to Lucille — poems he had memorized. At night before they went to sleep, Art would whisper the lines of one of Shakespeare's sonnets. After a while, he began to write verse of his own. Their friends in Yuma couldn't imagine that the talented, witty man they knew had ever been shy and lonely.

It wasn't until after my own parents died that I became acquainted with this "new" Uncle Art. It was after my own fifty-fifth birthday and my husband had just filed for divorce. I was heartbroken, and felt as if my life had ended. *I'm too old to start over,* I thought.

In an effort to escape from my pain, I drove down to Durango for a visit with Uncle Art and Lucille. And it was there, as we sat in their comfortable living room, that Art told me the story of his fifty-fifth birthday.

"You started your life at fifty-five?" I said with a slight gasp. I looked from Art to Lucille, who had her arm twined lovingly with his.

"You're never too old to begin again," she said with quiet conviction. Art nodded. "For some of us, fifty-five is the time we start," he said in his deep, twinkly voice.

That visit was twenty-two years ago. Now Uncle Art has passed the century mark, and I'm in my seventies. And he was right. In the years since my divorce, I have become a book author and professional speaker. I moved back to the Midwest and found the warm gift of friendship that exists among women. And I met Jim, a wonderful man and the partner of my happy older years.

Although there was pain in my divorce transition, there was also self-discovery. Any time I got discouraged, I would think of Uncle Art.

Lucille passed on five years ago, but I'm planning to celebrate Uncle Art's 103rd birthday. Who knows? There may still be more I can learn from him.

— Barbara Bartocci —

90

Repairing Brokenness

Blessed are the hearts that can bend;
they shall never be broken.
~Albert Camus

I n 2001, just a few months before 9/11, my future wife Lucy went to New York with her mom. They saw several Broadway shows and bought a snow globe filled with the city's top landmarks and signs from the more popular Broadway shows. She always enjoyed collecting snow globes from her travels.

Then five years ago, when we'd just gotten married and had moved to a new house, Lucy left the snow globe on the garage floor while searching for something in a trunk we had out there. She should have put it back where it belonged, but she didn't. I saw it there the next day. I was somewhat peeved that she'd left it there. I should've picked it up and put it back in its proper place, but I didn't. I was wrong for that.

That snow globe remained on the floor of the garage for several days. Each of us saw it and had multiple opportunities to pick it up and do the right thing, but both of us failed.

One night, I turned on the light in the garage, but the bulb blew. It didn't faze me. I continued to do whatever it was I was doing. Several seconds later, I accidentally kicked the snow globe over and it shattered into seemingly a million pieces.

My heart started racing. I knew she'd be upset. I picked everything up the best I could, discarded the glass, put the base in a box, and set it aside. It was something special, so I vowed to get it repaired one day. In my heart and soul, I knew it could be fixed.

Less than a year later, Lucy and I were divorced. We argued, fought, and even suffered a devastating miscarriage. We were broken. She took her stuff, and I took mine. I also took the broken snow globe. I knew it could be fixed.

We didn't see each other for a year and half, although we texted from time to time. Sometimes it was nice; other times, not so much.

Before her, I was alone yet never felt lonely. When I lost her, I was a mess. I served in the U.S. Army for many years, including three yearlong tours of duty in Iraq. My body hurt. My mind hurt. My soul hurt. My heart hurt. I was broken from head to toe.

There were times I turned to extreme amounts of alcohol to escape the hurt. I only hurt more. On one occasion, I went with three of my best friends to the Georgia Dome in Atlanta to see our beloved Auburn Tigers play the Louisville Cardinals. I watched the first series of the game and then disappeared. I sat on the floor in a corner away from everyone and never watched another snap. I was so alone. I hurt so much.

Finally, in early December, I stopped in at my local VA hospital to ask for some help. I could've walked in to the mental health clinic and seen a doctor right then, but it wasn't urgent. I wasn't going to do anything stupid. I knew I could be fixed. I just didn't know how.

The first available appointment was the last slot of the day on Christmas Eve. I thought that was quite special. What a gift! I saw a doctor for my physical pain and a counselor for my mental pain. I was well on my way to repairing my own personal brokenness.

I needed to cut Lucy loose. I had to. I needed to move on. "If you love something, set it free," they say, and I did.

Besides an occasional text, we didn't communicate at all for the better part of a year... until we did.

She was going through her own hard times, trying to deal with her own brokenness. One day, she felt that she'd hit rock bottom. Her mom, sister, and daughter told her to talk to me, because "Jody was the only guy who really ever loved her."

So, she called me. I was shocked. She's not someone who likes talking on the phone. We talked for a while. She said she was in the area, so I asked her to stop by if she wanted. The funny thing is that we lived in a small town, so she was always "in the area."

We spent the rest of that day just hanging out in my back yard. I had a bountiful garden, so we picked fresh vegetables and ate them raw. I think we cooked something later that night.

From that night on, we saw each other frequently. We were just friends enjoying each other's company; we were trying to get to know each other better than before.

Inevitably, we started talking about a possible future but knew we had to fix some things. When I saw the writing on the wall that we indeed could be fixed, I sent the broken snow globe to a shop in Colorado to be repaired.

I'd hoped to get it back by Valentine's Day. I had a speech and a romantic presentation laid out for her. I wanted to use the snow globe as a symbol for our failed marriage and how we both contributed to it but also as a symbol of how something so special could be repaired. Unfortunately, the repairs on the globe took longer than expected so I didn't have it in time for Valentine's Day.

It turned out that we didn't need the snow globe to symbolize our brokenness or our repairs. We made a decision to give our relationship another go while the repairs were still taking place.

When I finally surprised her with the repaired snow globe, she was blown away. It looked brand new — better than ever. She had no idea that I had sent it off and had no idea that it could be salvaged. I did. I knew it could be fixed.

Upon further review, it wasn't perfect. The Statue of Liberty's torch had broken off, but that was okay. It wasn't perfect, but it was close enough.

We've been back together for more than two years. We've truly never been happier. We live in my family home, which sits on fifty-eight acres of land in the country near a river just two miles down the road from my mother. Her mother lives a whopping nine miles away. It's quiet, and we love it. My late father was born in our house. It's special.

We're in a good place, figuratively and literally.

Speaking of babies, we have our own. Her name is Abigail. She was born seven and a half weeks early, in the back of an ambulance on Friday the 13th. Just your typical birth, I guess. She's perfect in every way.

When something is special and you know it, you don't throw it away. You keep it. You hold onto it the best you can, and when the timing is right, you fix it.

—Jody Fuller—

91

A Little Birdie Told Me

Life is not about waiting for the storms to pass. It's
about learning how to dance in the rain.
~Vivian Greene

Four days after my twenty-seventh birthday, I felt sad and empty. It wasn't getting older that bothered me, but rather the point that I was at in my life. I was struggling financially, about to lose my house, and was facing unemployment. I had pounded the pavement every day in search of work, but I hadn't received a call back. "It's all going to be okay! I promise!" my best friend Meghan said on the phone when I cried and shared my worry.

"How can you be sure?" I asked between sobs.

"We've all had low points in our lives," she said. "I always ask for a sign that everything is going to be okay. Trust me, it works!"

I was hesitant to believe her. She was just trying to make me feel better, after all. And the last thing I wanted to do was depress her. "Okay, I'll give it a try," I promised before we hung up.

"Good, I'll talk to you tomorrow," she said. I disconnected, knelt beside my bed and bowed my head. I wasn't sure what to say, so I just started talking. "Please, show me a sign that everything is going to be okay. Let me be positive that whatever sign it is, it's for me."

That night as I climbed into bed, I felt a sense of peace wash over me. For the first time in months, I slept soundly.

I woke up the next morning, though, still feeling discouraged. When I collected the mail I found bills with the words URGENT in big, red letters on the envelopes. I remembered what Meghan had said, and I whispered, "Show me a sign! Please! Anything to let me know it's going to be okay!"

I walked around to the back of the house when a flurry of motion suddenly caught my eye. On the ground near the corner of the shed, I saw a tiny baby bird. I put down the mail and stopped in my tracks. I had no idea what to do. Should I pick it up? Shouldn't I? I couldn't just leave it there alone and stranded. Thoughts raced through my mind, and my brain finally sprang into action. I went to the shed and fished out a pair of gloves, a cardboard box, and some clean rags. I picked up the tiny bird and gently placed it in the box. "It's going to be okay," I said out loud and looked around for a nest, but there wasn't one that I could see. I remembered hearing that if one touches a bird, its mother won't come back for it, so I prayed that I had done the right thing.

I brought the bird into the house and flipped through the phone-book to find an animal rescue. I called one after another until I was finally connected with an agent. "I found a baby bird in my yard, and I think it might be hurt!" I said to the woman on the other end.

"Where is the bird now?" the woman asked.

"It's in my kitchen in an old shoebox on the counter," I answered.

"It may take some time before we can send someone out. There's only one person on duty at the moment, but we'll send him as soon as we can."

"What should I do in the meantime?" I asked nervously. I knew nothing about birds or how to care for them.

"It sounds like the bird is in good hands for now. See you in a bit."

I gave her my address, and she disconnected. I turned my attention back to the bird. "I guess it's just you and me for a while," I said. I stuck out my finger and gently stroked his feathers. "You'll be okay. Help is coming soon," I said. All of a sudden, it hit me. I was telling the bird exactly what I needed to hear. Tears flowed down my cheeks, and I knew that finding this bird was my sign that everything was going to be okay.

A few hours later, the animal-control officer came and took the bird into his care. "You did a great job," he said, smiling. "This little fella has a broken wing. We'll get him fixed up and set him free."

Two days later, my phone rang, and I received a job offer that would allow me to cover my bills and more. I called my best friend, thanked her for her advice, and told her about the little bird. From that day on, I knew that everything was going to be okay.

—Lacey L. Bakker—

92

The Right Dream

The clearer you are when visualizing your dreams,
the brighter the spotlight will be to lead you
on the right path.
~Gail Lynne Goodwin

After working for nearly a decade at the same dead-end job with no advancement and no pay increases, I was contemplating leaving the profession for good when I got a job offer I couldn't pass up. I was offered the position of Office Manager for a struggling company that had been operating at a loss for over a year. My job would be to organize the office, hire and fire as needed, and help turn a losing operation into a profitable one. The owner knew that would be no easy task and because of same, he offered me a salary I had only dreamed of, paid vacation, sick leave and a 401K. Since my current job offered zero benefits, it took me only two seconds to accept.

I had colleagues in the business who were willing to come aboard for the benefits alone, and with the owner's permission, hired friends and family (including my husband) who shared the same vision I did: to make the firm the biggest and best in the business.

When we became profitable, I was promoted to State Manager with a substantial salary increase. I managed two offices with forty-four employees working in five separate departments, with plans to open a third office on the drawing board.

As sometimes happens when one goes from rags to riches, as our income increased, so did our spending. My husband and I moved from our small apartment to a large, beautiful home near my office. Since the job entailed a considerable amount of entertaining, our house was filled to overflowing with high-end quality furniture which I had purchased on the installment plan to improve my credit rating. We had two beautiful cars in the driveway.

By all appearances, we were living the American Dream.

I'll never forget the Friday that I was walking around the office, looking forward to the weekend, and encountered our company attorney. He wordlessly handed me a sealed envelope.

The letter inside was brief. It stated that due to the recent downturn in the economy, the company had reorganized and my position had been eliminated. Effective immediately, I was to leave the premises.

When I looked up after reading it, I noticed that seven other employees had been given the same envelope — including my husband.

The aftermath was devastating. We got new jobs, but in a different profession and only making minimum wage. We were forced to move out of our house into a tiny apartment. The furniture and one of our cars were repossessed.

Even worse than the loss of our possessions was the loss of self-esteem. Somewhere along the way, I had equated my identity with my job; i.e. since I had such an important job, then that made me important. And somewhere along the way, I measured personal success by how many big and expensive things I owned; the more possessions, the more successful I was. Without that important job and without all those possessions, I thought of myself as unimportant and unsuccessful.

> *We had sacrificed time with our friends, families and even each other.*

The sudden loss of our jobs was heartbreaking but as with most misfortunes, it turned out to be a blessing in disguise. It forced us to come to a complete stop and analyze what we really wanted out of life and what we needed to do to get there.

We realized we had worked 24/7, 365 days a year to keep that company afloat and profitable. We had sacrificed time with our friends, families and even each other to advance in a corporate world that in the end, didn't appreciate, deserve or value our efforts. We had missed important births, funerals, graduations and weddings.

It's been years now since we both lost our jobs. And our lives did change — for the better.

Now, our home is modest but fully paid for. We don't have a lot of things that need dusting and maintenance — only the necessities. We don't finance or use credit cards anymore. If we don't have the cash, we don't buy it.

Now I can honestly say my husband and I are truly living — and enjoying — the American Dream.

— Pam Phree —

Make a Difference

93

Mindfulness Matters

*Mindfulness is a way of befriending ourselves
and our experience.*
~Jon Kabat-Zinn

My great-grandfather inspired me to make a positive difference in the world. He was a very mindful person, and he taught me about positive thinking. He used to say things like "Think well to be well," and "Every day, we have a new choice to make, so choose to be happy."

Most of all, Grandpa Jack was always kind. He believed that a smile is not just a smile. It's a road to peace, one that kids can learn in pre-kindergarten, and something that can change the world. And he taught me that if we smile, even if we don't feel like it, our bodies get a positive signal from our brains, and the smile comes true! Grandpa knew then what scientists have since proven: Smiling is contagious.

When Grandpa Jack passed away, I wanted to honor him by teaching his messages of positivity, kindness, and happiness to other kids. I believe that the key to ending violence is teaching kids to be mindful when they're young. That's why I started the Wuf Shanti Children's Wellness Foundation, to teach kids to live a healthy and happy life, using his wisdom.

Wuf Shanti is a dog character that teaches mindfulness, social and emotional learning, kindness, and positivity to kids from three to ten years old. Wuf Shanti has produced seven books; a free mobile app with signature games; and 100 videos, which have run on local PBS stations, the Children's TV Network (the station in children's hospitals across the nation), Adventure to Learning (health and fitness video programming in 25,000 schools) and Kidoodle.TV (safe streaming network for kids).

In my Wuf Shanti dog costume, I traveled to schools and children's hospitals to visit the kids and share our message with them. When Wuf would walk into the hospitals and meet the kids, especially the kids who had cancer — many of them bald from treatment or hooked up to tubes — they'd forget all that for a few minutes. They would smile and run up to Wuf to hug him, dance, or give a high-five.

Parents would cry with joy at seeing their kids smiling and happy. It had an impact on me. I felt sad seeing them like this, but happy about how my being there was helping their lives, even for a few minutes. It made me realize how good my life is and how so many people need help to be happier.

One time, my little sister was crying, and I was able to share Grandpa Jack's message. I told her that she had a choice to make. She could choose to be upset about not getting what she wanted, or she could choose to be happy for what she did have. About five minutes later, I overheard her calming herself down by repeating "think well, be well," while tapping her fingers one at a time against her thumb, one of the exercises Wuf Shanti teaches. You don't realize how much of an impact you're making until you witness a five-year-old control her own temper tantrum and bring positivity back into her life.

I've used my grandpa's teaching often. For example, when I became a teenager, I got self-conscious when some of my friends teased me about being a dog character. So, I did what Grandpa taught me to do: I laughed. They stop teasing you if they see it doesn't bother you.

And I took action by expanding our curriculum for older kids, ages eleven to seventeen (minus the dog character). My mission is to provide kids and teens with coping tools so they grow up less depressed and anxious. I want them to become happy, peace-loving adults who solve their problems in productive ways. I consider these techniques to be life skills. My goal is to get these mindful, social-and-emotional-learning programs into schools across the country as part of their core curriculums.

We live near Parkland, Florida and the tragic shooting that happened at Marjory Stoneman Douglas High School. That made me want to do even more, so I founded the Kids' Association for Mindfulness in Education for teens to collaborate and figure out ways to work together to make the world a better place. I also founded the international online Mindful Kids Peace Summit for middle schools and high schools. More than fifty subject-matter experts spoke about diversity, kindness, anti-bullying, communication, mindfulness, positivity, learning to interact with others, compassion, collaboration, positive psychology, and more.

Through working on all of this, I've learned that even when you feel like giving up (like when you see yet another shooting on the news), you have to work even harder. I've also learned that collaboration is key. We can't change the world alone. Even though I'm a mindful kid, I get sad or upset sometimes. Sometimes, I find it hard to put down my phone and look up, but I force myself to do it. I now tell people that if they can just practice mindfulness for five minutes every day, it can help them.

Science has proven that mindfulness helps us relax, stay focused, do better in school and sports, stay healthy, heal faster, get along better with others, and live a happier life. There will always be stress in life that we'll have to deal with, so we need to stop thinking negatively and start focusing on the positive. We need to connect with each other and smile. "Think well to be well," as my grandpa would say. It can change our lives and change the world. It's a lesson that I take to heart every day.

—Adam Avin—

Editor's note: You can watch Adam's TEDx Talk at https://www.tedxkc.org/adam-avin-kcyouth or on YouTube at https://youtu.be/2r6TWTqr8FM.

94

Happy Thankful Thursday!

The more you praise and celebrate your life,
the more there is in life to celebrate.
~Oprah Winfrey

As part of my upbringing, I was taught to smile and say, "Thank you." My mother always advised, "Don't look mean. Smile and look or act like you're happy!"

Years after my mother passed away, when social media was becoming a new phenomenon, I decided to publicly express why I was thankful. I would share a motivational message that could touch others at least once a week. My favorite day became "Thankful Thursday" on Facebook. It made me happy to share in a manner that the introvert in me probably would not use if I were in public view. So, for more than six years, I've written weekly messages to share via social media. Here is a sample of some of my Thankful Thursday thoughts:

> *We all have our dry seasons, but they don't stay that way.*

- *If you do more than just exist, you will not only make a positive change in your life, you will also change the life of someone else in the world. Happy Thankful Thursday! Be a life-changer! (11-19-11)*

- *Even though I initially settled, something greater was offered. God knows what's best and HE delivers! Happy Thankful Thursday! (5-3-12)*

- *I have decided that I'd rather host a "thank you party" over a "pity party." All things happen for a reason, and perhaps it was not my season... yet! As it is often stated, we can turn lemons into lemonade. There is no sugar in pity, but oh how sweet it is to be thankful! Have a blessed Thankful Thursday! Enjoy your party! (9-6-12)*

- *I was driving to work this morning in a sleepy, dreary-type mood. Still feeling a void and not even realizing that I had driven miles without noticing the streets. Have you ever wondered how you got somewhere so quickly? It seemed as if my life was like the cold ground, with dried brown grass and no leaves on the branches. Then, I saw one little tree that was as green as could be. It reminded me that in a few weeks the season is going to change, and everything around me will have vibrant color. Life is going to wake up! So, that is what I needed to do. We all have our dry seasons, but they don't stay that way. Therefore, I am so thankful that there are brighter days ahead! Have a blessed Thankful Thursday, and cheers to your brighter days! (3-14-13)*

- *Good morning! Still no power or running water, and another tree went down yesterday. The night was by candlelight. But I woke up this morning blessed — not stressed, because I know my real power source. So I am going to my car to charge this phone and listen to the radio, with some fruit. Thank God for options. Happy Thankful Thursday! (7-11-13)*

- *Oh, happy day! It's Thankful Thursday! I was thinking about TRUE friendship because of something that was said to me this week. It made me think of friendship as a math equation. Friends add to, not take away. We build up, not tear down. We make each other smile, not frown. We wipe tears, not create tears. We celebrate one another because we are more than, not less than. All of that equals (=) TRUE friendship, plus more! Think about a true friend, and he or she should make you smile. It did for me. It's a blessing. Have a wonderful day! (2-20-14)*

- *I had to learn that if I didn't like the taste of life, I had to stir in new ingredients. Be your own chef, and change the flavor of life to your desired taste. It may take time, but some things are worth simmering until perfection. Have a blessed Thankful Thursday! Can you taste it? (4-17-14)*

- *On Wednesday, I was gliding up the highway on cruise control. It's a nice feature that allows comfort to set in while driving. Well, after about 65 miles, I had to snap out of comfort on a sunny day and stop to get more gas. It made me reflect on life and why it's not good, nor smart, to remain in a comfortable position. It is always necessary to stop and refill, re-group, re-position... and stretch! Our bones are made to move, and our mind is made to develop. It truly makes a difference. #LessgasLessdistance #MoregasMoredistance Happy #ThankfulThursday! (5-18-17)*

After a few years of sharing Thankful Thursday messages, I considered stopping, thinking that maybe my Facebook friends had had enough of my thoughts. Oh, dear, was I wrong. There were responses like, "I look forward to your messages," and "I love Thankful Thursday!" These wonderful responses made me decide to keep going and even extend the messages via Instagram and Twitter. The feedback has been fantastic, and people are honestly happy. Friends often share their comments each week when they can identify with the message or it motivates them to do something. The sharing of comments makes me happy because the weekly messages are not about me; it's about public expressions of gratitude, which ignite the chain of happiness among hundreds of people.

When we realize that happiness comes from within, and being thankful is an expression from the heart, we unleash an attitude of gratitude. Making it a habit to say "thank you" to all the people who have made a difference in our lives can catapult us into a state of happiness. Happiness is contagious!

— LaTonya Branham —

95

A Bethany Blessing

Experience is not what happens to you. It is what you
do with what happens to you. Don't waste your pain;
use it to help others.
~Rick Warren, The Purpose Driven Life

December 12th should have been a day to celebrate. But after our daughter, Bethany, passed away from a brain tumor, it was a day of mourning. It was her birthday and I didn't know how I would survive it that first year after she was gone. It had only been two months and my grief was still so raw.

Bethany was our only daughter. She had brought the "pink" into our lives in a household with two boys. She was a fireball of activity and interests, but her most outstanding quality was her big heart. She was a friend to the friendless, the one who could speak to anybody and cheer them up. In high school, she began a group that visited the elderly in a nursing home. She called and made all the arrangements and rallied her friends at church to join the endeavor.

How would I get through that birthday? And then it occurred to me: I would celebrate another baby girl born on December 12th. I would go to our local hospital, where I used to work as a nurse, and find a baby girl in the maternity wing. I worked as a school nurse now, but my friend Sarah still worked at the hospital.

I put together a bag with a pink toy and a gift card for a local store. The note on the outside said: "For the first baby girl born on December 12th." The card was signed, "A Bethany Blessing."

Make a Difference |

I took it to Sarah and asked, "Can you deliver this to the mother/baby unit?"

Sarah had been Bethany's close friend, and we both fought back tears. "Of course," she said with a brave smile.

We hugged, and I was amazed I made it back to the elevator, through the foyer and out to my car with my blurred vision.

Through the years, I've continued the tradition. The money I would have used to buy my daughter a birthday gift is used instead as a blessing for another little girl and her mom. I started praying that the recipient would be someone who very much needed the help of that gift card.

After the first couple of years, I grew brave enough to deliver the gift bag to the nurses on the floor in person. I told them what it was and asked them to deliver it to the right mom. With patient privacy, I did not wish to intrude on the patient. Besides, I wanted to remain anonymous to the recipient.

The head nurse remembered me for several years. She'd greet me with a sympathetic hug and thank me. "I know just who this is going to," she'd say. I'd smile, fight back the tears and thank her.

One year took me completely by surprise. As I approached the desk of the maternity unit — which by now had greater security — I handed the gift bag to the clerk. "This is a Bethany Blessing for the first baby girl born today."

"Wait. This is for you." She grinned and handed me an envelope.

"For me?" Stunned, I took the thick envelope and thanked her. She just kept smiling, and I turned to go. All the way down in the elevator, I wondered what on earth it was. I trudged through the snow and ice in the parking lot, climbed in my freezing car, and opened the envelope.

The card read: "You don't know me, but your Bethany Blessing was so special to my daughter and me." The young mom expressed how she had been going through a very difficult time when her baby was born and how the gift card was truly a blessing for them. She included several photos of her now three-year-old daughter. The child's contagious smile put a smile on my own face.

"I just wanted to say thanks," the card continued.

I'm so grateful that I was able to look past my own pain to reach out to others. This note reminded me that we may never know the impact of a kindness, however small, but our action can be the answer to a prayer for someone else.

I survive every December 12th with another "Bethany Blessing," knowing my daughter's legacy of giving lives on.

— Elaine Marie Cooper —

96

Operation Sunshine

Your abundance is not measured by what you have;
it is created by what you share.
~Heidi Catherine Culbertson, Wisdom and Recipes

I was a single mother of two preteens, working three part-time jobs so I would have the flexibility to take my mother to the dialysis clinic for treatments three times a week. One day, as we sat in the waiting room at the clinic, my mother leaned closer to me and said, "You know, honey, barring getting a kidney transplant, every single person in this room is terminal."

Immediately, I understood what she was saying. The average lifespan for a dialysis patient is only about five to ten years, although some people can take treatments for decades. Once treatment is initiated, however, it is extremely unlikely that a person's kidney function will ever improve to the point at which he or she will be able to discontinue the treatments and live.

Glancing around the room again, I thought about the people who were there. There was "Aunt Tootsie," a retired schoolteacher who loved to talk to everyone. And Colonel Hooper, a retired military hero. There was Mr. Coble, a retired police detective from Detroit. When he found out that my late father had been a police officer, he loved to sit beside me and tell me about some of his more interesting cases. There was also Mr. Miller, a Mennonite man, who came from a small community an hour and fifteen minutes away from the clinic for his treatments.

The dialysis patients weren't all older people, however. There was Jimmy, a thirtyish man, who was not a viable candidate for a transplant because his body produced too many antibodies. Talking to him was an even younger man, a relatively new patient whose name I hadn't learned yet, who had already undergone a heart/double lung transplant and was now waiting for a new kidney. Each one of these people came into the clinic and endured a physically demanding three- to four-and-a-half-hour dialysis treatment.

My mother was gently pointing out to me that at least I still had my entire life ahead of me, unlike most of these wonderful people whom we had come to know.

I mulled over her words during her entire four-hour treatment. I kept thinking that I wanted — no, I needed — to do something to let these patients know that someone realized their struggles and cared about what happened to them.

Later, I went to the dollar store and a craft store, looking for some inspiration. It was September, so I bought some miniature apples, pumpkins, and leaves for a fall theme. When I arrived home, I put them into small, individual Ziploc bags.

The next time I took Mom to dialysis, I waited until after she had gone to the back for her treatment. Then I snuck back to my car and retrieved the bags of treats from where I had hidden them on the back seat. I rang the door buzzer, and when a nurse came to the door, I handed her the bags and asked her to pass them out among the patients.

"What's this?" she asked with a surprised smile.

"I'm calling it… Operation Sunshine," I said, smiling in return.

In October, I made non-edible treat bags for Halloween. In November, there was something for Thanksgiving. For Christmas, I gave all of the patients on Mom's shift a Christmas ornament chosen specifically for them.

If a patient's port was blocked, requiring him or her to go to Nashville for surgery and post-operative dialysis, I sent a card to them. If a patient passed away, the family received a card or an angel Christmas ornament. These were always sent from "Operation Sunshine" — I never signed my real name.

It was several months before my mother realized who was behind Operation Sunshine. She had recognized my handwriting on a card given to someone else and asked pointblank if it was me. I admitted that it was, but I asked her to keep my secret, as the nurses who came to the door to take my gifts back to the patients were the only ones who knew my identity.

Sometime after the first of the year, one of the nurses pulled me aside and said that some of the patients on other shifts had heard about Operation Sunshine. They wanted to know why only one shift was getting these treats.

So, I expanded my project to include the later shift on Mom's Monday–Wednesday–Friday rotation and both shifts on the alternating days. I bought kids' paper Valentines, gold "coins" for St. Patrick's Day, flag-themed items for the Fourth of July, and something for all of the major holidays. If a month didn't have a holiday, such as August, I bought items to represent the season. The challenge became being able to buy so many treats without spending a lot of money that I did not have. But by buying when items were on clearance one year for use on next year's Operation Sunshine, I was able to keep things affordable.

Five years after I began this project, my mother passed away suddenly. It was the first weekend in May. The very next week, I showed up at the dialysis clinic with artificial roses for Mother's Day Operation Sunshine.

The nurse who greeted me at the door had tears in her eyes.

"You didn't have to, Jan. No one expected you to do it this month," she said as she took the large shopping bag from me.

"This was the most important one," I said determinedly. "Otherwise, I might not be able to come back in here."

My mother has been gone twelve years, but I still continue to do Operation Sunshine at the same dialysis clinic. Due to the HIPAA Privacy Rule, I can no longer send cards to patients in the hospital, and it is impossible to find out when a patient dies so I can send a sympathy card. In fact, I don't know if anyone who was a patient while my mother was there is still living, but I continue to try to do what I can to brighten these patients' days because they showed me what courage is and the importance of making a difference in people's lives.

—Jan Hopkins-Campbell—

#MakeaStrangersDay

As we work to create light for others,
we naturally light our own way.
~Mary Anne Radmacher

P hysically, emotionally and mentally exhausted, I pushed my cart like a zombie. After a double shift on my feet at a job that made me miserable, my day ended with a text message from my boss informing me that he was letting me go. No reason was given — just "goodbye." All I wanted to do was crawl into bed and cry. However, as the matriarch of a household of six, I knew that since I'd been gone the majority of the day, none of my family had eaten dinner. Wiping the tears from my eyes, I faced the dreaded grocery store.

Shopping for what could be our last solid meal for a while, I walked around trying to pick up whatever staples would get us through. My cart contained eggs, milk, ramen and the makings for a casserole to fill the hungry masses I would encounter when I returned home. Passing the meat, wistful that it was not in the budget, I noticed a package of ground beef that was marked half off because it was due to expire. Snatching it up, I headed toward the checkout. Not two steps away, something yellow buried in the meat section caught my eye. Curious, I went to investigate. It was an envelope that read: "Open Me." So I did. Inside, I found a small piece of paper with the words: "Everything is going to be okay. Just continue to be a good person. Keep strong, and you will be fine."

I began to cry right there. Somehow, the universe was giving me a pep talk after such a horrid day. I rushed to the customer-service station with the note. "Did you do this? Do you know who did?" I asked, showing them the piece of paper. The teenagers behind the counter looked at me blankly.

> *Somehow, the universe was giving me a pep talk after such a horrid day.*

"How can I help you, ma'am? We are about to close," said the pimple-faced kid.

"Do you have an envelope and a piece of paper?" I asked in hopes of returning the favor.

"Stationery is in aisle 8," he responded with a bored tone. With the wind slightly taken out of my sails, I let him ring up my items so that he could go home.

Waking up the next morning, I was not quite sure if the letter had been a dream. Then I settled down at my computer, and there it was — that bright yellow envelope. It did happen. And it did affect me. The note was right. Everything was going to be okay. No longer was I feeling like my world was caving in. Instead, I was inspired to reach higher. I knew then and there what I had to do.

Quickly, I went to social media to share the story. People were touched, and comments of "I'm going to do that" filled my heart. I gathered up the rest of my quarters to buy envelopes and note cards. I wrote out one hundred inspirational notes and announced loudly to anyone who would listen that April was now national #makeastrangersday month. A woman on a mission, it felt good to think that I could help others for even a second. If even one of these one hundred cards helped even one person, then it was worth doing.

Everywhere I went for the next month — stores, restaurants, parks — I left a note. When I took a road trip, I left a note at every stop. I was determined to build positive energy at every turn.

"Did you leave this for me?" I once overheard a waitress asking a regular.

"I don't know what you are talking about," he responded.

I had left a note in the server station reading simply: "You are doing a good job in a difficult field. Keep it up. #makeastrangersday."

Make a Difference |

I went to the drugstore and left a letter in the feminine-hygiene area stating, "Don't forget to get yourself some chocolate and something to make you feel pretty. You deserve it!" I actually went out once and forgot one of my pre-written notes, so I asked the waitress for a pen and a piece of paper and left a note in the women's bathroom, only to see the same note again in the same bathroom a few weeks later with replies of "Thank you."

I began texting my friends daily asking, "Did you make a stranger's day?" The answer was usually "yes," and they would tell me excitedly about what they had done, where they had left a note, or how they had paid for the coffee of the person behind them in line or helped an elderly woman with her groceries.

Within a few weeks, I started getting letters or comments about a friend of a friend who had found a #makeastrangersday note, not just in my area, but all over the country. My heart swelled with joy as I listened to all the stories of others boosting morale. I may not have started the kindness, but I was confident that I had helped inspire others to pay it forward.

The month of April ended, and we all went back to our normal lives — now (hopefully) with a little more compassion toward our fellow humans. Once in a while, I would still leave notes for strangers, but admittedly I was not as vigilant about it as I was during those first thirty days.

One day, my phone rang. "Jodi, I have someone on the line you are going to want to talk to," my friend said.

"Hi, Jodi. My name is Nancy," the unknown voice began.

"Hi, Nancy," I replied, confused.

"I'm the woman who wrote that note in the grocery store," her voice continued. She described the color of the envelope, where it was and what it had said, just to make it clear she really was my benefactor. "I just had a feeling that someone needed a pep talk that day," she finished. Tears welled in my eyes as I thanked her for her kindness and gushed over how much it had affected me. "I heard you turned it into quite a movement," she complimented.

"I just tried to take what you did and help others with the same idea," I replied, embarrassed at the praise.

"Personally, I can't wait until next April for 'Make a Stranger's Day Month.' Let me know how I can help," she said in closing. I put down my phone in awe of what had just happened. Not only did I get to meet the stranger who had lifted me up when I was so down, but I had made a new friend in the process. One stranger had lifted my spirits twice.

A week ago, I sent my daughter to get a bag of rice. The gentleman in front of her paid for it. "You didn't have to do that," she said, showing him that she had money.

"Ah, it's nothing. Make a stranger's day, right?" he replied as he walked away.

In return, my daughter took the money I had given her and paid for the person's milk behind her. The woman looked confused. "You're welcome," my daughter reassured her. "Just be sure that you take the time on occasion to make a stranger's day." I couldn't have been prouder.

—Jodi Renee Thomas—

98

Warm from the Inside Out

You will find as you look back upon your life that the moments when you have truly lived are the moments when you have done things in the spirit of love.

~Henry Drummond

T he wind and rain made it feel like a cold December day, and yet it was already spring. I sloshed through the puddles as I walked as fast as I could to the huge arena. *Why am I doing this?* I thought to myself. *I am so tired, up too early, and I want to be huddled under the covers. This is crazy!*

When I got inside, it was still cold, and I was grateful that I had remembered to wear a toque, two pairs of gloves, and three layers of clothing, plus a vest and warm jacket.

Then a cheery voice called out, "Hi, Fran."

"Hello, Lindy. Hi, Pippa. How are you, Diana?" I replied with a smile. It was so nice to see them, knowing that they too were braving the cold to fulfill their volunteer commitments. The vast arena buzzed with activity. The gentle nickering of a horse mingled with the sound of a child's laughter. Volunteers led horses, while moms tended to their children with special needs, zipping up jackets, tightening riding helmets, securing gloves on tiny, wiggling fingers, preparing them for their riding lesson.

I couldn't help smiling. These beautiful children all faced daily mental and physical challenges, and their parents' love was evident. Just the tiniest sign of improvement — a wide grin, a loud laugh, a child managing a simple exercise — was a major milestone for the instructor, parent and child.

I knew now why I got up early to come to this place. It was for the children's smiles and laughter, the devoted parents, the instructors patiently teaching, the volunteer staff, and the beautiful horses gently carrying their precious cargoes. Despite the inclement weather outside, I felt like I had found a piece of heaven.

Few people realize the army of volunteers that it takes for one young child to have a half-hour riding lesson. I volunteer at Valley Therapeutic Equestrian Association in Aldergrove. B.C., close to the Washington State border. It takes a few paid staff and an army of volunteers — approximately eighty — to take care of a dozen horses and help with eighty or more children during the week. There is a large barn to clean, and hay nets and water buckets to scrub and fill. Specific feeds for each horse must be prepared twice daily. Paddocks and stalls need daily cleaning and new shavings brought in by wheelbarrow.

The horses need daily grooming, plus their vetting and shoeing requirements attended to. There is the endless cleaning of tack and complex administrative work, funds to be raised, volunteer and riding schedules prepared, and ongoing property maintenance. The list is endless.

To prepare a horse for a ride, someone has to bring it in from the pasture, at times sinking into inches of black, clinging mud during the winter months. Usually, two volunteers groom the horse and put on the special saddle and bridle. Then they lead the horse to the arena for the lesson. There, one volunteer leads the horse, and usually two walk alongside for safety, one on each side. Then the horse must be returned to the barn, unsaddled, groomed and fed.

Yet so many people willingly give their time — because the children need us. Ranging in age from two upwards, the children have varying degrees of autism or mental disabilities. Some have severe physical handicaps. Riding strengthens their muscles and bones or helps to straighten spines, enabling them to enjoy a more fruitful life.

Throughout my past life as an accountant, business author and speaker, I volunteered on many levels and in many organizations.

However, a terrible motor-vehicle accident changed my life in a split second when my car was hit — as was my head — causing traumatic brain injury. The journey back has been painful. Now, fourteen years later, I am a different, more simplified person. It took a long time to accept this new "me" and her often-frustrating limitations.

As many brain-injury and trauma survivors know, clinical depression can be a common, major side effect of life-changing damage. Many of us experience terrible, dark moments. Not left unscathed, I often face this demon. It took many years to discover that I needed to do something that I have a passion for. I'd loved horses from childhood, and working with them and with the children has helped turn my life around.

> *It took many years to discover that I needed to do something that I have a passion for.*

That day, as I walked beside the horses and those beautiful, angelic children looked down at me from atop their steeds and smiled — or grunted or squealed in joy, as many cannot speak — my heart was filled to overflowing. I didn't notice the cold, or the rain, or the mud. I was warm from the inside out.

— Frances R. McGuckin —

99

Leading the Fire Drill

And though she be but little, she is fierce.
~William Shakespeare

My six-year-old daughter came home from school and asked, "Why do boys get to do everything and girls don't?" Fire drills were held at the school on a regular basis and they had just had one. Each room had a plastic fireman's hat, and a boy was always picked to lead the class safely away from the building. "Why can't a girl be the leader?" my little girl asked.

Girls were not reared to be independent women when I grew up in the 1950s. At the age of eighteen, I married and went from my parents' home to living with my husband. I had never spent the night alone. When my husband was drafted a short time later, my two younger brothers thought it was great fun to spend the night with me, make fudge and popcorn, watch TV, stay up late, and sleep on my sofa. But the fun soon wore off, and I was left alone for the first time in my life.

I was alone when the electricity went off in the middle of the night, and I had no flashlight. I was alone when the water heater blew up, and water covered my kitchen floor. I was alone when the fuel line froze. I had no heat, and the temperature was below freezing. I was alone when the car wouldn't start and I had no way to get to work. I was alone when a Peeping Tom was caught looking in my window, and when there was not enough money to pay the bills and only enough food to keep from starving. And I was alone during the first seven months of my pregnancy, through morning sickness and doctors' visits.

When my daughter was born, I resolved that she would not be like me. I would raise her to be a self-confident, independent woman. From the very beginning, I encouraged her potential, praised her efforts, and exposed her to ideas and dreams. I was determined that I would help her explore the possibilities that were available.

She showed leadership in kindergarten. Her first-grade teacher said she was a born leader. A move shortly thereafter didn't faze her. As we registered at the new school, I was told that my daughter could attend that day in the stylish little pantsuit that I had made for her, but that pants thereafter were inappropriate. She had to wear a dress or be sent home. The principal believed that children behaved better when they wore their Sunday clothes.

The boys, however, did not have to wear suits, shirts and ties because they liked to hang upside down from the monkey bars on the playground. I suggested that perhaps little girls might like to hang upside down as well without their underwear showing. "My daughter will wear Sunday dresses to school when the boys wear suits and ties," I said. Within a week, every little girl at school was wearing pants.

When my daughter mentioned that she might like to be a nurse when she grew up, I agreed that nursing was a wonderful profession. "But if you want to go into the medical field, you might also think about becoming a doctor," I said.

When she said she wanted to be a teacher, I praised her choice, but I suggested that if she wanted to go into education, she should think about administration, too. She could be the principal of an entire school or the head of a college or university.

When she said she wanted to be a flight attendant and travel all over the world, I agreed that flying would be an exciting career. "But if you want to fly," I said, "think about becoming the pilot. The pilot gets to fly the plane."

Neil Armstrong walked on the moon. When my little girl took exaggerated steps like she saw him do on television, she said she wanted to be an astronaut. I told her that she could be the first woman to walk on the moon if that was what she wanted.

Of course, little girls change their minds often, but whatever she thought she wanted to be at any given time, I supported and then challenged her to dream even bigger and to think outside traditional gender roles.

After my daughter asked why a girl couldn't lead the fire drill, I spoke to the teacher. She said, "It's never been done by a girl, but I suppose if she really wants to..." My daughter wore the red plastic firefighter's hat and led the class safely away from the building during the next fire drill.

The school my six-year-old attended was innovative in encouraging the children to work independently at their own speed. Assignments were given, and as each child finished, she or he could go to various stations around the room for stimulating activities. There were puzzles to work, books to read, and games to play.

At one station, a tape recorder held a tape of *Casey at the Bat*. My little daughter saw the excitement of her male classmates as they donned headphones and listened to the classic baseball tale. They were having fun. She finished her work and made a beeline for the vacant play station, only to be directed by the teacher to an activity she deemed more suited for girls. My daughter came home and asked me why she could not hear the story of *Casey at the Bat*.

After I made another trip to the school, the teacher agreed there was no reason why the stations should be designated by gender. She never thought that little girls might want to hear about baseball or play with building materials or that little boys might want to put on a boa and read *Cinderella* or string necklaces from fruit-flavored cereal and macaroni. When my daughter finished her assignment the next day, she headed straight for the play station, put on the headphones and heard *Casey at the Bat* for the first time.

Times were changing. Each time I went to school, I wanted equal opportunity for my daughter — nothing more and nothing less. I never confronted a teacher in front of anyone else. I handled each situation pleasantly. I was never critical or angry.

I simply wanted my child to be exposed to possibilities and opportunities. She could then decide what she liked or did not like. I wanted her to study academics based on interests and not gender, to have dreams and a non-traditional career if she chose one.

And I wanted her and the other girls to lead the fire drill just as often as the boys.

—Judy Lee Green—

100

90,000 Doughnuts

We cannot live only for ourselves. A thousand fibers
connect us with our fellow men.
~Herman Melville

I t was a day just like any other in our small country town. My youngest, Tyler, and I stopped by our corner store to grab a drink and snack after school. A few police cars caught Tyler's attention, and when we walked inside, we saw the police officers were having lunch in the back corner. "Mom, you know cops' favorite drink is coffee, and their favorite food is doughnuts, right?" I laughed and agreed. "Can I use my allowance money and buy them some mini doughnuts to say 'thank you'?"

"Of course!" I said.

As I watched Tyler thank them and witnessed their gratitude, I felt pride and reassurance that I was fulfilling my purpose to raise my children to be kind and compassionate.

After a few minutes, we left the store, and I thought to myself, *What a beautiful moment.* But then Tyler asked a question that would change our lives and the lives of countless others forever.

"Why were the police so happy about that snack?"

I went on to explain that some people judge a whole by a few. Consequently, they are not always kind to police officers and have even hurt them. Tyler was very sad to hear this, and instead of shrugging it off, he exclaimed that he was going to thank every cop in America and buy them each a doughnut!

I was quite shocked by his response, but it never occurred to me to say "no." In fact, I thought it was a fabulous — but unachievable — idea. I suggested many other options, such as doing a local thank-you event for police, but nothing I said was enough for this young, passionate child on a newfound mission.

> He was going to thank every cop in America and buy them each a doughnut!

I had no idea how to put all of this passion into action, but I knew one thing… Tyler had found his purpose, and it was my duty as his parent to help him fulfill it. I sent an e-mail to our local sheriffs' office and asked if Tyler could host a thank you event for them. They were delighted. At the event, the sheriff introduced Tyler as "The Donut Boy," a name that has become known throughout the nation.

Within a couple of weeks, we had our second event scheduled and then an unexpected phone call — the Liz and Reilly radio show from Eugene, Oregon. This call led to a trip to Oregon to thank the police.

I will never forget the plane ride. Tyler had never flown before and he was so nervous, yet so excited to meet more of his heroes. We had just taken off and were ascending when he looked over at me with the most serious of faces and proclaimed, "See Mom, I told you I could go across America."

By the time we left Oregon, Tyler's mission had been discovered by *Inside Edition* and then *Steve Harvey*. We kept planning thank you events and before we knew it we were on a plane to Chicago to meet Steve in person.

The mission was in full swing and Tyler was working hard to fulfill his dream of giving every officer in America a thank you and an oh so delicious "Power Ring." In May 2017, we headed off to Washington, D.C. for National Police Week, having no idea what to expect. To say this was the most humbling experience of our lives is an understatement; there were 40,000-plus police officers from across the country, all in one city to honor their fallen brothers and sisters. Tyler spent three incredible days thanking these brave men and women and hearing their stories of sacrifice, bravery, loss and passion for their job. By the time we left, our original two-week summer road trip to thank the police had evolved into a six-week delivery mission.

The years that have followed have been incredible. Tyler has spent nights in cars, hotels, campgrounds and even a covered wagon. He has turned his mission into an official nonprofit "I DONUT Need a Reason to THANK a Cop, Inc." and he has worked hard to purchase needed equipment for agencies that are underfunded.

As a mother, it has been an honor to watch Tyler grow and mature and gain an even better understanding of the struggles and rewards of a police officer's duties. I find the utmost joy in watching him sit down with an officer and ask a million questions as he is eager to learn everything about the job that he also hopes to do someday. This program has shaped Tyler into the young man he now is and will continue to shape him into the man he will become, the officer he will be someday, and the husband and father he will be.

Fast-forward to July 2019. It's been three years since a simple act of kindness sparked a wonderful idea in an eight-year-old boy, and it has been one amazing ride. As Tyler is gearing up to complete a smaller goal of his mission — to thank police in every state at least once — I have taken time to reflect on these past years and the impact this one small person has had on the lives of thousands. There have been many happy tears, many hugs, many thank-yous back to Tyler, and many laughs and wonderful memories. We have documented this entire journey on Facebook @idonutneedareasontothankacop and cannot wait to see what the future holds for Tyler and his mission.

In forty-eight states, more than 90,000 doughnuts have been delivered so far, with no end in sight. We have made memories that will last a lifetime, have stories that are almost unbelievable, have laughed and cried, but most importantly, we have served those who serve us daily and made our mark on this world. This is Tyler's legacy.

— Sheena Carach —

A Place to Call Home

Take the first step in faith. You don't have to see the
whole staircase, just take the first step.
~Martin Luther King, Jr.

When Joyce saw the little trailer, she said, "I can't do this. There is no way I could live here."

Admittedly, it didn't look promising. Sitting empty in a dusty storage yard for several years, the tiny trailer desperately needed a good cleaning and a lot of freshening up. The stale smell that greeted us as we stepped inside was disheartening enough, but the years of neglect seemed overwhelming.

Grime covered the walls. The floor creaked and sagged beneath our feet. The dirt and accumulated pet hair in the tiny bedroom were at least half an inch thick. The toilet in the bathroom was filled with dead flies. And all of this I was presenting to Joyce as a possible home for her and her young son. I couldn't blame her for despairing.

But Joyce needed someplace to live, and this was being offered to her for free. Joyce and her son Robbie had been living with a relative, but it had been a strained arrangement, and change was needed desperately. A neighbor had offered Joyce this trailer, but it needed, in the neighbor's words, "a little bit of cleaning." Joyce and I had driven to the storage yard to take a look and were seeing with our own eyes that it certainly needed cleaning... more than just a little.

Turning to Joyce, I mustered enthusiasm and said, "We can clean this up and fix it up very nicely. With some fresh paint and new curtains, this can be very charming. Trust me, we will transform this place… Think of it as our own home-makeover show! This will be fun." I don't know if I really convinced Joyce, but she needed a home, and this was the only one being offered for free. So, with a hesitant hope bordering on skepticism, she agreed.

After convincing Joyce that we could pull off a miracle, I tried my best to convince myself.

Joyce, who became and remains one of my dear friends, had already had a lifetime of overcoming obstacles. Her past included a drug addiction and jail time. At the time we began work on the little trailer, I was just getting to know her, but I knew Joyce had been sober for several years. Still, the trials of her past required some encouragement. After such a rough life, Joyce needed reassurance of her own value and capabilities.

For my part, I needed to learn to look past her past, which was difficult for me. I had very little positive experience with anyone who had battled addiction or served time incarcerated. Previously, during the time I volunteered for the Inland AIDS Project, I had encountered one man who had dealt with both. He was a good man, an inspiring individual who used his life experiences to help others. But he was a rarity among the multitudes, and I knew, or knew about, far more people with such challenges who couldn't be trusted.

Given all of this, Joyce was going to be a lesson to me in more than just the test of a trailer makeover and turning it into a suitable home. I was going to learn a lot about myself in the process. Was I up to the challenge of seeing past someone's "past"? But there was more to think about here — Joyce had an eight-year-old son who needed a stable home life. For both Joyce and myself, the opportunity to help Robbie have that stability overcame our hesitation.

And so we began, with more *chutzpah* than ability, and took on the job of turning the musty, little trailer into something livable.

I had a little experience in such things. I had helped paint several homes before, and I had painted many theater sets, but none of those had presented much difficulty because they were simple, straightforward jobs. Painting a flat wall in a house or painting a flat for theater scenery is relatively easy because you have a lot of space to work with, and they are generally clean enough to not require much attention before setting to work.

But the trailer was small, cramped and incredibly filthy. Joyce and I spent a week just cleaning, and it didn't appear much better after we had cleaned than before we had started. Surveying our work, Joyce asked doubtfully, "Is it just because it needs to be painted?" I looked at the dingy walls before answering brightly, "Oh, yes! A new coat of paint will fix everything right up!" But I spoke with more hope than assurance.

In truth, the new paint did help a lot. The dead flies were cleaned up, the counters were scrubbed, and new curtains were hung. All of the dirt and pet hair was removed. Joyce's cousin put in new flooring, and the place began to look livable. We rejoiced the day we attached the water line and water flowed from the kitchen tap. I even managed to light the cantankerous propane water heater. The furnace turned out to work perfectly, and a window air conditioner was more than adequate to cool the entire trailer.

A person is more than just a chapter from the story of her life.

But even more inspiring than the blossoming trailer was Joyce's growing confidence. She began to see possibilities where before she had seen only dead ends. And I found that she was someone I really liked. She was funny and caring and would do anything for her son. The Joyce of the past had been replaced by a mother willing to work to make a future for her family. The little trailer became more than just a place to live. It became a symbol of rebirth.

And through it all, I learned that a person is more than just a chapter from the story of her life. It's the entire story of that life that matters, along with the authorship of that life story, which lies in each of our hands.

Now, years later, Joyce and Robbie no longer live in the little trailer, but it was there for them when they needed it. Joyce's life has reaped the rewards of a faith in God and a faith in herself. Today, she is an office manager and medical sales representative. Her past gives her a unique compassion and ability to see the good that sometimes lies deeply buried in people. She sees the possibilities in people, where others only see dead ends.

And along the road of this journey was a little trailer asking only to be given a chance, to be seen as a possibility. That little trailer, neglected and dirty, fly-strewn and forlorn, blossomed with a little attention, love, and elbow grease. Against all the odds, it helped a mother and her son when they needed it most. It helped a woman reach inside herself and find who she could be for both herself and her son. It started a new and better chapter in someone's life.

It became a place to call home.

—Jack Byron—

Meet Our Contributors

Heidi Allen is the founder of the Positive People Army. What began as a blog has rapidly become a positive social media global movement with thousands of people from all over the world working together to make a positive difference.

Monica A. Andermann lives and writes on Long Island where she shares a home with her husband Bill and their little tabby Samson. Her work has appeared in such publications as *Sasee*, *Woman's World* and *Guideposts* as well as many editions in the *Chicken Soup for the Soul* series.

Fifteen-year-old **Adam Avin** created Wuf Shanti to teach mindfulness so kids can live in health, wellness, peace and positivity and to help them cope with emotions, stress and to interact with kindness. He founded the Kids' Association for Mindfulness in Education, and the Mindful Kids Peace Summit. Adam gave a TEDxYouthTalk about mindfulness.

Lacey L. Bakker has always been an avid reader. She loves reading all genres, spending time with her cats Simba and Sebastien, and with her husband Adam. She enjoys traveling, movies, and playing with her nephews and niece.

Kerrie R. Barney is a full-time student at Central New Mexico Community College where she is working towards earning a business degree. Her book, *Life, the Universe, and Houseplants*, about her humorous adventures growing houseplants, is available for sale online.

Barbara Bartocci is the author of nine published books and many articles in major national magazines such as *Good Housekeeping, Woman's Day, Reader's Digest*, etc. She is a nationally known speaker and also leads memoir-writing workshops. E-mail her at bhbartocci@icloud.com.

Brenda Beattie is a retired letter carrier, chaplain, and self-published author. Her books, *Finding Sacred Ground In The Daily Grind* and *The Case Of The Missing Letter*, are available online. She feels blessed and is enjoying retirement life in sunny Florida with her husband.

Stephanie Blank is a writer, artist, business owner and storyteller. She resides in Marina del Rey, CA where she runs her home-accessory business appropriately named Blankety Blank Designs.

Joan M. Borton is passionate about strengthening families affected by disability. She has been married to Jerry since 1995. When faced with a little downtime you will find Joan reading in her hammock, swimming, biking, or working on a jigsaw puzzle. Follow her blog at www.joanborton.com.

Lori Kempf Bosko has two grown sons, two lovely daughters-in-law and four funny, amazing grandchildren. She graduated, with honors, from the Journalism Program at Grant MacEwan College in 1990 and enjoys writing, traveling, photography, and spending time with family and friends. Lori lives in Edmonton, Canada.

LaTonya Branham was born in Dayton, OH. She received a Ph.D. in Leadership and Change, two M.A. degrees, and a B.S. degree. She is an administrator, educator, and author. Dr. Branham has previously been published in the *Chicken Soup for the Soul* series. She is happily married to Morton. Learn more at LaTonyaBranham.com.

Jack Byron received his degree in commercial illustration and has published art criticism in addition to his writing for the *Chicken Soup for the Soul* series. Always one to encourage others to write, he believes that the best writing is written first in our day-to-day lives before ever being committed to paper.

Kristine Byron worked for Tupperware Home Parties for over twenty-two years. Many of those years were spent as a motivational trainer for their distributorship. She has tried to pass on her positive attitude to her children and grandchildren.

Leah Cano received her B.A. in Spanish at UC Irvine and Masters of Education at UC Santa Cruz. She is retired and lives in Laguna Beach, CA. In addition to writing, she is a textile artist with an Etsy shop named Sweptaway. E-mail her at leahmc@hotmail.com or visit her shop at www.sweptaway.etsy.com.

Amy Michels Cantley received her Bachelor of Arts in English from Rollins College and is completing her MLIS degree at the University of South Florida. She works as a librarian and leads a writing group. She enjoys a good hike with her husband, reading, and painting. She writes memoir, poetry, and nonfiction essays.

Sheena Carach is the mother of three amazing children, Naudia, Zach and Tyler, and the wife to Jacob. She is a dedicated mom and president of I DONUT need a reason to THANK a cop, Inc. a nonprofit founded by her youngest child. She enjoys writing, photography and living life to the fullest. She loves a good adventure.

Eva Carter is a freelance writer and amateur photographer. She has a twenty-three-year background in finance. Born in Czechoslovakia but raised in New York, Eva is now living in Dallas, TX.

Matt Chandler is a graduate of Buffalo State College where he earned a B.A. in Communication Studies. He is a writer and author of forty-five books for children. He lives in New York with his wife Amber and his children Oliver and Zoey. Learn more at www.mattchandlerwriting.com.

Jen Chapman is a freelance writer and blogger at girlmeetsgrace.com. She earned her Bachelor of Arts in Print Journalism from Marshall University. Jen and her husband Shawn have an eighteen-year-old son, Noah. Her ideal day would include pajamas, books and *Gilmore Girls*. E-mail her at jchapman0427@gmail.com.

Claire Chargo is a writer living in Atlanta, GA. When not working on her latest project, she enjoys time with her family and her two rescue dogs. She loves coffee, peonies, and painted furniture.

Melanie Chartoff is a life-long actor from New Haven, now residing in Los Angeles, CA with her husband. She currently voices Didi Pickles, mother of the Rugrats, in their eighth season and in a new feature film.

M. Scott Coffman lives in Central Illinois with his wife, daughter, dog, and two cats. He writes to fend off middle-age decrepitude and plays the piano for as long as his arthritis will allow. This is his fourth story published in the *Chicken Soup for the Soul* series.

Jamie Coombs is a single mother of an eight-year-old son. She works in human services and writes short stories and poetry in her spare time.

Elaine Marie Cooper has written eight novels about the American Revolution. Her only nonfiction title, *Bethany's Calendar*, is about her daughter. Her writing has also appeared in several anthologies and periodicals. She does not mind being called a "history geek," but loves being called "GiGi." Learn more at elainemariecooper.com.

Gwen Cooper received her B.A. in English and Secondary Education in 2007, and completed the Publishing Institute at Denver University in 2009. In her free time she enjoys krav maga, traveling, and backpacking with her husband and Bloodhound rescue in the beautiful Rocky Mountains. Follow her on Twitter @Gwen_Cooper10.

Married with dogs, **Amanda Sue Creasey** holds a Master of Liberal Studies from University of Denver and a Bachelor of Arts from Michigan State. She teaches English and loves to write, read, run, and walk her dogs, Jack and Sadie. She is a member of James River Writers, Poetry Society of Virginia and Virginia Outdoor Writers Association.

Karen Haueisen Crissinger writes about memorable parenting moments like teaching her twins to plunge a toilet, which birthed the book *Big Kids Flush*. She is also a professional seamstress and all-around rabble-rouser. Find Karen on Facebook at facebook.com/BigKidsBooks and feel free to start some digital shenanigans.

Tracy Crump has enjoyed publishing twenty-two stories in the *Chicken Soup for the Soul* series. She co-directs Write Life Workshops, speaks at writers' conferences, and edits a popular writers' newsletter. Visit TracyCrump.com or find her course on her experience writing for Chicken Soup for the Soul at SeriousWriterAcademy.com.

Denise Del Bianco is a retired widow living in her hometown of Bischwiller, France, after traveling the world with the love of her life, Pietro. After meeting in France, he and Denise raised two children in Italy and Canada. She enjoys cooking, reading, and cuddling her furry grandkids. Find her on twitter @DeniseBecht.

Lindsay Detwiler is an international bestselling author of romance and thriller novels. Her debut thriller, *The Widow Next Door*, is a *USA TODAY* Bestseller. She is also a high school English teacher in her hometown in Pennsylvania. E-mail her at lindsayanndetwiler@gmail.com.

Dana Drosdick is a Digital Advertising Project Manager by day, a writer, reluctant runner, and avid reader by night. Dana graduated from Calvin College with a degree in Digital Communication and Spanish and has been previously published in *Chicken Soup for the Soul: Grandparents* and various online editorials.

Mindi Susman Ellis is a writer, artist and adventurer from the Midwest. She adores her two adult-ish children. She owns a marketing and communications business. Mindi loves yoga, travel, hiking, gardening, water sports, and almost anything outdoors. E-mail her at mindicreates@gmail.com.

Celeste Bergeron Ewan works full-time as a supervisor in a pipe manufacturing plant. If that isn't busy enough, she is also a proud mother of two and a newly wed wife to her husband John. Celeste enjoys spending time with her family, camping, treasure hunting, and of course, writing. She plans to write an autobiography one day.

Carole Brody Fleet is a multi-award winning author, media contributor and four-time contributor to the *Chicken Soup for the Soul* series. An expert in life-adversity recovery, Ms. Fleet has made over 1,200 radio show appearances and additionally appears on numerous television programs as well as in worldwide print and web media.

Victoria Otto Franzese has degrees from Smith College and New York University. She owned, operated and wrote for an online travel guide for fifteen years before selling it to a major media outlet. Now she writes on a variety of topics and all of her travel is for fun. She lives in New York City with her husband, two sons, and a Goldendoodle named Jenkins.

Jody Fuller is a comedian, speaker, writer and soldier with three combat tours in Iraq. He is also a lifetime stutterer. In 2018, *Alabama* magazine named Jody one of Alabama's top 40 men and women over 40 whose lives and careers are characterized by great levels of giving and achievement.

Cher P. Garman received her Bachelor of Arts from the University of Manitoba in 1997. She writes about her experiences and observations as a Canadian living in "The Windy City" on her blog, "The Chicago

Files," at www.thechicagofiles.com. Cher is currently working on her first children's book entitled *Laura and the Disappearing Stars*.

Kathleen Gerard's writing has been widely published, anthologized and broadcasted on NPR (National Public Radio). She is the author of three novels: *In Transit, Cold Comfort* and *The Thing Is*. Learn more at kathleengerard.blogspot.com.

Jim Grayson retired from careers in law enforcement and security consulting. As a Gemini, his hobbies have varied from SCUBA diving, sailing, snow skiing and flying, to now working at his home and garden along with fiction writing. He and his wife also experience great joy as docents at the Autry Museum in Los Angeles, CA.

Judy Lee Green is an award-winning writer and speaker whose spirit and roots reach deep into the Appalachian Mountains. Tennessee-bred and cornbread-fed, she has been published hundreds of times and received dozens of awards for her work. As her inspiration, she often writes about her large colorful family.

R'becca Groff is a freelance writer who resides in Cedar Rapids, IA. She has been published in national anthologies and magazines, and recently completed her first novel. Rebecca has two daughters and five grandchildren who keep her in the know. Her favorite writing time takes place in the company of music and nature.

Judythe Guarnera is comforted by the fact that having reached the age of eighty, she is now too old to die young. Connection is key in her life and she accomplishes that through her volunteering, especially as a mediator, and through her writing. E-mail her at follow.yourheart@sbcglobal.net.

An award-winning speaker, **Tom Guetzke** engages audiences around the globe. Traveling to over sixty-five countries, Tom studied the psychological similarities and differences of happiness. Today Tom is on a mission to change minds, hearts, and lives by helping others discover how they can create more happiness in their own lives.

Wendy J. Hairfield has a B.A. degree in Journalism, with honors, from Temple University. After a rewarding career in public relations promoting environmental programs, she now enjoys writing, tennis, photography, and gardening. She has a daughter and stepson and lives in the Seattle area with her husband and two tortoises.

Jan Hopkins-Campbell is a children's book author/illustrator who received her Bachelor of Science degree in Early Childhood Education from Tennessee State University in 2012. She enjoys reading, antiquing, painting, and spending time with her pets Smokie and Duchess in the home she and her late husband Bracey decorated.

Darrell Horwitz is a writer, sports talk radio host, aspiring motivational speaker, and is nearing completion of his self-help book, *Guess Whose Turn It Is*. He's now using the phrase "beyond fresh" to replace "thinking outside the box." You can reach him at darrellhorwitz@gmail.com.

Vicki L. Julian, a University of Kansas alumnus, is an award-winning writer, and editor whose works have appeared in myriad newspapers and magazines. She is the author of six books with two additional to be released soon; and included in ten anthologies. Learn more at www.vickijulian.com.

Jennifer Kennedy is a freelance writer specializing in marketing and public relations content and a senior writer for *Story Terrace*. This is her second story published in the *Chicken Soup for the Soul* series, but it is extra special because she is published alongside the best writer she knows — her dad. E-mail her at jenniferkennedypr@gmail.com.

Mary Potter Kenyon lives in Dubuque, IA, where she is Program Coordinator for the Shalom Spirituality Center. Mary graduated from the University of Northern Iowa and is a certified grief counselor, public speaker, and workshop presenter. She is the author of seven books, including one on creativity to be released by Familius in 2020.

Lori Ann King is the author of *Come Back Strong: Balanced Wellness after Surgical Menopause*. She is a 2019 U.S. IsaBody Challenge Finalist with a passion for helping others transform physically and financially. When she's not writing or coaching, you'll find her with her husband Jim on their bikes, paddle boards, or kayaks.

Mimi Greenwood Knight is a freelance writer and mama of four living on a small hobby farm in South Louisiana. Mimi has thousands of articles, devotionals, and essays in print, including in more than two-dozen *Chicken Soup for the Soul* books. She and her husband, David, are anxiously awaiting their empty nest years.

Samantha LaBarbera received her Bachelor of Arts degree from Franklin & Marshall College and her J.D. from Villanova University Charles Widger School of Law. An attorney in the pharmaceutical industry, she lives in Pennsylvania with her husband and two children.

Carol C. Lake received her MBA and MA in Geography from SUNY at Buffalo. She and her husband have three daughters and she works in finance for the University of California. Carol enjoys reading and everything family. She plans to write a collection of stories to share successes of overcoming life's challenges. Read her blog at uniquelytold.com.

Lisa Leshaw is thrilled to be re-launching her empowerment workshops for women throughout the U.S. Her latest endeavor involves a series of videos/books addressing the empty nest phase of parenting, one she is all too familiar with and is still graciously adjusting to.

Ina Massler Levin was a middle school teacher and, later, the editor-in-chief at an educational publishing house. In retirement she has been indulging her love of travel and ballroom dancing with her husband Michael. Ina loves spending time with her family including her granddaughter Elianna Mae.

Bobbie Jensen Lippman is a professional writer who lives in Seal Rock, OR with her cat Purrfect and a robot named Waldo. Bobbie's work has been published nationally and internationally. She writes a weekly human-interest column for *The News-Times* in Newport, OR. E-mail her at bobbisbeat@gmail.com.

Joyce Lombardi is a nonfiction writer and nonprofit lawyer/lobbyist who lives in Baltimore, MD, aka Charm City, with her two teenaged children. She writes about power, gender, race, and sometimes water. Her work has been published in Salon.com, *The Village Voice*, the *Chicken Soup for the Soul* series, and several local outlets.

Frederick Loomis received his Bachelor of Arts degree from Temple University and Master's and Doctoral degrees from Penn State University. He is a retired associate professor of education and continues to teach and mentor students. He wakes up each day for his devoted wife, two grown children and four wonderful grandchildren.

Diana Lynn is a freelance writer and business owner in Washington State. This is a milestone for her as it's her tenth story published in the *Chicken Soup for the Soul* series.

Carol L. MacKay is a freelance writer who lives in the picturesque town of Qualicum Beach on Vancouver Island. This is her second story published in the *Chicken Soup for the Soul* series. Carol is currently busy at work on a mystery novel set in the Alberta Parkland.

Mark Mason is a freelance illustrator living in Whittier, CA. His work has appeared in magazines, children's books and greeting cards. He is passionate about life and living in the moment. When he isn't at the drawing table, he can be found at the local bakery indulging in a pecan roll. E-mail him at got.mark@verizon.net.

Frances R. McGuckin is the author of the bestseller, *Business for Beginners*. After a life-altering car accident in 2005 and serious brain injury, she resumed writing in 2015, with two stories published in *Chicken Soup for the Soul: The Spirit of Canada* in 2017. She loves horses, gardening, and fitness. E-mail her at franmcg@telus.net.

Kim Johnson McGuire received her Bachelor of Arts in Literature from University of California, Santa Barbara in 1983. She works as a Pilates instructor and enjoys traveling, reading, and playing golf. She joyfully recalls many travel and golfing adventures she shared with her husband.

Jennifer McMurrain has won numerous awards for her short stories and novels, including hitting #1 on the Amazon Best Seller list with her book, *Quail Crossings*. She has sixteen novels and collaborations published. She lives in Bartlesville, OK with her family. Learn more at www.jennifermcmurrain.com.

Nancy Merczel lives in Illinois with her husband and (senior) cat. She is currently writing a book for tween girls.

Sarah E. Morin is a kid wrangler at a history museum in Indiana. She writes poems, short stories, and unruly fairy tales, including two books: *Waking Beauty* and *Rapunzel the Hairbrained*. When she grows up she wants to be a child prodigy.

Ann Morrow is a writer, humorist, and frequent contributor to the *Chicken Soup for the Soul* series. She and her husband live in the Black Hills of South Dakota. Ann is currently at work on a collection of humor essays that she hopes to have published in the near future.

Diane Morrow-Kondos writes a weekly blog about grandparenting at www.tulsakids.com/Grand-Life/. Her book, *The Long Road to Happy:*

A Sister's Struggle Through Her Brother's Disabilities, will be released fall 2019. Diane is also a triathlete and open water swimmer. Learn more at www.dianemorrowkondos.com.

A recent, self-described escapee of the corporate world, **Lauren Mosher** now enjoys a career with a dog-walking company. She is devoted to her volunteer work with animal-rescue nonprofits and human-welfare organizations. She believes that living life in service to others is paramount. Her favorite color is pink.

Brian Narelle's career has spanned film, television and theater. A cartoonist at heart, his political cartoons can be found in textbooks worldwide. Starring in the cult film *Dark Star* in deep space, he has since confined his flying to 10,000 feet. If you need cartoons e-mail him at briannarelle@comcast.net.

S.K. Naus has enjoyed writing since grade school and likes to enter contests on a lark. Words are important and arranging them in the right order can create wonderful stories, which is her favourite part of writing.

Marcus A. Nelson is a prolific writer. His debut novel, *Born from Weeds & Rats*, has received high praise from an audience awaiting his next release. You can find him blogging at www.mafoombay.com with a mix of relevant commentaries, short stories and book reviews. Raised in New Jersey(land), he now lives in Connecticut.

Dr. Noelle C. Nelson is a psychologist, speaker, and author of over a dozen books empowering individuals to be happier, healthier and more successful at work, at home and in relationships. Her passion for inspiring people led her to create @MeetTheAmazings. A competitive ballroom dancer, she also loves reading and travel.

Laura Niebauer Palmer received her graduate degree in English from DePaul University and currently lives in Austin, TX with her husband

and son. She enjoys writing, traveling, pool days, and sharing her adventures at palmerpathtoparenthood.com.

Perry P. Perkins' work has appeared in hundreds of magazines from *Writer's Digest*, to *Bass Master*, to *Guideposts*, as well as twenty-two *Chicken Soup for the Soul* titles. The author of over a dozen books he currently writes a monthly column, "Renaissance Dad," for *Vancouver Family Magazine*. Learn more at www.perryperkinsbooks.com.

Kristen Mai Pham is delighted to be an eight-time contributor to the *Chicken Soup for the Soul* series. She is also a screenwriter and her ultimate dream is to see her stories produced for television and film. Follow her on Instagram @kristenmaipham or e-mail her at kristenmaipham3@gmail.com.

Pam Phree retired from Social Service in 2017 to become a full-time writer. She is nearing completion on her latest novel about life in heaven. She lives in Ellensburg, WA with her dog, Bella.

Connie K. Pombo is an inspirational speaker, freelance writer, and frequent contributor to the *Chicken Soup for the Soul series*. When not speaking or writing, she enjoys traveling internationally where she volunteers her time for causes important to her heart. Learn more at www.conniepombo.com.

Staying positive — and healthy — comes easier with happiness, so that's what **C. L. Pryor** strives to do daily: fill her life with joy. Her heart is happiest when she's writing, spending time with her husband, playing with her pets, traveling (especially cruising), reading, or playing puzzle games on her phone.

Donna L. Roberts is a native upstate New Yorker who lives and works in Europe. She is a university professor and holds a Ph.D. in Psychology. Donna is an animal and human rights advocate and when she is researching or writing she can be found at her computer buried in rescue cats. E-mail her at donna_roberts13@yahoo.com.

It is rumored that the first word **Sue Ross** uttered gave her such satisfaction that she said it twice. "Author! Author!" Finding stories all around her, Sue revels in language that lifts and inspires. With a B.A. in English, she is editing her first novel, *Golanski's Treasures*. E-mail her at kidangel@me.com.

Award-winning speaker, educator, author and musician **Linda Ruescher's** life and career came to a grinding halt with acute onset of systemic lupus. During four years on disability, Linda tried to make sense of what happened to her life. Her research opened the doors to new possibilities and the creation of her own new normal.

Cheryl M. Scott is a nonprofit executive in Bakersfield, CA where she "connects the dots" between businesses, educators, and the community. She enjoys running and hiking, writing, and wine tasting—not necessarily in that order! She and her husband have two sons, two dogs, and an occasional brood of backyard hummingbirds.

Heather Spiva is a freelance writer from Sacramento, CA. She loves reading and writing and hanging out with her two boys and husband. When she's not doing these things, she's probably shopping for vintage clothing or drinking coffee… or doing both simultaneously. Learn more at www.heatherspiva.com.

Glenda Standeven is an adventurer, amputee, author, and inspirational speaker. She lives with her husband, Rick, three hours north of Seattle, WA in Chilliwack, BC. Her books, *I Am Choosing to Smile* and *What Men Won't Talk About... And Women Need to Know* are available online.

Suzette Martinez Standring is syndicated with GateHouse Media and wrote *The Art of Column Writing* and *The Art of Opinion Writing*. The unseen world sends powerful messages and she listens. Learn more at www.readsuzette.com.

Judee Stapp is an author and speaker for Stonecroft Ministries, retreats, and women's events. She is a wife, mother of three, and grandmother of four, including precious Kelly (from this story). Judee hopes to inspire people to find happiness through a personal relationship with God. E-mail her at judeestapp@roadrunner.com.

Diane St. Laurent is a wife, mother of three and grandmother of seven. She enjoys swimming, writing, reading, and planning adventures with her family.

Lisa Swan is a University of Texas at Austin graduate who lives in New York City. She has written for a variety of publications, including *Guideposts*, the *New York Daily News*, and *The Washington Post*. Lisa is also a back-of-the-pack runner, triathlete, and eight-time marathoner whose goal is to run marathons in all fifty states.

Jodi Renee Thomas likes to write stuff, and sometimes people like to read it. She is an avid advocate for equal rights for all and has even spoken on the steps of our nation's capitol. She lives happily in Florida with her husband, best friend, and a dog that likes to sit next to her while she types.

Ingrid Tomey received her MFA from University of Michigan in 1983. She and Paul have a son, daughter, and three grandchildren. Ingrid is a mediator in northern Michigan. She also enjoys yoga, biking, and sitting on her porch and watching the changing weather over Lake Michigan.

"Sunny" Esther Valenzuela is a writer/speaker and Realtor. In between real estate transactions, Sunny and her mom, Charlotte, speak about her mom's experiences in a concentration camp during WWII. Sunny and her mom speak at civic, church and community events. For more info e-mail her at sunnymarie522@yahoo.com.

Sarah Wagner lives in West Virginia with her husband, sons, dogs, and lizards. Her work has appeared in several anthologies and magazines including *Flashquake*, *Chronogram*, and the *Sigurd Journal*. She has four paranormal novels and a science fiction short story collection available. Learn more at www.sarahewagner.com.

Nick Walker is an on-camera meteorologist on *The Weather Channel*, a voice over narrator, speaker, writer and The Weather Dude®, educating young people about weather through music. He writes the "Tales from a Weathered Man" blog and podcast at nickwalkerblog.com.

Jude Walsh is a writer and a creativity and life coach. Her writing is published in numerous literary magazines and anthologies, including three titles in the *Chicken Soup for the Soul* series. She is the author of *Post-Divorce Bliss: Ending Us and Finding Me* (Morgan James Press, 2019). Learn more at www.secondbloomcoaching.com.

David Warren and his wife of twenty-eight years reside in Kettering, OH. They have one daughter Marissa. David's stories have been in multiple titles in the *Chicken Soup for the Soul* series. He is Vice President of Lutz Americas and continues to inspire with positive views on life!

Jodi Whitsitt is a blogger, widow, and proud mom of three. She's a mix of optimism, tenacity, and anxiety. Life has tried to knock her down a few times, but with faith, family, and friendship she continues to rise up. It's her mission to turn her pain into purpose by keeping it real with her readers at ExtraGraceRequired.com.

Arthur Wiknik, Jr. served in Vietnam with the 101st Airborne Division and was featured on the *History* channel and the *Military* channel (currently known as *American Heroes Channel*) for his participation in the battle of Hamburger Hill. Arthur frequently shares his military experiences at schools and civic organizations. Learn more at www.namsense.com.

Courtney Wright attended Concordia College New York and then earned her Master's in multi-cultural education from Iona College. She lives in Northern New Jersey where she enjoys hiking, fishing, running, and binge watching Netflix. But her biggest passion is blogging and helping busy women build confidence.

Meet Amy Newmark

Amy Newmark is the bestselling author, editor-in-chief, and publisher of the *Chicken Soup for the Soul* book series. Since 2008, she has published 160 new books, most of them national bestsellers in the U.S. and Canada, more than doubling the number of Chicken Soup for the Soul titles in print today. She is also the author of *Simply Happy*, a crash course in Chicken Soup for the Soul advice and wisdom that is filled with easy-to-implement, practical tips for enjoying a better life.

Amy is credited with revitalizing the Chicken Soup for the Soul brand, which has been a publishing industry phenomenon since the first book came out in 1993. By compiling inspirational and aspirational true stories curated from ordinary people who have had extraordinary experiences, Amy has kept the twenty-six-year-old Chicken Soup for the Soul brand fresh and relevant.

Amy graduated *magna cum laude* from Harvard University where she majored in Portuguese and minored in French. She then embarked on a three-decade career as a Wall Street analyst, a hedge fund manager, and a corporate executive in the technology field. She is a Chartered Financial Analyst.

Her return to literary pursuits was inevitable, as her honors thesis in college involved traveling throughout Brazil's impoverished northeast region, collecting stories from regular people. She is delighted to have come full circle in her writing career — from collecting stories "from the people" in Brazil as a twenty-year-old to, three decades later, collecting stories "from the people" for Chicken Soup for the Soul.

When Amy and her husband Bill, the CEO of Chicken Soup for the Soul, are not working, they are visiting their four grown children and their grandchildren.

Follow Amy on Twitter @amynewmark. Listen to her free podcast — "Chicken Soup for the Soul with Amy Newmark" — on Apple Podcasts, Google Play, the Podcasts app on iPhone, or by using your favorite podcast app on other devices.

Meet Deborah Norville

Bestselling author Deborah Norville credits many of the successes in her life to a positive mental attitude. She is the anchor of *Inside Edition*, the nation's top-rated daily news magazine, a two-time Emmy winner, and serves on the Board of Directors for the Viacom Corporation, the global provider of entertainment content.

Deborah is also the author of a half-dozen books including the New York Times bestseller, *Thank You Power: Making the Science of Gratitude Work for You*. That book brought together for the first time the growing body of academic research proving the benefits of gratitude. Similarly, *The Power of Respect* presented research detailing the benefits of respectful behavior, with real-life stories. She also coauthored *Chicken Soup for the Soul: Think Possible* and *Chicken Soup for the Soul: The Power of Gratitude* and wrote the forewords for *Chicken Soup for the Soul: Think Positive* and *Chicken Soup for the Soul: Find Your Happiness*.

Deborah Norville is a summa cum laude (4.0) graduate of the University of Georgia. She is married and the mother of three.

Get in touch with Deborah on social media or via her website at www.DeborahNorville.com.

Thank You

We owe huge thanks to all of our contributors and fans. We were overwhelmed with thousands of submissions on this very popular topic, and we had a team that spent months reading all of them. Laura Dean, Crescent LoMonaco, Barbara LoMonaco, and D'ette Corona read all of them, and then Amy Newmark narrowed down the semifinalists for Deborah Norville to make the final selections.

Susan Heim did the first round of editing, D'ette chose the perfect quotations to put at the beginning of each story, and Amy edited the stories and shaped the final manuscript.

As we finished our work, Associate Publisher D'ette Corona continued to be Amy's right-hand woman in creating the final manuscript and working with all our wonderful writers. Barbara LoMonaco and Kristiana Pastir, along with Elaine Kimbler, jumped in at the end to proof, proof, proof. And yes, there will always be typos anyway, so feel free to let us know about them at webmaster@chickensoupforthesoul. com, and we will correct them in future printings.

The whole publishing team deserves a hand, including our Senior Director of Marketing Maureen Peltier, our Vice President of Production Victor Cataldo, and our graphic designer Daniel Zaccari, who turned our manuscript into this beautiful book.

Sharing Happiness, Inspiration, and Hope

Real people sharing real stories, every day, all over the world. In 2007, *USA Today* named *Chicken Soup for the Soul* one of the five most memorable books in the last quarter-century. With over 100 million books sold to date in the U.S. and Canada alone, more than 250 titles in print, and translations into nearly fifty languages, "chicken soup for the soul®" is one of the world's best-known phrases.

Today, twenty-six years after we first began sharing happiness, inspiration and hope through our books, we continue to delight our readers with new titles, but have also evolved beyond the bookshelves with super premium pet food, television shows, a podcast, video journalism from aplus.com, licensed products, and free movies and TV shows on our Popcornflix and Crackle apps. We are busy "changing the world one story at a time®." Thanks for reading!

Share with Us

We all have had Chicken Soup for the Soul moments in our lives. If you would like to share your story or poem with millions of people around the world, go to chickensoup. com and click on Submit Your Story. You may be able to help another reader and become a published author at the same time. Some of our past contributors have launched writing and speaking careers from the publication of their stories in our books!

We only accept story submissions via our website. They are no longer accepted via mail or fax. Visit our website, www.chickensoup. com, and click on Submit Your Story for our writing guidelines and a list of topics we are working on.

To contact us regarding other matters, please send us an e-mail through webmaster@chickensoupforthesoul.com, or fax or write us at:

Chicken Soup for the Soul
P.O. Box 700
Cos Cob, CT 06807-0700
Fax: 203-861-7194

One more note from your friends at Chicken Soup for the Soul: Occasionally, we receive an unsolicited book manuscript from one of our readers, and we would like to respectfully inform you that we do not accept unsolicited manuscripts, and we must discard the ones that appear.

Changing your life one story at a time®
www.chickensoup.com